GRAMMAR FOR LANGUAGE LEARNING

ELEMENTS *of* SUCCESS

ANNE M. EDIGER

RANDEE FALK

MARI VARGO

JENNI CURRIE SANTAMARIA

1 B

OXFORD
UNIVERSITY PRESS

SHAPING learning TOGETHER

We would like to thank the following classes for piloting *Elements of Success*:

University of Delaware English Language Institute
Teacher: Kathleen Vodvarka
Students: Ahmad Alenzi, Bandar Manei Algahmdi, Fadi Mohammed Alhazmi, Abdel Rahman Atallah, Anna Kuzmina, Muhanna Sayer Aljuaid, Coulibaly Sita

ABC Adult School, Cerritos, CA
Teacher: Jenni Santamaria
Students: Gabriela A. Marquez Aguilar, Yijung Chen, Laura Gomez, Terry Hahn, EunKyung Lee, Subin Lee, Sunmin Lee, Jane Leelachat, Lilia Nunezuribe, Gina Olivar, Young Park, Seol Hee Seok, Kwang Mi Song

---

During the development of *Elements of Success*, we spoke with teachers and professionals who are passionate about teaching grammar. Their feedback led us to create *Elements of Success: Grammar for Language Learning*, a course that solves teaching challenges by presenting grammar clearly, simply, and completely. We would like to acknowledge the advice of teachers from

USA • BRAZIL • CANADA • COSTA RICA • GUATEMALA • IRAN • JAPAN • MEXICO • OMAN • RUSSIA

SAUDI ARABIA • SOUTH KOREA • TUNISIA • TURKEY • UKRAINE • THE UNITED ARAB EMIRATES

Mehmet Abi, Mentese Anatolian High School, Turkey; **Anna-Marie Aldaz**, Doña Ana Community College, NM; **Diana Allen**, Oakton Community College, IL; **Marjorie Allen**, Harper College, IL; **Mark Alves**, Montgomery College, Rockville, MD; **Kelly Arce**, College of Lake County, IL; **Irma Arencibia**, Union City Adult Learning Center, NJ; **Arlys Arnold**, University of Minnesota, MN; **Marcia Arthur**, Renton Technical College, WA; **Alexander Astor**, Hostos Community College, NY; **Chris Atkins**, CHICLE Language Institute, NC; **Karin Avila-John**, University of Dayton, OH; **Ümmet Aydan**, Karabuk University, Iran; **Fabiana Azurmendi; John Baker**, Wayne State University, MI; **Sepehr Bamdadnia; Terry Barakat**, Missouri State University, MO; **Marie Bareille**, Borough of Manhattan Community College, NY; **Eileen Barlow**, SUNY Albany, NY; **Denise Barnes**, Madison English as a Second Language School, WI; **Kitty Barrera**, University of Houston, TX; **Denise Barsotti**, EID Training Solutions, FL; **Maria Bauer**, El Camino College; **Christine Bauer-Ramazani**, Saint Michael's College, VT; **Jamie Beaton**, Boston University, MA; **Gena Bennett**, Cornerstone University, NE; **Linda Berendsen**, Oakton Community College, IL; **Carol Berteotti; Grace Bishop**, Houston Community College, TX; **Perrin Blackman**, University of Kansas, KS; **Mara Blake-Ward**, Drexel University English Language Center, PA; **Melissa Bloom**, ELS; **Alexander Bochkov**, ELS, WA; **Marcel Bolintiam**, University of Colorado, CO; **Nancy Boyer**, Golden West College, CA; **T. Bredl**, The New School, NY; **Rosemarie Brefeld**, University of Missouri, MO; **Leticia Brereton**, Kingsborough Community College, NY; **Deborah Brooks**, Laney College, CA; **Kevin Brown**, Irvine Community College, CA; **Rachel Brown**, Center for Literacy, NY; **Tracey Brown**, Parkland College, IL; **Crystal Brunelli**, Tokyo Jogakkan Middle and High School, Japan; **Tom Burger**, Harris County Department of Education, TX; **Thom Burns**, Tokyo English Specialists College, Japan; **Caralyn Bushey**, Maryland English Institute, MD; **Gül Büyü**, Ankara University, Turkey; **Scott Callaway**, Community Family Centers, TX; **Adele Camus**, George Mason University, VA; **Nigel Caplan**, University of Delaware, DE; **Nathan Carr**, California State University, CA; **Christina Cavage**, Savannah College of Art and Design, GA; **Neslihan Çelik**, Özdemir Sabancı Emirgan Anatolian High School, Turkey; **Shelley Cetin**, Kansas City Kansas Community College, KS; **Hoi Yuen Chan**, University of Wyoming, WY; **Esther Chase**, Berwyn Public Library, IL; **Suzidilara Çınar**, Yıldırım Beyazıt University, Turkey; **Diane Cirino**, SUNY Suffolk, NY; **Cara Codney**, Emporia State University, KS; **Catherine Coleman**, Irvine Valley College, CA; **Jenelle Collins**, Washington High School, AZ; **Greg Conner**, Orange Coast Community College, CA; **Ewelina Cope**, The Language Company, PA; **Jorge Cordon**, Colegio Montessori, Guatemala; **Kathy Cornman**, University of Michigan, MI; **Barry Costa**, Castro Valley Adult and Career Education, CA; **Cathy Costa**, Edmonds Community College, WA; **Julia Cote**, Houston Community College NE, TX; **Eileen Cotter**, Montgomery College, MD; **Winnie Cragg**, Mukogawa Fort Wright Institute, WA; **Douglas Craig**, Diplomatic Language Services, VA; **Elizabeth Craig**, Savannah College of Art and Design, GA; **Ann Telfair Cramer**, Florida State College at Jacksonville, FL; **R. M. Crocker**, Plano Independent School District, TX; **Virginia Cu**, Queens Adult Learning Center, CT; **Marc L. Cummings**, Jefferson Community and Technical College, KY; **Roberta Cummings**, Trinidad Correctional Facility, CO; **David Dahnke**, Lone Star College-North Harris, TX; **Debra Daise**, University of Denver, CO; **L. Dalgish**, Concordia College, NY; **Kristen Danek**, North Carolina State University, NC; **April Darnell**, University of Dayton, OH; **Heather Davis**, OISE Boston, MA; **Megan Davis**, Embassy English, NY; **Jeanne de Simon**, University of West Florida, FL; **Renee Delatizky**, Boston University, MA; **Sonia Delgadillo**, Sierra Community College, NY; **Gözde Burcu Demirkul**, Orkunoglu College, Turkey; **Stella L. Dennis**, Longfellow Middle School, NY; **Mary Diamond**, Auburn University, AL; **Emily Dibala**, Bucks County Community College, PA; **Cynthia Dieckmann**, West Chester East High School, PA; **Michelle DiGiorno**, Richland College, TX; **Luciana Diniz**, Portland Community College, OR; **Özgür Dirik**, Yıldız Technical University, Turkey; **Marta O. Dmytrenko-Arab**, Wayne State University, MI; **Margie Domingo**, Intergenerational Learning Community, CO; **Kellie Draheim**, Hongik University, South Korea; **Ilke Buyuk Duman**, Sehir University, Turkey; **Jennifer Eick-Magan**, Prairie State College, IL; **Juliet Emanuel**, Borough of Manhattan Community College, NY; **David Emery**, Kaplan International Center, CA; **Patricia Emery**, Jefferson County Literacy Council, WI; **Eva Engelhard**, Kaplan International Center, WA; **Nancey Epperson**, Harry S. Truman College, IL; **Ken Estep**, Mentor Language Institute, CA; **Cindy Etter**, University of Washington, WA; **Rhoda Fagerland**, St. Cloud State University, MN; **Anrisa Fannin**, Diablo Valley College, CA; **Marie Farnsworth**, Union Public Schools, OK; **Jim Fenton**, Bluegrass Community Technical College, KY; **Lynn Filazzola**, Nassau BOCES Adult Learning Center, NY; **Christine Finck**, Stennis Language Lab; **Mary Fischer**, Texas Intensive English Program, TX; **Mark Fisher**, Lone Star College, TX; **Celeste Flowers**, University of Central Arkansas, AR; **Elizabeth Foss**, Washtenaw Community College, MI; **Jacqueline Fredericks**, West Contra Costa Adult Education, CA; **Patricia Gairaud**, San Jose City College, CA; **Patricia Gallo**, Delaware Technical Community College, DE; **Beverly Gandall**, Coastline Community College, CA; **Alberto Garrido**, The Community College of Baltimore County, MD; **Debbie Garza**, Park University, MO; **Karen Gelender**, Castro Valley Adult and Career Education, CA; **Ronald Gentry**, Suenos Compartidos, Mexico; **Kathie Madden Gerecke**, North Shore Community College, MA; **Jeanne Gibson**, Colorado State University, CO; **A. Elizabeth Gilfillan**, Houston Community College, TX; **Melanie Gobert**, The Higher Colleges of Technology, UAE; **Ellen Goldman**, West Valley College, CA; **Jo Golub**, Houston Community College, TX; **Maria Renata Gonzalez**, Colegio Montessori, Guatemala; **Elisabeth Goodwin**, Pima Community College, AZ; **John Graney**, Santa Fe College, FL; **Karina Greene**, CUNY in the Heights, NY; **Katherine Gregorio**, CASA de Maryland, MD; **Claudia Gronsbell**, La Escuelita, NY; **Yvonne Groseil**, Hunter College, NY; **Alejandra Gutierrez**, Hartnell College, CA; **Eugene Guza**, North Orange County Community College District, CA; **Mary Beth Haan**, El Paso Community College, TX; **Elizabeth Haga**, State College of Florida, FL; **Saeede Haghi**, Ozyegin University, Turkey; **Laura Halvorson**, Lorain County Community College, OH; **Nancy Hamadou**, Pima Community College, AZ; **Kerri Hamberg**, Brookline Community and Adult Education, MA;

Katia Hameg, L'Envol Des Langues, Québec, Canada; **Sunsook Han**, King Abdulaziz University, Saudi Arabia; **Aniko Harrier**, Valencia College, FL; **James M. Harris**, University of Texas-Pan American, TX; **Susan Haskins-Doloff**, Pratt Institute, NY; **Olcay Havalan**, Bursa Anadolu Erkek Lisesi, Turkey; **Marla Heath**, Sacred Heart University, CT; **Jean Hendrickson**, SUNY Stony Brook, NY; **Tracy Henninger-Willey**, Lane Community College, OR; **Emily Herrick**, University of Nebraska, NE; **Jan Hinson**, Carson Newman University, TN; **Lisa Hockstein**, SUNY Westchester, NY; **Sarah Hodge**, Defense Language Institute, TX; **Kristie Hofelich**, Brown Mackie College, KY; **Harry Holden**, North Lake Community College, TX; **Elke Holtz**, Escuela Sierra Nevada, Mexico; **Hirofumi Hosokawa**, Fukuoka Jo Gakuin University, Japan; **Elisa Hunt**, North Dakota State University, ND; **Lutfi Hussein**, Mesa Community College, AZ; **Curt Hutchison**, Leeward Community College, HI; **Elizabeth Iannotti**, LaGuardia Community College, NY; **Barbara Inerfeld**, Rutgers University, NJ; **Julie Ingber**, Columbia University, NY; **Debbie Janysek**, Victoria College, TX; **Joan Jarrett**, Feather River College, CA; **Shawn Jarvis**, St. Cloud State University, MN; **Justin Jernigan**, Georgia Gwinnett College, GA; **Melanie Jipping**, Tokyo International University of America, OR; **Catherine Jones**, Excellent Interpreting, CO; **Jackie Jones**, Wayne State University, MI; **Irene Juzkiw**, University of Missouri, MO; **Aysegul Liman Kaban**, Gedik University, Turkey; **Vivian Kahn**, Long Island University, NY; **Eleanor Kamataris**, Harris Middle School, TX; **Gursharan Kandola**, University of Houston, TX; **Emily Kaney**, Northern Michigan University, MI; **Krystal Kaplan**, Pace University, NY; **Linda Karlen**, Oakton Community College, IL; **Katherine Katsenis**, Lyceum Tutorial Services, LLC, CA; **Martha Kehl**, Ohlone College, CA; **Scott Keller**, Literacy Volunteers of Leon County, FL; **Robert Kelso**, Miami Dade College, FL; **Alicia N. Kenter**, City College of San Francisco, CA; **Paul Kern**, Green River Community College, WA; **Mignon Kery**, H-B Woodlawn Secondary Program, VA; **Candace Khanna**, Laney College, CA; **Joy Kidstry**, University of Phoenix, AZ; **Cynthia Kilpatrick**, The University of Texas at Arlington, TX; **Doe-Hyung Kim**, Georgia Gwinnett College, GA; **Kindra Kinyon**, Los Angeles Trade-Technical College, CA; **James Kirchner**, Macomb Community College, MI; **Renee La Rue**, Lone Star College-Montgomery, TX; **Marjorie Labe**, Montgomery County Community College, PA; **Peter LaFontaine**, Alexandria Adult Learning Center, VA; **Katie Land**, St. Giles International, Canada; **Renee Lane**, Oxnard Adult School, CA; **Alan Lanes**, The Higher Colleges of Technology, UAE; **Stephanie Lange**, Cuyamaca College, CA; **T. Jonathan Lathers**, Macomb Community College, MI; **Margaret Vera Layton**, University of Nevada, NV; **Susan Leckart**, Middlesex County College, NJ; **Suzanne Leduc**, The New America College, CO; **Judy Lee**, Central Connecticut State University, CT; **Joy Leventhal**, Cuyahoga Community College, OH; **Helen Lin**, University of Florida, FL; **Amy Lindstrom**, University of New Mexico, NM; **Gytis Liulevicius**, Wellstone International High School, MN; **Robyn Lockwood**, Stanford University, CA; **Victoria Loeb**, Houston Community College, TX; **Janet Long**, University of Missouri, MO; **Roland Lopez**, Santa Monica College, CA; **Alexandra Lowe**, Westchester Community College (SUNY), NY; **Mary Lozano**, Pierce College, CA; **Gail Lugo**, Trine University, IN; **Joanna Luper**, Liberty University, VA; **Jaime Lyon**, University of Northern Iowa, IA; **Doris Macdonald**, Northern Illinois University, IL; **Bridgette MacFarlane**, Brewster Technical Center, FL; **Kevin Mackie**, Austin Community College, TX; **Mercedes Martinez**, Global Language Institute, MN; **Tetiana Maslova**, Kyiv Polytechnic Institute, Ukraine; **Terry Masters**, American School for Women and Children, OH; **Maryann Matheny**, Campbellsville University, KY; **Jennifer Maxwell**, Daytona State College, FL; **Halina Mazurak**, Cleveland State University, OH; **Susan McAlister**, University of Houston, TX; **Luke McCarthy**, Norwalk Community College, CT; **Marlo McClurg**, Cosumnes River College, CA; **Deb McCormick**, Doña Ana Community College, NM; **Chris McDaniel**, Yale University, CT; **Bridget McDonald**, Independent Learning Services, MA; **Deborah McGraw**, Syracuse University, NY; **Lisa McHenry**, GEOS Languages Plus, CA; **Deirdre McMurtry**, University of Nebraska at Omaha, NE; **Aziah McNamara**, Kansas State University, KS; **Ellen Measday**, Middlesex County College, NJ; **Nancy Megarity**, Collin College, TX; **Diane Mehegan**, Harvard University, MA; **Michelle Merritt**, Harmony School of Innovation, TX; **Nila Middleton**, Lone Star College-Cypress, TX; **Brandon Mills**, ELS Language Center, ND; **Malgorzata Moll**, St. Louis Community College, MO; **Kathleen Molzan**, Cuyahoga Community College, OH; **Adrienne Monaco**, Erie 1 BOCES, NY; **Beth Montag**, University of Nebraska at Kearney, NE; **Elisabete Montero**, Val Hala escola de idiomas, Brazil; **Do Sik Moon**, Hanyang Cyber University, South Korea; **Diane Mora**, Johnson County Community College, KS; **Micheline Morena**, College of the Desert, CA; **Gloria Munson**, University of Texas, TX; **Gino Muzzatti**, Santa Rosa Junior College, CA; **Myo Myint**, Mission College, CA; **Kathy Najafi**, Houston Community College, TX; **Patricia Nation**, Miami Dade College, FL; **Elizabeth Neblett**, Union County College, NJ; **Karen Nelson**, Pittsburgh State University, PA; **Marley Nelson**, English Center USA, IL; **Anastasia Nizamova**, New York University, NY; **Sharon Nunn**, Englishdom; **Karla Odenwald**, Boston University, MA; **Tina O'Donnell**, Language Center International, MI; **Ann O'Driscoll**, Southern Oregon University, OR; **Donna Ogle**, Arkansas Tech University, AR; **Nastaran Ohadi**, Ganjineh Danesh, Iran; **Iris Oriaro**, Arkansas State University, AR; **Fernanda Ortiz**, University of Arizona, AZ; **Susan Osuch**, Englishworks, Inc., TX; **Kris Oswald**, Kansas State University, KS; **Stephanie Owens**, ELS, CT; **Gorkem Oztur**, Özel Manavgat Bahcesehir Anadolu Lisesi, Turkey; **Ümit Öztürk**, İzmir-Torbalı Anatolian Teacher Training High School, Turkey; **Murat Ozudogru**, Maltepe University, Turkey; **Marilyn Padgett**, Calhoun Middle School, NY; **Bilsev Pastakkaya**, Yalova University, Turkey; **Angela Pastore-Nikitenko**, Embassy English, CA; **Wendy Patriquin**, Parkland College, IL; **Irina Patten**, Lone Star College, TX; **Jennifer Paz**, Auburn University, AL; **Mary Peacock**, Richland College, TX; **Randi Lynn Peerlman**, Texas A&M University, TX; **Jeanne Peine**, University of Houston, TX; **Nuran Peker**, Nazilli High School, Turkey; **Susan Pelley**, Doña Ana Community College, NM; **Jorge Perez**, Southwestern College, CA; **Kim Perkins**, Boston University, MA; **William Phelps**, Southern Illinois University, IL; **Tom Pierce**, Central New Mexico Community College, NM; **Jennifer Piotrowski**, Language Center International, MI; **Carole Poppleton-Schrading**, Johns Hopkins University, MD; **Valentina Portnov**, Kingsborough Community College, NY; **Nancy Price**, University of Missouri, MO; **Catherine Ramberg**, Albany Adult School, CA; **Brian Ramey**, Sehir University, Turkey; **Steven Rashba**, University of Bridgeport, CT; **Victoria Reis**, Language Studies International, NY; **Amy Renehan**, University of Washington, WA; **Elizabeth Reyes**, Elgin Community College, IL; **Kathleen Reynolds**, Harper College, IL; **Tom Riedmiller**, University of Northern Iowa, IA; **Dzidra Rodins**, DePaul University, IL; **Ana Rodriguez**, Elliston School of Languages, FL; **Ann Roemer**, Utah State University, UT; **Margot Rose**, Pierce College, WA; **David Ross**, Houston Community College, TX; **Robert Ruddy**, Northeastern University, MA; **Peter Ruggiero**, Boston University, MA; **Phil Ruggiero**, The University of Missouri, MO; **Anne Sadberry**, The Language Company, OK; **Jessica Saigh**, University of Missouri-St. Louis, MO; **Irene Sakk**, Northwestern University, IL; **Kamila Salimova**, TGT, Russia; **Chari Sanchinelli**, Colegio Valle Verde, Guatemala; **Christen Savage**, University of Houston, TX; **Boutheina Sayadi**, Virtual University of Tunis, Tunisia; **Rosemary Schmid**, University of North Carolina, NC; **Diana Schoolman**, St. John's University, NY; **Myrna Schwarz**, La Roche College, PA; **Karen Schwenke**, Biola University, CA; **Dilek Batur Secer**, Toros University, Turkey; **Diana Sefchik**, Raritan Valley Community College, NJ; **Ertan Selimoglu**, Yildiz Technical University, Turkey; **Rene Serrano**, Universidad Nacional Autónoma de México, Mexico; **Gul Shamim**, Amir Sharifi, California State University, CA; **Caroline Sharp**, University of Maryland, MD; **Shixian Sheng**, Boston Chinatown Neighborhood Center, MA; **Oksana Shevchenko**, Horlivka Language School, Ukraine; **A. Shipley**, Academy of Art University, CA; **D. H. Shreve**, University of North Texas, TX; **Meire Silva**, Celebration Language Institute, FL; **Fiore Sireci**, Hunter College, NY; **Anita Teresa Smith**, Majan College, Oman; **Jacqueline Smith**, The New School, NY; **Jeff Smith**, Ohio Northern University, OH; **Lorraine Smith**, Queens College, NY; **Barbara Smith-Palinkas**, Hillsborough Community College, FL; **Kimberly Spallinger**, Bowling Green State University, OH; **James Stakenburg**, Rennert International, NY; **Katrina Tamura**, Palomar College, CA; **Dan Tannacito**, Indiana University of Pennsylvania, PA; **Jamie Tanzman**, Northern Kentucky University, KY; **Tara Tarpey**, New York University, NY; **Amy Tate**, Houston Community College, TX; **Rose Tauscher**, Skyline High School, TX; **Tamara Taylor**, University of North Texas-IELI, TX; **Cihan Tekin**, İMKB 24 Kasım Anadolu Lisesi, Turkey; **Kelly Tennison**, Roseville Area High School, MN; **Abby Thomas**, Northern Essex Community College, MA; **Brett Thomas**, Sacramento City College, CA; **Linda Thomas**, Lone Star College-Montgomery, TX; **Edith Thompson**, Purdy R-II School District, MO; **Sylwia Thorne**, Kent State University, OH; **Donna Tooker**, Miramar College, CA; **Beth Topping**, Auburn University, AL; **Carolyn Trachtova**, Webster University, MO; **William Trudeau**, Ohio Northern University, OH; **Kathy Truman**, Haverford High School, PA; **Karen Tucker**, Georgia Institute of Technology, GA; **Gretchen Twohig**, ASC English, MA; **Blanca Ugraskan**, Del Mar Community College, TX; **Serkan Ülgü**, Air Force Academy, Turkey; **Mecit Uzun**, Gaziosmanpaşa, Turkey; **Cynthia Valdez**, Palisade High, CO; **Kanako Valencia Suda**, De Anza College, CA; **Michelle Van de Sande**, Arapahoe Community College, CO; **Sharon Van Houte**, Lorain County Community College, OH; **Sara Vandenberg**, University of Colorado, CO; **Lillian Vargas**, University of Florida, FL; **Tara Vassallo**, Pace University, NY; **Stephanie Viol**, Palm House; **Kathleen Vodvarka**, University of Delaware, DE; **Kerry Vrabel**, GateWay Community College, AZ; **Carol Wachana**, ELS Language School; **Christine Waddail**, Johns Hopkins University, MD; **Christina Wade**, Liberty University, VA; **Wendy Walsh**, College of Marin, CA; **Colin Ward**, Lone Star College-North Harris, TX; **Mary Kay Wedum**, Colorado State University, CO; **Linda Wesley**, Pennsylvania State University, PA; **Lynne Wilkins**, The English Center, CA; **Betty Williams**; **Jeff Wilson**, Irvine Community College, CA; **Lori Wilson-Patterson**, Ivy Tech Community College, IN; **Kirsten Windahl**, Cuyahoga Community College, OH; **Aleasha Winters**, Lingo TEFL Language Institute, Costa Rica; **Jing Zhou**, Defense Language Institute, CA; **Yelena Zimon**, Fremont Adult School, CA; **Koraljka Zunic**, Grossmont College, CA

Contents

8 | Simple Past

Warm-Up 194

8.1 Positive Statements with the Simple Past 196

Spelling Note: *-ed* Verb Endings 197

Pronunciation Note: *-ed* Verb Endings 199

8.2 Simple Past Irregular Verbs 202

8.3 Negative Statements with the Simple Past 204

8.4 Questions with the Simple Past 206

8.5 Simple Past of *Be*: Positive and Negative Statements 209

Pronunciation Note: *Were* vs. *Weren't* 211

8.6 Simple Past Questions with *Be* 213

8.7 *There Was/There Were* 216

Wrap-Up 218

Grammar in Reading 218

Grammar in Speaking 219

8.8 Summary of the Simple Past 219

9 | Adjectives

Warm-Up 220

9.1 Placement of Adjectives 222

9.2 Adverbs of Degree 226

9.3 Questions with *How* + Adjective 231

9.4 Adjectives with *-er* and *More* 233

Spelling Note: Adjectives + *-er* 234

9.5 Using Adjectives to Compare 236

9.6 *Less* + Adjective 239

9.7 Adjectives with *-est* and *Most* 242

Spelling Note: Adjectives + *-est* 244

Usage Note: Prepositional Phrases after *-est/Most* Forms 246

Wrap-Up 248

Grammar in Reading 248

Grammar in Writing 249

9.8 Summary of Adjectives 249

10 | Future Forms

Warm-Up...250

10.1 **Positive and Negative Statements with *Be Going To***................252

Pronunciation Note: *Gonna*..253

Usage Note: *There Is/There Are Going to Be*............................255

10.2 **Future Time Expressions**..256

Usage Note: *I Think* and *Probably*..258

10.3 ***Yes/No* Questions and Short Answers with *Be Going To***..........259

10.4 ***Wh-* Questions with *Be Going To***....................................261

10.5 **Using the Present Progressive to Talk about Future Plans**..........263

10.6 ***May* and *Might* for Future Possibility**................................266

10.7 **Statements with *Will***..269

Pronunciation Note: *'ll*..271

10.8 **Questions with *Will***..274

Wrap-Up..276

Grammar in Reading..276

Grammar in Writing..276

10.9 **Summary of Future Forms**..277

11 | Modals I

Warm-Up..278

11.1 ***Can* for Ability and Possibility**......................................280

Usage Note: *Very Well*, *Pretty Well*, and *Not at All*....................281

Pronunciation Note: *Can* vs. *Can't*......................................282

11.2 **Questions with *Can***..283

11.3 ***Could* for Past Ability**..286

11.4 ***Be Able To***..290

11.5 **Permission with *Can*, *Could*, and *May* + *I/We***....................293

11.6 **Requests with *Can*, *Could*, and *Would* + *You***......................295

Usage Note: *Borrow*, *Have*, *Lend*, and *Give*..........................298

11.7 ***Would Like* for Desires, Offers, and Invitations**.....................299

Pronunciation Note: *Would You*..300

Usage Note: *Would Like* vs. *Want*..302

Pronunciation Note: *D'you Wanna*..302

Wrap-Up..304

Grammar in Reading..304

Grammar in Speaking..304

11.8 **Summary of Modals I**..305

12 | Modals II

Warm-Up..306

12.1 **Advice and Opinions with *Should* and *Shouldn't***....................308

Pronunciation Note: Stress with *Should* and *Shouldn't*................308

Usage Note: *I (Don't) Think* and *Maybe* in Statements with *Should*....310

12.2 **Questions with *Should***..311

12.3 **Suggestions with *Why Don't You/We***..................................314

12.4 **Necessity with *Have To* and *Need To***................................318

Pronunciation Note: *Have To* and *Need To*..............................319

12.5	Questions with *Have To* and *Need To*	321
12.6	Necessity and Prohibition with *Must*	323
	Usage Note: *Must Not* vs. *Not Have To*	324
12.7	Comparing Modals: *Can* vs. *Should* vs. *Have To*	326
	Wrap-Up	329
	Grammar in Reading	329
	Grammar in Speaking	330
12.8	Summary of Modals II	331

13 | Types of Verbs

	Warm-Up	332
13.1	Overview of Past, Present, and Future Verb Forms	334
	Usage Note: Action Verbs and Non-Action Verbs with Present Forms	336
13.2	Verb + Object	340
	Usage Note: Common Phrases with *Make* and *Take*	341
13.3	Verbs with No Object	343
	Usage Note: Verb + Object vs. No Object	344
13.4	Be and Other Linking Verbs	345
13.5	Comparing Different Types of Verbs	346
13.6	Be + Adjective Phrase + Preposition	348
13.7	Multi-Word Verbs (Part 1)	351
13.8	Multi-Word Verbs (Part 2)	353
	Wrap-Up	355
	Grammar in Reading	355
	Grammar in Writing	357
13.9	Summary of Types of Verbs	357

14 | Sentence Patterns

	Warm-Up	358
14.1	What Is a Sentence?	360
14.2	Subjects and Verbs in Questions	362
	Pronunciation Note: Statements as Questions	364
14.3	Common Sentence Patterns	365
	Usage Note: Placement of Adverbs of Frequency	368
14.4	Connecting Clauses with *And*, *But*, and *So*	370
14.5	Clauses with *Because*	373
14.6	Past and Present Time Clauses	375
14.7	Future Time Clauses	378
14.8	Using Sentence Patterns in Writing	381
	Wrap-Up	382
	Grammar in Reading	382
	Grammar in Writing	382
14.9	Summary of Sentence Patterns	383

Resources	R-2
Index	I-1

GO ONLINE For the Class Audio tracks and scripts, go to the Online Resources.

OXFORD
UNIVERSITY PRESS

198 Madison Avenue
New York, NY 10016 USA

Great Clarendon Street, Oxford, OX2 6DP, United Kingdom

Oxford University Press is a department of the University of Oxford. It furthers the University's objective of excellence in research, scholarship, and education by publishing worldwide. Oxford is a registered trade mark of Oxford University Press in the UK and in certain other countries.

First published in 2015
2019 2018 2017 2016 2015
10 9 8 7 6 5 4 3 2 1

Director, ELT New York: Laura Pearson
Head of Adult, ELT New York: Stephanie Karras
Publisher: Sharon Sargent
Senior Development Editor: Andrew Gitzy
Senior Development Editor: Rebecca Mostov
Development Editor: Eric Zuarino
Executive Art and Design Manager: Maj-Britt Hagsted
Content Production Manager: Julie Armstrong
Image Manager: Trisha Masterson
Image Editor: Liaht Pashayan
Production Artists: Elissa Santos, Julie Sussman-Perez
Production Coordinator: Brad Tucker

Special thanks to Electra Jablons and Rima Ibrahim for assistance with language data research.

ISBN: 978 0 19 402822 6 Student Book 1B with Online Practice Pack
ISBN: 978 0 19 402841 7 Student Book 1B as pack component
ISBN: 978 0 19 402879 0 Online Practice website

Printed in China

This book is printed on paper from certified and well-managed sources.

ACKNOWLEDGEMENTS

Illustrations by: Mark Duffin: 33, 34, 86 (desk), 127, 131, 135. Dermot Flynn: p. 110. John Kaufmann: p. 91. Jerome Mireault: p. 80, 132, 133, 151, 158, 159, 160. Joe Taylor: p. 8, 13, 19, 32, 33, 86, 87, 150, 157, 171, 181, 188, 205, 226, 229, 230, 253, 254, 287, 288, 293, 294, 295, 312, 313, 349, 350. 5W Infographics: p. 20, 21, 30, 35, 41, 82, 91, 128, 129, 138, 139, 144, 149, 169, 196, 201, 233, 239, 242, 256, 258, 266, 287, 314, 323, 324.

We would also like to thank the following for permission to reproduce the following photographs: Cover: blinkblink/shutterstock; back cover: lvcandy/Getty Images; global: Rodin Anton/shutterstock; p. 2 Jim Craigmyle/Corbis; p. 3 Robert Deutschman /Getty Images, NicoElNino/shutterstock; p. 4 paulista/shutterstock, Thomas Bethge/shutterstock, OUP/Digital Vision, Mark Hunt/Huntstock/Corbis, michaeljung/shutterstock.com, Nikada/istockphoto, OUP/Image Source, Beau Lark/Corbis, OUP/Corbis, OUP/Thinkstock, GSPhotography/Shutterstock.com; p. 5 EricFerguson/istockphoto, OUP/Okea, Corbis, adventtr/istockphoto, wavebreakmedia/shutterstock, Steve Debenport/Getty Images, OUP/Dennis Kitchen Studio, Inc., Chris Howey/shutterstock, Mrsiraphol/shutterstock, OUP/Mark Mason, mphillips007/istockphoto, Tom Wang/shutterstock; p. 10 Ocean/Corbis, OUP/Asia Images RF, OUP/Beau Lark, OUP/Luminis; p. 12 DJTaylor/shutterstock, CORBIS RM/CUSP/Inmagine, ostill/shutterstock, wavebreakmedia/shutterstock, Radius Images/Alamy; p. 14 Goodluz/shutterstock, Tetra Images/Alamy, Moncherie/Getty Images, Aletia/shutterstock, gchutka/istockphoto, Lithiumphoto/shutterstock; p. 18 OUP/Photodisc; p. 26 guvendemir/istock, Jack Hollingsworth/Getty Images; p. 27 OUP/LePZ, Monkey Business Images/shutterstock, Justin Kase zsixz/Alamy, Brejeq/istockphoto, Joe Gough/shutterstock; p. 28 imagebroker/Alamy; p. 29 Naho Yoshizawa/Aflo/Corbis, Africa Studio/shutterstock, age fotostock/SuperStock, Julia Davila-Lampe/Getty Images, JTB Photo/SuperStock, harikarn/shutterstock; p. 31 cynoclub/shutterstock, Andrew Scherbackov/shutterstock, photobank.ch/shutterstock, karen roach/shutterstock; p. 35 mozcann/istockphoto.com, Ziva_K/istockphoto, vasabii/shutterstock, skodonnell/istockphoto, pockygallery/shutterstock; p. 36 blyjak/istockphoto, Sergii Korolko/shutterstock, OUP/LePZ, haveseen/shutterstock, muharrem öner/istockphoto; p. 39 szefei wong/Alamy; p. 40 Cusp/SuperStock, Henry Westheim Photography/Alamy, Christian Kober/age fotostock; p. 42 r.nagy/shutterstock; p. 46 Johanna Goodyear/shutterstock, Martin Harvey/Getty Images, Craig Dingle/istockphoto, Gleb Tarro/shutterstock, OUP/Corel, OUP/Ingram; p. 47 kickstand/istockphoto, Willie B. Thomas/istockphoto, Stanislaw Pytel/getty Images, OUP/Cultura; p. 48 almgren/shutterstock, Hellen Sergeyeva/shutterstock; p. 49 OUP/Jim Reed, OUP/Digital Vision, OUP/Tom Wang, Minerva Studio/shutterstock; p. 50 Jose Luis Pelaez, Inc./Blend Images/Corbis, OUP/Fuse, bjdlzx/istockphoto, OUP/Digital Vision, Dmitry Kalinovsky/shutterstock, Monkey Business Images/shutterstock; p. 51Minerva Studio/shutterstock, BJI/Blue Jean Images/Getty Images, Alexander Raths/shutterstock, Dave & Les Jacobs/Blend Images/Corbis, Tony Gentile/Reuters/Corbis, Alina Solovyova-Vincent/Getty Images; p. 54 LWA/Getty Images, Radius Images/Alamy; p. 61 shaunl/istockphoto; p. 67 Montreal_Photos/istockphoto; p. 70 OUP/Digital Vision, OUP/Corbis, Konrad Mostert/shutterstock, OUP/Photodisc, Heiko Kiera/shutterstock, skilpad/istockphoto, Matthias Breiter/Minden Pictures/Corbis; p. 71 Ralph Lee Hopkins/National Geographic Society/Corbis; p. 74 arek_malang/shutterstock, Robert Crum/shutterstock, takayuki/shutterstock, ArtisticCaptures/istockphoto; p. 75 Monkey Business Images/shutterstock, Tetra Images/Alamy, Viktor Gladkov/shutterstock, Andrey Arkusha/shutterstock; p. 77 Don Mason/Blend Images/Corbis, Justin Horrocks/Getty Images, Jose Luis Pelaez, Inc./Blend Images/Corbis, Keith Brofsky/Blend Images/Corbis, wavebreakmedia/shutterstock; p. 78 bumihills/shutterstock, OUP/Ocean, Planet Observer/Universal Images Group/Getty Images, Noppasin/shutterstock.com, Blaine Harrington III/Corbis, OUP/Photodisc, Marco Rubino/shutterstock, Celia Mannings/Alamy, Roger De La Harpe; Gallo Images/Corbis, Steven Vidler/Eurasia Press/Corbis; p. 80 Fine Art Photographic Library/SuperStock, Corbis; p. 81 Corbis; p. 83 Yagi Studio/Getty Images, KidStock/Blend Images/Corbis, Hero Images/Corbis, Ocean/Corbis; p. 87 Harvey Silikovitz; p. 88 Rodrigo Reyes MarÃn/AFLO/Nippon News/Corbis; p. 94 OUP/Photodisc; p. 97 Juniors Bildarchiv GmbH/Alamy, blickwinkel/Alamy; p. 102 Olympus/shutterstock, Jinxy Productions/Blend Images/Corbis, Hans-Peter Merten/Robert Harding World Imagery/Corbis, Chad McDermott/shutterstock, Spiderplay/Getty Images, Pichi/shutterstock; p. 103 Klaus Tiedge/Corbis, JDC/LWA/Corbis, Andersen Ross/Blend Images/Corbis, OUP/Mikhail Kokhanchikov, OUP/Andres Rodriguez, OUP/Photodisc, Ensuper/shutterstock, Ed Kashi/VII/Corbis; p. 106 OUP/Mark Mason, OUP/Gareth Boden, Enrique Soriano/Bloomberg/Getty Images; p. 107 lilly3/istockphoto, Jochen Tack/imagebrok/age fotostock; p. 109 Blaine Harrington III/Alamy, Li Muzi/Xinhua Press/Corbis; p. 112 Roobcio/shutterstock, OUP/Photodisc, sandr2002/shutterstock, OZaiachin/shutterstock, Amos Chapple/Getty Images; p. 113 Ted Dayton Photography/Beateworks/Corbis, Hoberman Collection/UIG via Getty Images, Clive Rose/Getty Images; p. 117 Lena Pantiukh/shutterstock; p. 123 Mikulich Alexander Andreevich/shutterstock; p. 124 OUP/Imge Source, djem/shutterstock; p. 136 Jose Luis Pelaez Inc/Blend Image/Blend Images/Corbis, David Wall Photo/Getty Images, Mark Bolton/Getty Images, chsherbakova yuliya/shutterstock; p. 137 JAG IMAGES/age fotostock, Don Mason/Blend Images/Corbis, Turba/Corbis, Erik Mandre/shutterstock, Corepics VOF/shutterstock, Aaron Amat/shutterstock; p. 148 Adam Pass Photography/cultura/Corbis, OUP/Vulkanette; p. 152 OUP/Photodisc; p. 153 Christophe Testi/shutterstock, Vector Market/shutterstock; p. 164 Michael Hall Photography Pty Ltd/Corbis, Stephen Stickler/Getty Images, lithian/shutterstock; p. 165 Sergey Nivens/shutterstock, John Fedele/Getty Images, PhotoTalk/istockphoto, jcarillet/istockphoto; p. 167 michaeljung/shutterstock, urbandevill/istockphoto, Stephen Dalton/Getty Images; p. 172 Brent Winebrenner/Getty Images; p. 185 Reuters/STR New; p. 190 Beau Lark/Corbis, Marcelo Santos/Getty Images, Ariel Skelley/Getty Images, Image Source/Getty Images, Alexander Raths/shutterstock, Moxie Productions/Blend Images/Corbis; p. 191 www.joshneufeld.com. p. 194 P. Coen/Corbis, antos777/shutterstock, Ferenc Szelepcsenyi/shutterstock.com; p. 195 OUP/Photodisc, zhu difeng/shutterstock.com, ImageegamI/istockphoto, Cavan Images/Getty Images; p. 197 cinemafestival/shutterstock.com(2), K2 images/shutterstock.com, DFree/shutterstock.com, Helga Esteb/shutterstock.com, Featureflash/shutterstock.com, LaCameraChiara/shutterstock.com, JStone/shutterstock.com; p. 203 OUP/Dave Crombeen, mbbirdy/istockphoto; p. 204 Ansis Klucis/shutterstock, Myibean/shutterstock, Mike Flippo/shutterstock; p. 211 Underwood & Underwood/Corbis, Oxford Science Archive/Print Collector/Getty Images; p. 212 Erik Isakson/Tetra Images/Corbis; p. 215 Eric Audras/Onoky/Corbis; p. 218 Michael Ochs Archives/Getty Images, Paul Schutzer/Time Life Pictures/Getty Images, Chris Jackson/Getty Images; p. 220 OUP/StockbrokerXtra, SIHASAKPRACHUM/shutterstock, Jean-Paul Ferrero/age fotostock, Tracy Packer Photography/Getty Images; p. 221 John Harper/Corbis, OUP/Songquan Deng, OUP/Corbis/Digital Stock, Whiteway/istockphoto, isoft/istockphoto; p. 222 David Haring/DUPC/Getty Images; p. 223 Mint Images - Frans Lanting/Getty Images, Kazakov Maksim/shutterstock, Christian Musat/shutterstock, Eric Isselee/shutterstock; p. 224 Steve Hickey/Alamy, Sean Nel/shutterstock, LianeM/shutterstock, ollyy/shutterstock; p. 225 OUP/Purestock, Ocean/Corbis, Phase4Studios/shutterstock; p. 230 Foodio/shutterstock; p. 232 OUP/Photodisc; p. 234 OUP/Ingram, Kletr/shutterstock; p. 235 Todor Tsvetkov/istockphoto; p. 240 Jorge Salcedo/shutterstock; p. 241 karamysh/shutterstock, Patrick Poendl/shutterstock.com; p. 243 Tuan Tran/Getty Images; p. 245 TommL/istockphoto, Petar Chernaev/istockphoto; p. 248 Nick Tzolo/Getty Images, Myroslava/shutterstock; p. 250 OUP/LePZ, OUP/Digital Vision, littleny/shutterstock.com, OUP/Blue Jean Images; p. 251 IS_ImageSource/istockphoto, Goodluz/shutterstock, Terrafugia Inc., Universal Images Group Limited/Alamy, Jupiterimages/Getty Images, Pinkcandy/shutterstock; p. 254 Syda Productions/shutterstock, Joshua Dalsimer/Corbis, Tifonimages/shutterstock, James Baigrie/Getty Images, Konstantin Sutyagin/shutterstock, Stokkete/shutterstock, Thomas Kienzle/Getty Images, Corbis; p. 255 Kim Nguyen/shutterstock; p. 262 Flashon Studio/shutterstock; p. 265 Ron Niebrugge/Alamy; p. 268 OUP/HAWKEYE, OJO_Images/istockphoto, Michael Pettigrew/shutterstock, Fotokostic/shutterstock; p. 270 IS_ImageSource/istockphoto; p. 271 Margoe Edwards/shutterstock; p. 276 iconeer/istockphoto; p. 278 Dirk Lindner/Getty Images, Petrified Collection/Getty Images, Tomas Rodriguez/Corbis, incamerastock/Alamy; p. 279 Izabela Habur/Getty Images, Johner Images/Johnér Images/Corbis, mediaphotos/istockphoto, skynesher/istockphoto; p. 280 sampics/Corbis, Christian Hartmann/Reuters/Corbis, Liao Yujie/xh/Xinhua Press/Corbis, Smirnov Vladimir/ITAR-TASS Photo/Corbis, Jewel Samad/AFP/GettyImages, Alex Livesey/Getty Images, Richard Heathcote/Getty Images, PCN/Corbis; p. 284 BlueSkyImage/shutterstock, Marko Tomicic/shutterstock, Art Wolfe/Getty Images, Gillian Holliday/shutterstock, dmvphotos/shutterstock, OUP/Digital Stock, Brian J. Skerry/National Geographic Creative, c-foto/istockphoto, OUP/White, OUP/Amazon-Images, Anton_Ivanov/shutterstock, OUP/Corbis; p. 287 Bloomimage/Corbis, mandygodbehear/istockphoto; p. 291 Josie Elias/Getty Images, Dimitrios Kambouris/Getty Images, Jerry Lodriguss/Science Photo Library; p. 297 Image Source/Getty Images, YinYang/Getty Images, Dmitry Kalinovsky/shutterstock, DAJ/Getty Images; p. 302 Alex Mares-Manton/Getty Images, OJO_Images/istockphoto; p. 304 REUTERS/Danny Moloshok; p. 306 Joshua Blake/Getty Images, Benoit Daoust/shutterstock, Paul Bradbury/Getty Images, Kris Ubach and Quim Roser/cultura/Corbis; p. 307 Topic Photo Agency/Corbis, wavebreakmedia/shutterstock, Bogdan VASILESCU/shutterstock, Fuse/Getty Images; p. 319 Andresr/shutterstock; p. 325 Baloncici/shutterstock, Sonja Pacho/Corbis, pio3/shutterstock, Steve Debenport/istockphoto; p. 326 AP Photo/Paul Sakuma; p. 327 Martina I. Meyer/shutterstock; p. 329 koh sze kiat/shutterstock, Gareth Brown/Corbis; p. 332 Popperfoto/Getty Images, XXLPhoto/shutterstock, olaser/istockphoto, Courtesy Aptera/ZUMA Press/Newscom; p. 333 VOISIN/phanie/Phanie Sarl/Corbis, Justin Horrocks/istockphoto, Subbotina Anna/shutterstock, Jose Azel/Aurora Photos/Corbis, Jess Yu/shutterstock, OJO_Images/istockphoto; p. 336 Bettmann/Corbis; p. 337 Hulton Archive/Getty Images, CB2/ZOB/WENN.com/Newscom; p. 339 Radharc Images/Alamy, muzsy/shutterstock.com; p. 343 wavebreakmedia/shutterstock; p. 345 urii Kachkovskyi/shutterstock; p. 351 INTERFOTO/Alamy, OUP/Photographers Choice, OUP/Art Explosion; p. 356 Gino's Premium Images/Alamy; p. 358 Helen King/Corbis, Photodisc/Getty Images; p. 359 HamsterMan/shutterstock, Grisha Bruev/shutterstock; p. 361 Leonello Calvetti/Stocktrek Images/Corbis, Pablo Corral Vega/Corbis; p. 362 Hurst Photo/shutterstock; p. 363 OUP/Photodisc; p. 366 Jenny Matthews/Alamy, Dennis MacDonald/Alamy; p. 369 Veronica Louro/shutterstock; p. 371 Danilo Ascione/shutterstock; p. 376 Science Source/Science Photo Library, Keystone Pictures USA/Alamy; p. 377 violetblue/shutterstock; p. 379 michaeljung/shutterstock.

8

Simple Past

WARM-UP 194

8.1 Positive Statements with the Simple Past 196

Spelling Note: *-ed* Verb Endings 197

Pronunciation Note: *-ed* Verb Endings 199

8.2 Simple Past Irregular Verbs 202

8.3 Negative Statements with the Simple Past 204

8.4 Questions with the Simple Past 206

8.5 Simple Past of *Be*: Positive and Negative Statements 209

Pronunciation Note: *Were* vs. *Weren't* 211

8.6 Simple Past Questions with *Be* 213

8.7 *There Was/There Were* 216

WRAP-UP 218

Grammar in Reading 218

Grammar in Speaking 219

8.8 Summary of the Simple Past 219

GO ONLINE

For the Unit Vocabulary Check, go to the Online Practice.

IN THIS UNIT, WE USE the simple past to:

Talk about past events and situations

1. We **cooked** dinner last night.

2. We **didn't do** the dishes.

3. I **went** to a concert last weekend.

4. There **were** a lot of people there.

5. My parents **moved** to Seattle ten years ago.

6. They **opened** a restaurant in 2012.

7. I **was** a shy child.

8. My sister **had** a lot of books.

Think about It Read these sentences. Check (✓) *True* or *False*.

	TRUE	FALSE
1. I cooked dinner last night.	☐	☐
2. I did the dishes last night.	☐	☐
3. I went to a concert last weekend.	☐	☐
4. I moved to a new city a few years ago.	☐	☐
5. I was a shy child.	☐	☐

8.1 Positive Statements with the Simple Past

A

To form the **simple past**, we add *-ed* or *-d* to the base form of most verbs*.

	BASE FORM	SIMPLE PAST FORM
1 I **worked** yesterday.	work	work**ed**
2 Jack **called** the doctor this morning.	call	call**ed**
3 We **enjoyed** the movie a lot.	enjoy	enjoy**ed**
4 You **exercised** three times last week.	exercise	exercise**d**

Notice: The simple past form is the same for all subjects (*I*, *he*, *they*, etc.).

*Simple past verbs that end in *-ed* are called **regular** simple past verbs. For irregular verbs, see Chart 8.2.

B

TIME EXPRESSIONS

We often use **time expressions** to refer to a specific time in the past.

MON	TUE	WED	THU	FRI	SAT	SUN
			last Thursday	a week **ago**	**last** weekend	
on Monday		two days **ago**	**yesterday** **last** night	TODAY		

	6:00–11:00 a.m.	1:00–5:00 p.m.	6:00–9:00 p.m.	10:00 p.m.
TODAY	**this** morning	**this** afternoon	**this** evening **tonight**	NOW

5 I **talked** to Leila **yesterday**.	**yesterday**	
6 She **applied** for the job **last week**.	**last** +	**night / week / Tuesday / weekend / month / year**
7 They **replied** **this morning**.	**this** +	**morning / afternoon / evening**
8 I **worked** **on Saturday**.	**on** +	**Wednesday / Friday / Saturday**
9 My sister **arrived** **at noon**.	**at** +	**8 a.m. / noon / 4:30**
10 I **finished** my paper **around 10:00**.	**around** +	**10:00 / noon / 6:45**

11 Mark **moved** to Boston **three years ago**.	**two days / a week / five years** + **ago**

GO ONLINE

1 | Noticing the Simple Past of Regular Verbs Underline the simple past verbs that end in *-ed*. Then complete each fact with the correct celebrity on page 197. [8.1 A]

BEFORE THEY WERE FAMOUS

1. _____Madonna_____ worked at a donut shop. She started her singing career in the 1980s.

2. _____ dressed up as a chicken for a fast-food restaurant. Now he's an actor.
   He performed[1] in the films *Fight Club* and *World War Z*.

   [1] **perform (past form *performed*):** to be in something such as a play, movie, or other show

3. _____ served ice cream at an ice cream shop. Now he's a politician[2].

4. _____ performed for children at birthday parties. He was a clown. Now he's an actor. He played Wolverine in the *X-Men* movies.

5. _____ studied business at the London School of Economics. He also worked in a hospital. He earned about $7.80 per hour. Now he's a singer. He joined the Rolling Stones (the band) in 1962.

6. _____ fixed airplanes for the U.S. Air Force. Now he's an actor. He starred[3] in *Driving Miss Daisy* and the *Batman* movies.

7. _____ worked at her mother's hair salon. Now she's a very famous singer.

8. _____ worked in a hotel. He carried people's suitcases to their rooms. Now he's an actor. He starred in *Top Gun, Minority Report,* and the *Mission: Impossible* movies.

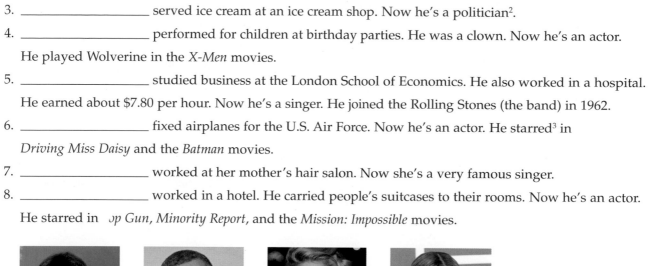

 Mick Jagger    Barack Obama    Madonna    Beyoncé

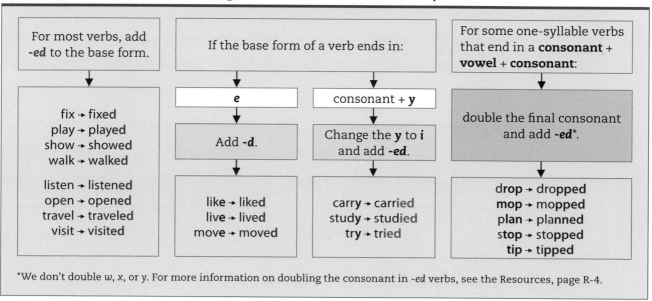

 Hugh Jackman    Tom Cruise    Brad Pitt    Morgan Freeman

Talk about It Which facts in Activity 1 surprise you?

2 | Spelling Note: *-ed* Verb Endings Read the note. Then do Activity 3.

For most verbs, add *-ed* to the base form.	If the base form of a verb ends in:		For some one-syllable verbs that end in a **consonant + vowel + consonant**:
↓	*e*	consonant + **y**	↓
fix → fixed play → played show → showed walk → walked	↓ Add *-d*.	↓ Change the **y** to **i** and add *-ed*.	double the final consonant and add *-ed**.
↓	↓	↓	↓
listen → listened open → opened travel → traveled visit → visited	like → liked live → lived move → moved	carry → carried study → studied try → tried	drop → dropped mop → mopped plan → planned stop → stopped tip → tipped

*We don't double *w, x,* or *y*. For more information on doubling the consonant in *-ed* verbs, see the Resources, page R-4.

[2] **politician:** someone who works in politics (government)

[3] **star (past form *starred*):** to be the main actor in a play or movie

3 | Spelling Regular Simple Past Verbs Write the simple past form of these verbs in the correct part of the chart below.

add	call	drop	finish	hurry	need	shave	stop	tip	wait
apply	carry	dry	fix	learn	plan	smile	study	try	want
arrive	cry	enjoy	grade	live	practice	start	talk	visit	watch
ask	decide	explore	help	mop	reply	stay	taste	vote	work

Add -*ed*	Add -*d*	Change the *y* to *i* and add -*ed*	Double the final consonant and add -*ed*
added			

Write about It Write three sentences about things you did recently. Use the verbs in the chart above and the time expressions in this box.

| last night | this morning | yesterday |

I called my parents last night.

4 | Using the Simple Past Complete this email with the simple past form of the verbs in parentheses.

`8.1 A`

To: Stella

Subject: Thanks for everything!

Hi Stella,

Thanks for letting me stay here this weekend. I ___*spilled*___ orange juice all over the carpet this
(1. spill)

morning. Sorry! I _____ to clean the carpet, but there's a stain⁴. I _____ the sofa
(2. try)   (3. move)

to cover the stain.

I _____ the kitchen this morning. I _____ the dishes and _____
(4. clean)   (5. wash)   (6. mop)

the floor. I _____ breakfast for you, too! It's in the oven. I _____ some eggs
(7. cook)   (8. drop)

behind the oven. Sorry! But I _____ the sink for you!
(9. fix)

I don't need a ride to the airport. I know you're tired. I _____ a taxi for 6 a.m. Oh, and I
(10. call)

_____ $40 from your wallet. I hope that's OK.
(11. borrow)

⁴ **stain:** a spot or a mark

I really _____ the weekend! Let's do this again sometime soon!
(12. enjoy)

See you soon,

Samantha

P.S. Someone _____ you yesterday. I don't remember who. Your boss, maybe? Also, a
(13. call)

package _____ for you two days ago. It's in the kitchen.
(14. arrive)

Talk about It Do you think Stella wants Samantha to come to her house again soon? Why or why not?

5 | Pronunciation Note: -ed Verb Endings Listen to the note. Then do Activity 6.

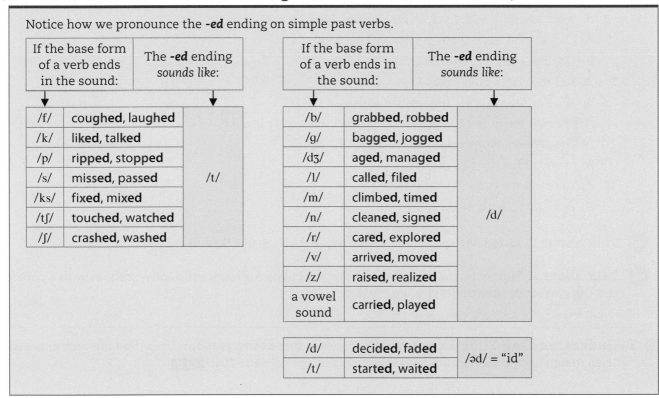

Notice how we pronounce the **-ed** ending on simple past verbs.

If the base form of a verb ends in the sound:		The **-ed** ending *sounds like:*
/f/	coughed, laughed	
/k/	liked, talked	
/p/	ripped, stopped	
/s/	missed, passed	/t/
/ks/	fixed, mixed	
/tʃ/	touched, watched	
/ʃ/	crashed, washed	

If the base form of a verb ends in the sound:		The **-ed** ending *sounds like:*
/b/	grabbed, robbed	
/g/	bagged, jogged	
/dʒ/	aged, managed	
/l/	called, filed	
/m/	climbed, timed	
/n/	cleaned, signed	/d/
/r/	cared, explored	
/v/	arrived, moved	
/z/	raised, realized	
a vowel sound	carried, played	

/d/	decided, faded	/əd/ = "id"
/t/	started, waited	

6 | Pronouncing Regular Simple Past Verbs Underline the simple past verbs in these conversations. Check (✓) the correct pronunciation for each *-ed* ending. **8.1 A**

	/t/	/d/	/əd/

1. A: How's work? ☐ ☐ ☐
   B: Not great. I <u>applied</u> for a new job last week.
   A: Oh, no! Why?
   B: I don't feel comfortable there. The people are unfriendly.

2. A: Is Marcus OK? ☐ ☐ ☐
   B: I think so. Why?
   A: He seemed sad this morning.

	/t/	/d/	/əd/

3. A: Are you ready for the history midterm?

    B: I think so. I studied all night long.

    A: Me too.

☐ ☐ ☐

4. A: How are you?

    B: I'm really busy. I started school last week.

☐ ☐ ☐

5. A: I'm so tired today.

    B: Why?

    A: I watched a movie until 3 a.m.

☐ ☐ ☐

6. A: Where's your car?

    B: It's at home. I walked to work today.

☐ ☐ ☐

7. A: Hey there. You're late.

    B: I know. I missed my bus this morning.

☐ ☐ ☐

8. A: Are you sick?

    B: Yeah, I have a cold. I stayed home from work today.

☐ ☐ ☐

9. A: I have good news. I passed my driving test!

    B: Oh, that's great! Congratulations!

☐ ☐ ☐

10. A: You're a great guitar player.

    B: Thanks. Do you play any instruments?

    A: I played the guitar in high school. I don't really play it now.

☐ ☐ ☐

11. A: The coffeemaker works!

    B: I know. I fixed it this morning.

☐ ☐ ☐

12. A: You're home early. It's only 3:00.

    B: Yeah, our class ended early today.

☐ ☐ ☐

Talk about It Listen and repeat the verbs from Activity 6. Check your answers.

Talk about It Now listen to the conversations in Activity 6. Practice the conversations with a partner. Use the correct pronunciation for -*ed* endings.

7 | Understanding Time Expressions Listen to these conversations. Underline the time expressions. Then match each conversation with the correct image on page 201. **8.1 B**

1. A: Do you want to watch this show with me?

    B: No, I watched it <u>last Monday</u>.

2. A: Do you want to go to the gym with me later?

    B: No, thanks. I worked out⁵ this morning.

3. A: You sound great! You're really good.

    B: Thanks! I practiced that song a lot yesterday.

4. A: Is your sister here?

    B: Yes, she arrived two days ago.

5. A: Do you want to work on our papers⁶ together?

    B: I finished my paper on Sunday night.

6. A: Are you hungry?

    B: No, my roommate cooked dinner for me tonight.

7. A: Oh, Kelly called me.

    B: When?

    A: Around 5:00.

8. A: Where do you live?

    B: I live in LA. I moved there two months ago.

---

⁵ **work out:** to do exercise, such as running, jogging, or lifting weights

⁶ **papers:** pieces of writing that you do for school

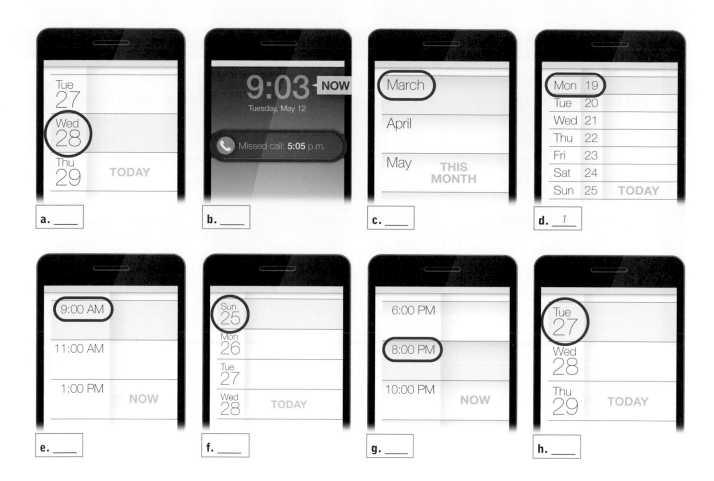

a. ____   b. ____   c. ____   d. _1_

e. ____   f. ____   g. ____   h. ____

Talk about It Tell a partner three interesting facts about your past. Use the phrases in this box or your own ideas. Use past time expressions.

| live in   move to   start English classes   study   travel to   work for |

"I lived in Dubai three years ago."

8 | Using Past Time Expressions Read these statements. Check (✓) *True* or *False*. 8.1 B

	TRUE	FALSE
1. I cleaned my bedroom yesterday.	☐	☐
2. I studied for a test three days ago.	☐	☐
3. I called a friend last night.	☐	☐
4. I started English lessons in 2013.	☐	☐
5. I visited a friend last weekend.	☐	☐
6. I arrived at school around 9:00 this morning.	☐	☐
7. I finished a book last month.	☐	☐
8. I washed dishes this morning.	☐	☐
9. I worked out on Monday.	☐	☐
10. I ate lunch at noon yesterday.	☐	☐

Write about It Rewrite the false statements above to make them true for you. Use different time expressions.

I cleaned my bedroom two weeks ago.

8.2 Simple Past Irregular Verbs

Many common verbs have **irregular simple past forms**. We don't add *-ed / -d* to these verbs.

A

BASE FORM	SIMPLE PAST FORM
be*	was / were
buy	bought
choose	chose
come	came
do	did
drink	drank
eat	ate

BASE FORM	SIMPLE PAST FORM
get	got
give	gave
go	went
have	had
make	made
say	said
take	took

BASE FORM	SIMPLE PAST FORM
hurt	hurt
put	put
quit	quit
read	read**

Notice: For some verbs, the simple past form is the same as the base form.

For more irregular verbs, see the Resources, page R-4.

*For more information about *was / were*, see Charts 8.5 and 8.6.
**The simple past form *read* is pronounced "red."

9 | Learning Irregular Verbs Listen and repeat the simple past verbs in Chart 8.2. **8.2 A**

Talk about It Work with a partner. Close your book. Your partner reads a base form verb from Chart 8.2. You say and write the simple past form. Take turns. Practice all of the verbs.

A: drink
B: drank

10 | Noticing Irregular Simple Past Forms Underline the irregular simple past verbs in this article. Then write each of these verbs in the correct part of the chart on page 203. (Look on page R-5 for more irregular verbs.) **8.2 A**

iPad App Saves Kidnapped Boy

A car thief stole a car and kidnapped[7] a boy in Harris County, Texas, earlier this week. At 6 p.m., the boy's father drove to a local store. He parked his car, and he left his five-year-old son in the car. The father went inside the store for a few minutes. At 6:05, he came out of the store. His car was gone.

Police arrived quickly. The father was lucky: he had his iPad. His iPhone was in the car. The father used the iPad app "Find My iPhone." The app gave him the location of the iPhone, and the father gave the information to the police. The police quickly found the boy and the car. They arrested[8] the thief. An ambulance took the boy to the hospital. Luckily, the boy was OK.

FYI

When we tell a story, we often use a time expression at the beginning of a sentence.

At 6 p.m., the boy's father drove to a local store.

[7] **kidnap (past form *kidnapped*):** to take a person away and hide them

[8] **arrest (past form *arrested*):** to take a person away to ask them questions about a crime (and maybe take them to jail)

Base form	Simple past form	Base form	Simple past form
1. be		6. go	
2. come		7. have	
3. drive		8. leave	
4. find		9. steal	*stole*
5. give		10. take	

Think about It Circle the regular simple past verbs in the article in Activity 10.

Talk about It Think about a news story you heard recently. Tell the story to a partner.

11 | Using Simple Past Forms Complete this story with the simple past form of the verbs in parentheses. Use regular and irregular past forms. [8.2 A]

THE PERFECT GIFT

Michael and Jane _____*got*_____ married five years ago.
(1. get)
Yesterday was their anniversary. Last week, Michael _____
(2. go)
shopping. He _____ to buy a special anniversary gift for Jane.
(3. want)
A few months ago, Jane _____ a new surfboard. So Michael
(4. buy)
_____ the perfect gift: a beach vacation in Aruba. But the
(5. choose)
tickets were very expensive. He _____ more money, so
(6. need)
he _____ to sell his new skis. He _____ an
(7. decide)   (8. put)
advertisement online. Someone _____ his skis
(9. buy)
that day, and Michael _____ the plane tickets.
(10. buy)
      Jane _____ to get a special anniversary gift for Michael,
(11. want)
too. Two weeks ago, she _____ Michael's brother Tom for
(12. ask)
ideas. Tom _____, "I know Michael wants to go skiing. He
(13. say)
bought new skis last month." Jane _____ the idea. So she
(14. like)
_____ the perfect gift: a skiing vacation in the Swiss Alps.
(15. choose)
But she _____ more money. . . .
(16. need)

a surfboard

skis

Write about It Write an ending to the story about Michael and Jane above. Write three to five sentences. Then share your ending with a partner. Use the verbs in this box or your own ideas.

ask	buy	give	sell

Think about It Put these events from Activity 11 in order. Add the time expressions from the box.

___ Michael sold his new skis _____.

___ Michael bought new skis _____.

_1_ Michael and Jane got married _____.

___ Jane asked Tom for ideas _____.

___ Jane bought a new surfboard _____.

last week
two weeks ago
last month
a few months ago
five years ago

8.3 Negative Statements with the Simple Past

A

For most verbs, we use *did not* (*didn't*) + the **base form of a verb** to form negative statements with the simple past.

subject	*did + not*	base form verb
I He She It You We They	did not didn't	go. work. start. finish.

Didn't is a **helping verb**.

This is the **main verb**.

WARNING! Don't use *didn't* + a past form of the main verb.

✓ I didn't work yesterday.

✗ I didn't **worked** yesterday.

GO ONLINE

🔊 **12 | Writing Negative Simple Past Statements** Listen and complete these conversations with the missing words. **8.3 A**

I DIDN'T DO IT!

1. A: Where's my soda? It was in the break room.

   B: I don't know. I _____*didn't drink*_____ it.

2. A: Someone left the TV on all night.

   B: Not me. I _____ TV last night.

3. A: Oh, no! My favorite mug is broken.

   B: I _____ it. I never use your mug.

4. A: There's a dent in the car door. What happened?

   B: We _____ the car! I think Dad drove it.

5. A: Someone ate my yogurt again! Where's Susan? She always eats my food.

   B: Susan _____ it. I think Sheila ate it. Go ask her.

6. A: Alex made a mess in the kitchen.

   B: He _____ it. He never cooks.

7. A: Someone used all my laundry detergent.

   B: I _____ it. I think José did laundry yesterday.

8. A: What happened to my shoes? They're really dirty.

   B: I don't know. I _____ them. They don't fit me.

a broken mug

a dent

laundry detergent

9. A: Where's my money? I'm missing $50.

   B: I _____ it! I promise.

10. A: Sam, there's a pizza delivery person at the door.

   B: I _____ a pizza. It was probably Jake. He's upstairs.

Talk about It Who are the people in the conversations in Activity 12—roommates, family members, or co-workers? Share your ideas with a partner.

13 | Writing Positive and Negative Simple Past Statements Look at the pictures. Complete the sentences with the positive or negative simple past form of the verbs in parentheses. 8.3 A

WHAT HAPPENED YESTERDAY?

1. Alex _____cleaned_____ the floor yesterday.
   (clean)
2. He _____ the laundry.
   (do)
3. He _____ the car.
   (wash)

4. Kylie _____ last night.
   (study)
5. She _____ asleep.
   (fall)
6. She _____ her homework.
   (finish)

7. Max _____ dinner last night.
   (cook)
8. He _____ chicken and rice.
   (make)
9. He _____ the dishes.
   (do)

Write about It Write three things that you did yesterday and three things that you didn't do yesterday. Use the verbs in this box or your own ideas. Then share your sentences with a partner.

call	cook	eat	see	talk to
clean	do	go	study	wash

I called my uncle. I didn't talk to my cousin.

8.4 Questions with the Simple Past

A

For most verbs, we use **did** to form *yes/no* questions and short answers with the simple past.

YES/NO QUESTIONS

	did	subject	base form verb	
1		I	forget	something?
2		you	work	last night?
3		he	start	school this week?
4	Did	she	go	out last night?
5		it	rain	yesterday?
6		we	pass	the test?
7		they	take	a vacation in June?

SHORT ANSWERS

	subject	*did (+ not)*
Yes,	you / I / he / she / it / you / we / they	did.
No,		didn't.

OTHER WAYS TO ANSWER *YES/NO* QUESTIONS

We often answer *yes/no* questions with more information.

8 A: Did you go out last night?
B: **No, I stayed home.**

9 A: Did she pass the test?
B: **Yes, she got an A!**

WARNING! Don't use *did* + a past form of the main verb.

✓ Did they go home? ✗ Did they **went** home?

B

WH- QUESTIONS

	wh- word	*did*	subject	base form verb	
10	What		I	forget?	
11	Where		you	go	last night?
12	When	did	he	come	home?
13	Why		she	arrive	late?
14	How		it	break?	
15	Who		they	go	with?

16 A: **What did** you **do** last night?
B: I went out with friends.

17 A: **When did** you **come** home?
B: Around midnight.

18 A: **Who did** they **go** with?
B: They went with Mina and Kim.

19 A: **How did** they **get** home?
B: They took a cab.

WH- QUESTIONS ABOUT THE SUBJECT

In these questions, *what* and *who* are the subject. We use just the **simple past form** of the main verb. We DON'T use *did*.

	wh- word	simple past verb	
20	What	**happened?**	
21	Who	**ate**	the last cookie?

14 | Forming *Yes/No* Questions with the Simple Past Complete these *yes/no* questions with the subject *you* and the verbs in parentheses. Use the simple past. `8.4 A`

SOCIAL LIFE

1. _Did you talk_ to your parents yesterday? (talk)
2. _____ your friends last night? (see)
3. _____ time with a friend last Saturday? (spend)

FOOD

4. _____ any vegetables today? (eat)
5. _____ coffee this morning? (drink)
6. _____ dinner last night? (cook)

TRAVEL

7. _____ the country last year? (leave)
8. _____ a vacation last summer? (take)
9. _____ a cousin last month? (visit)

SCHOOL

10. _____ any schoolwork last weekend? (do)
11. _____ something interesting last week? (learn)
12. _____ with a friend last week? (study)

FREE TIME

13. _____ a movie last weekend? (see)
14. _____ TV last night? (watch)
15. _____ something interesting yesterday? (read)

F Y I

Remember: Some questions and negative statements use a form of **do** as a **helping verb** and a **main verb**.

A: **Did** you **do** your homework last night?

B: No, I **didn't do** it yet.

Talk about It Ask and answer the questions above with a partner. Use short answers.

1. A: *Did you talk to your parents yesterday?*   B: *Yes, I did.*

Write about It Write positive and negative sentences about your partner.

Anna called her parents yesterday. She didn't talk to her sister.

15 | Forming *Wh-* Questions with the Simple Past Complete these conversations with the words in parentheses and the *wh-* words in the box. Then listen and check your answers. `8.4 B`

A PARENT'S QUESTIONS

1. A: _What did you do_ last night? (you/do)

   B: I went out with some friends.

2. A: _____? (you/go)

   B: We went downtown.

3. A: _____ there? (you/get)

   B: We took a taxi.

how	where
what	who
when	why

4. A: _____ out with? (you/go)

   B: Marissa and Clara.

5. A: _____ a taxi? (you/take)

   B: Because Marissa's car is in the shop⁹.

6. A: _____ home? (you/come)

   B: Around 11:30.

7. A: _____ this morning? (call)

   B: Clara called.

8. A: _____? (she/call)

   B: Because she left her wallet in my backpack.

how	where
what	who
when	why

Think about It Which question in Activity 15 is a question about
the subject (the subject is *who* or *what*)?

FYI

In conversation, we
can use prepositions
like **with**, **to**, or **about**
after the main verb in
wh- questions.

Who did you go **with**?

Who did you talk **to**?

What did you talk **about**?

🔊 **16 | Asking Questions with the Simple Past** Use the words in each box to complete the questions in
these conversations. Add *did* where necessary. Then listen and check your answers. `8.4 A–B`

1. A: _Who did you call_____ this morning?

   B: I called Gina. I didn't understand our homework.

2. A: _____ late last night?

   B: Eric. He lost his keys.

3. A: _____ last night?

   B: We went out with Sarah. We're exhausted!

| what/you/do |
| who/called |
| who/you/call |

4. A: _____ to Sam yesterday?

   B: No. Why?

   A: He has some interesting news.

5. A: _____ anywhere last weekend?

   B: Yeah, we went to San Diego. It was a lot of fun.

6. A: _____ last weekend?

   B: We went to the beach.

| where/you/go |
| you/go |
| you/talk |

7. A: I think I lost my phone.

   B: _____ it last?

   A: About an hour ago.

8. A: Are you OK?

   B: No, I think I hurt my leg.

   A: _____?

9. A: Guess what? My car broke down¹⁰ again.

   B: _____ to work?

   A: A friend gave me a ride.

| how/you/get |
| what/happened |
| when/you/have |

Talk about It Continue conversations 7–9 above with a partner.

⁹**in the shop:** (for a car) getting fixed   ¹⁰**break down (past form *broke down*):** to stop working

17 | Error Correction Find and correct the errors. (Some sentences may not have any errors.)

1. I ~~go~~ *went* home early yesterday.

2. Did you went to class yesterday?

3. Did Mike had fun?

4. How you do on your English test?

5. Marta didn't came to class this morning.

6. I didn't finish my homework.

7. Where did you get those shoes?

8. Stella buy a new car last week.

9. When did Stella arrive?

10. Why you get home so late?

11. We took Carla out to dinner last night.

12. Who gave you that book?

13. Did you finished your homework?

14. Who you study with?

15. What happen to David?

16. They didn't paid for their food.

8.5 Simple Past of *Be*: Positive and Negative Statements

The verb **be** in the simple past has two forms: **was** and **were**.

A

POSITIVE STATEMENTS

	subject	was / were	
1	I		a salesperson.
2	He	**was**	tired all the time.
3	She		in class on Monday.
4	It		really fun.
5	You		lonely.
6	We	**were**	in New York.
7	They		students here.

NEGATIVE STATEMENTS

	subject	was / were + not	
8	I		a good swimmer.
9	He	**was not wasn't**	athletic.
10	She		home often.
11	It		very good.
12	You		with your friends.
13	We	**were not weren't**	in school.
14	They		happy.

15 The movie **was** great! I loved it.

16 We **were** out of town last week.
We went to my mother's house.

17 Sheila **wasn't** in class yesterday.
She didn't feel well.

18 I called you, but you **weren't** home.

 GO ONLINE

---

18 | Noticing the Past of *Be* Read this passage. Underline the positive and negative forms of *was* and *were*. `8.5 A`

○ ○ ○

Famous Artists of the Past

Andy Warhol <u>was</u> a popular American artist. He was born in 1928 and he died in 1987. His parents were immigrants[11] from Slovakia. As a child, Warhol wasn't very healthy. He was sick a lot. He learned to draw when he was sick in bed. Warhol's art became very popular in the 1960s. His paintings were fun and very colorful. He often painted cans of soup, soda bottles, and famous people like Marilyn Monroe.

> **FYI**
>
> We use the phrase **was born in** to talk about someone's place or year of birth.
>
> Jack was born **in Korea**.
> (*in* + place)
>
> He was born **in 1994**.
> (*in* + year)

[11]**immigrants:** people who come from another country to live in a new country

Frida Kahlo was a famous Mexican artist. She was born in Mexico City in 1907. In 1925, she was in a terrible bus accident. Before the accident, Kahlo wasn't an artist. She wanted to be a doctor. But after the accident, she didn't walk for a few months. She started to paint. Her husband, Diego Rivera, was also an artist. Many of Kahlo's paintings were self-portraits[12]. She once said, "I paint myself because I am so often alone. . . ." She died in 1954. She was 47.

Johannes Vermeer and Vincent Van Gogh were both Dutch[13] painters. Vermeer painted in the seventeenth century[14]. Many of his paintings show everyday activities. For example, in one painting, a woman is writing a letter. In another painting, a woman is pouring milk into a bowl. Van Gogh was a painter in the nineteenth century. His paintings were very colorful. He often painted flowers and fields. He also painted many self-portraits. He made more than 2,000 paintings and drawings, but his paintings weren't popular. He sold only a few paintings. Today people pay millions of dollars for paintings by Vermeer and Van Gogh. But Vermeer and Van Gogh weren't wealthy at all. They were both poor all their lives.

Think about It Read these statements about the artists in the reading in Activity 18. Check (✓) *True* or *False*. Then rewrite the false statements to make them true.

	TRUE	FALSE
1. Andy Warhol's parents were from the United States.	☐	☑
2. Warhol's paintings were popular in the 1940s.	☐	☐
3. Kahlo was in a bus crash in 1925.	☐	☐
4. Many of Kahlo's paintings were self-portraits.	☐	☐
5. Van Gogh's work was popular in the nineteenth century.	☐	☐
6. Van Gogh and Vermeer were wealthy artists.	☐	☐

1. Andy Warhol's parents were from Slovakia.

Talk about It Go online. Find a painting by one of the artists in the reading in Activity 18. Describe the painting to a partner. Your partner tells you who made the painting.

A: This painting has eight pictures of Elvis Presley on a silver background.
B: Andy Warhol painted that.

Write about It Choose one the artists from this box. Go online to find information about the artist. Complete the sentences below. Share your information with the class.

Mary Cassatt	Abidin Dino	Kim Hong-do	Jackson Pollock
Salvador Dali	Nicola Facchinetti	Edvard Munch	Qiu Ying

1. _____ _____ born in _____ in _____.
   (artist's name)   (was / were)   (place)   (year)

2. _____ parents _____ from _____.
   (his / her)   (was / were)   (place)

3. _____ often painted _____.
   (he / she)

4. _____ died in _____.
   (he / she)   (year)

[12] **self-portraits:** pictures of yourself that you draw or paint
[13] **Dutch:** from the Netherlands (Holland)
[14] **century:** a 100-year period of time (The seventeenth century is the time period of 1601 to 1700.)

19 | Using the Simple Past of *Be* Complete these paragraphs with the correct past form of *be* or *be + not*. `8.5 A`

FAMOUS FIRSTS

The University of Al-Karouine and the University of Oxford

<u>   *were*   </u> two of the first universities in the world. The University
(1. be)

of Al-Karouine is in Morocco. Fatima al-Fihri started the university in the

year 859. The University of Oxford _____ the first university
(2. be)

in England. Students started learning there almost a thousand years ago.

Orville and Wilbur Wright _____ brothers. They invented[15]
(3. be)

the first successful airplane. Their first flight _____ very
(4. be / not)

long—it only lasted 12 seconds! Their first flight didn't get a lot of

attention. People _____ very excited about the airplane.
(5. be / not)

But later, the Wright brothers became famous around the world.

Neil Armstrong and Buzz Aldrin _____ the first people
(6. be)

on the moon. They landed on the moon in July 1969. Armstrong stepped

onto the moon first. But Aldrin _____ the first person to eat
(7. be)

or drink on the moon. The 1969 flight _____ their first time in
(8. be / not)

space. Armstrong's first space flight happened in March 1966. Aldrin's first

flight _____ in November 1966.
(9. be)

the Wright brothers

Neil Armstrong and Buzz Aldrin

Write about It Think of another "famous first" from history. Write a sentence with *was/were*.

20 | Pronunciation Note: *Were* vs. *Weren't* Listen to the note. Then do Activity 21.

Were and *weren't* often sound similar. Notice:

We usually DON'T stress *were*.	We usually stress *weren't*.
↓	↓
1 They were in CLASS yesterday.	**3** They WEREN'T in class yesterday.
2 We were LATE.	**4** We WEREN'T late.

21 | Pronouncing *Were* and *Weren't* Listen to these sentences. Circle the word you hear. `8.5 A`

1. We (were) / weren't) in Tokyo last spring.
2. You (were / weren't) in class on Monday.
3. Kim and I (were / weren't) roommates last year.
4. My brothers (were / weren't) born in Mexico.
5. The police (were / weren't) here this afternoon.
6. The stores (were / weren't) open on Sunday.

[15] **invent (past form *invented*):** to make or think of something for the first time

7. These shoes (were / weren't) very expensive.

8. Carl and Matthew (were / weren't) at soccer practice today.

9. My parents (were / weren't) born in China.

10. Eduardo and Josh (were / weren't) in my class last semester.

11. Alex and Jenna (were / weren't) here yesterday.

12. My classes (were / weren't) difficult this semester.

13. My neighbors (were / weren't) home this afternoon.

14. My roommates (were / weren't) really loud last night.

15. My family and I (were / weren't) in Asia last year.

16. My parents (were / weren't) on vacation last month.

Talk about It Listen to the sentences in Activity 21 again. Underline the stressed words in each sentence. Then practice the sentences with a partner.

"We were in <u>Tokyo</u> last spring."

Write about It Change sentences 9–16 above. Make them true for you. Then read your sentences to a partner.

My parents were born in Egypt.

22 | Writing about Your Past Think about your childhood. Complete these sentences with *was, wasn't, were,* or *weren't.* Then share your sentences with a partner. 8.5 A

AS A CHILD . . .

1. I _____ shy.

2. I _____ athletic[16].

3. I _____ a good student.

4. I _____ interested in languages.

5. I _____ in clubs at school.

6. My parents _____ home often.

7. My parents _____ strict[17].

8. My friends _____ similar to me.

9. My neighborhood _____ safe.

10. My school _____ close to my home.

Write about It Write four more simple past sentences about your childhood. Use subjects and verbs from these boxes or your own ideas. Write two sentences with *be* and two sentences with other verbs.

SUBJECT	VERB
My home	be (+ not)
My best friend(s)	

SUBJECT	VERB
I	(not +) like
	(not +) have

My best friends were Lisa and Ira.   *I didn't like bugs.*

Think about it In the sentences you wrote above, underline *not*. Where does *not* go in sentences with *be*? Where does *not* go in sentences with other verbs?

[16] **athletic:** good at sports   [17] **strict:** making people follow certain rules

212

8.6 Simple Past Questions with *Be*

A

YES/NO QUESTIONS

was / were subject

1	Was	I he she it	late?
2	Were	you we they	

SHORT ANSWERS

yes / no subject *was / were* (+ *not*)

3	Yes,	I he she it	was.
4	No,		wasn't.
5	Yes,	you we they	were.
6	No,		weren't.

7 A: **Was** the movie good?
B: Yes, it was. It was really funny!

8 A: **Were** your friends angry?
B: No, they weren't.

OTHER WAYS TO ANSWER *YES/NO* QUESTIONS

Remember: We often answer *yes/no* questions with more information. We can use *be* or other verbs in the answers.

9 A: Was Jack in class today?
B: **No, he was sick.**

10 A: Were you late this morning?
B: **No, I got here on time.**

B

WH- QUESTIONS

wh- word *was / were* subject

11	**Where**	was	Jim	yesterday*!*
12	**When**	were	you	in Tokyo?

13 A: **Where** was Jim yesterday?
B: He was at work.

14 A: **How** was the movie?
B: It was really good.

15 A: **What** was your favorite class last semester?
B: Psychology.

16 A: **How much** were the tickets?
B: They were $30 each.

17 A: **Why** were Karen and Will so late?
B: They got lost.

18 A: **Who** were they with?
B: They came with their parents.

WH- QUESTIONS ABOUT THE SUBJECT

> In these questions, the word **who** or **what** is the subject.
> In questions like these, we usually use the singular form **was**.

19 A: **Who** was there?   ✗ Who **were** there?
B: Luis and Carlos.

20 A: **What** was in the mail?
B: Just some bills.

C

PAST OF *BE* VS. OTHER VERBS

Remember: We often use *did* in questions with other verbs. We DON'T use *did* when the main verb is *be*.

BE		OTHER VERBS
✓**Was** she late?	✗ **Did** she late?	✓**Did** she **arrive**?
✓**Where were** you?	✗ **Where did** you?	✓**Where did** you **go**?

23 | Asking *Yes/No* Questions with *Was/Were* Write questions with *was* and *were* and the words in parentheses. Then listen and check your answers. `8.6 A`

    1. A: Hi. _*Were you asleep?*_____
                               (you / asleep)

       B: What? Uh, no. I wasn't asleep.

    2. A: _____
                     (your sister / here / last weekend)

       B: Yes, she just left.

       A: She's really messy!

    3. A: _____
                    (the test / hard)

       B: No, it was easy! I think I got an A!

    4. A: Hi. Sorry I missed your call. I was at a movie.

       B: That's OK. _____
                          (the movie / good)

       A: Yeah, I loved it!

    5. A: You look worried.

       B: I forgot to pay the electric bill again.

       A: Oh, no! _____
                     (your roommates / angry)

       B: Yes, they were. We have to pay a late fee.

    6. A: Hi, Jackie. _____
                       (you / in class / today)

       B: Yes, I was. Why?

       A: I missed class. I'm sick in bed. Can I borrow your notes?

    7. A: Hey! You found your wallet!

       B: Yes, finally.

       A: _____
                   (it / at / Gina's house)

       B: No, it was in my backpack. I just didn't see it!

    8. A: _____
                   (dinner / good)

       B: Yeah, it was great. I really like that new restaurant.

       A: What did you have?

       B: I had chicken. Here, I brought you some.

24 | Asking Questions with *Was/Were* Complete these conversations with simple past questions. Use *was/were* or a *wh-* word (*what, where, why, who,* or *how much*) + *was/were*. Then listen and check your answers. `8.6 A–B`

AT A JOB INTERVIEW

    1. A: _*Were*_____ you a manager at your last company?

       B: Yes, I was.

2. A: _____ your work responsibilities?

   B: I worked at the front desk of the hotel. I helped
      guests check in, and I answered their questions.

3. A: _____ you unemployed[18] for two years?

   B: I was in school.

check in

TALKING TO A FRIEND

4. A: _____ you last weekend?

   B: I was at the beach.

5. A: _____ there with you?

   B: James and Rico and a few other people.

6. A: _____ it fun?

   B: Yes, it was great!

TALKING TO A ROOMMATE

7. A: _____ the electric bill?

   B: It was $200! We need to use less electricity.

8. A: _____ the problem with the door?

   B: The lock was broken. But it's working now.

9. A: _____ the landlord here?

   B: He needed to fix the sink.

Talk about It Choose three of the questions in Activity 24. Give a different answer.

25 | Questions with *Did* and *Was/Were* Complete these questions with *did* or *was/were*. Think about your life at ages 5, 10, and 13. Write your answers in the chart. ▐ 8.6 C ▌

THE WAY YOU WERE

	At age 5	At age 10	At age 13
1. What ___*did*___ you do for fun?			
2. What _____ your three favorite foods?			
3. What food _____ you hate?			
4. Who _____ your best friends?			
5. What _____ your favorite hobbies?			
6. What _____ your favorite song?			
7. What _____ your favorite book?			
8. What _____ you afraid of?			

---

[18] **unemployed:** without a job

	At age 5	At age 10	At age 13
9. Where _____ you go on vacation?			
10. What _____ you do on the weekends?			
11. What _____ you do in the summer?			
12. _____ you like vegetables?			
13. _____ you a picky eater[19]?			
14. _____ you quiet?			
15. _____ you have a pet?			
16. _____ you ride a bike?			

Talk about It Ask and answer the questions in Activity 25 with a partner. Which answers change from age 5 to 10 and 13? Which answers stay the same?

A: *What did you do for fun at age 5?*
B: *I played with my cousins a lot.*

Write about It Compare your life in the past with your life now. Change the questions in Activity 25 to simple present questions. Ask and answer your questions with a partner.

What do you do for fun?

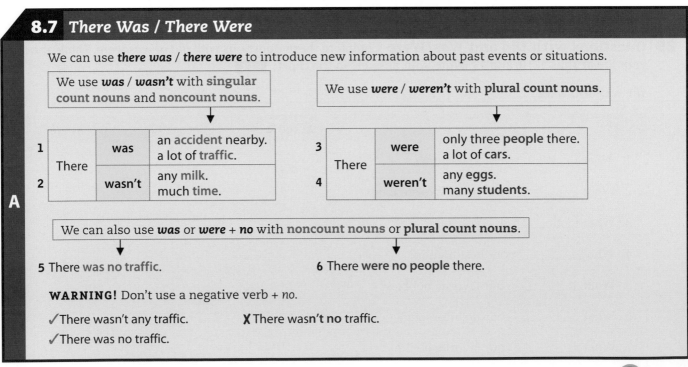

8.7 There Was / There Were

We can use **there was / there were** to introduce new information about past events or situations.

We use **was / wasn't** with **singular count nouns** and **noncount nouns**.

1	There	was	an **accident** nearby. / a lot of **traffic**.
2		wasn't	any **milk**. / much **time**.

We use **were / weren't** with **plural count nouns**.

3	There	were	only three **people** there. / a lot of **cars**.
4		weren't	any **eggs**. / many **students**.

A

We can also use **was** or **were** + **no** with **noncount nouns** or **plural count nouns**.

5 There **was no traffic**.   6 There **were no people** there.

WARNING! Don't use a negative verb + *no*.

✓There **wasn't** any traffic.   ✗There **wasn't no** traffic.
✓There **was no** traffic.

[19]**picky eater:** someone who doesn't like many foods

26 | Using *There Was* and *There Were* Complete these conversations with *there was, there wasn't, there were,* or *there weren't.* Then listen and check your answers. **8.7 A**

TALKING ABOUT EVENTS

1. A: _There was_____ a great event at the museum last weekend.

    B: I know. I tried to go to it.

    A: You didn't go?

    B: No, I got there too late. _____ any tickets left.

2. A: Did you go to the free concert?

    B: Yeah.

    A: How was it?

    B: It was really crowded. I think _____ about 20,000 people there.

    _____ no seats!

3. A: Where were you tonight?

    B: I was at a restaurant opening. My friend John opened a new restaurant.

    A: Oh, that's cool. How was it?

    B: It was great. _____ a lot of delicious food. _____

    a band, too.

4. A: Hey, did you do anything last weekend?

    B: Yeah, _____ an arts and crafts fair[20] downtown.

    A: How was it?

    B: It was really fun. _____ over 100 vendors[21]. I bought some homemade

    soap and a handmade sweater.

5. A: How was your sister's wedding?

    B: It was beautiful. It was in a garden, so _____ flowers everywhere.

    My sister was really happy. How was your dinner?

    A: It was terrible. My oven broke, so _____ much food. Everyone left early.

6. A: Did you enjoy your trip to France?

    B: Not really. We don't speak any French, so we decided to take a bus tour.

    A: What happened? Did you have a bad tour guide?

    B: No, _____ no tour guide! _____ just a bus driver!

    _____ also a lot of angry tourists.

Write about It Think about an event you went to recently. Write two sentences with *there was/were* or *there wasn't/weren't.*

I went to a wedding. There was a lot of food. There wasn't a band.

---

[20] **arts and crafts fair:** an event where people show and sell the things they make

[21] **vendors:** people who sell things, but not in stores

A | GRAMMAR IN READING Read these passages. Underline the simple past verbs.

DR. MARTIN LUTHER KING, JR. AND ROSA PARKS

Dr. Martin Luther King, Jr. <u>was</u> born in Atlanta, Georgia in 1929. He grew up in Atlanta, and later he got his PhD at Boston University. He became a famous civil rights[22] leader. His fight for civil rights began in 1955 in Montgomery, Alabama. There were segregation laws[23] in Alabama—African-American people did not have the same rights as white people. One day in 1955, an African-American woman named Rosa Parks got on a bus and sat down. A white man got on the bus, and the bus driver asked Ms. Parks to give her seat to the white man. She said no. The police arrested her.

   That night, Dr. King and other African-American leaders decided to boycott[24] the Montgomery buses. The boycott continued for 381 days. Then the U.S. Supreme Court ended the segregation laws in Alabama. Dr. King continued to fight for equal rights[25]. In 1968, someone shot and killed Dr. King in Memphis, Tennessee. Today people everywhere still remember his important work and his powerful words.

Dr. Martin Luther King, Jr.

Rosa Parks

NELSON MANDELA

Nelson Mandela was born on July 18, 1918 in Mvezo, South Africa. Mandela grew up in Mvezo. He studied at the University of South Africa. In South Africa, non-whites did not have the same rights as white people. As a young man, Mandela fought for equal rights for non-whites. He fought for their right to vote[26]. Because of his work, he went to prison in 1962 for 27 years. He got out of prison in 1990. In 1994, non-whites got the right to vote. Nelson Mandela ran for president in 1994, and he won. People around the world loved Mandela. He died on December 5, 2013 after a long illness. He was 95 years old. Nelson Mandela is gone, but he continues to be a symbol of peace.

Nelson Mandela

Write about It Write five questions about the people and events in the reading above. Then trade books with a partner. Write answers to your partner's questions.

1. When was Dr. King born?

Write about It How were Martin Luther King, Jr. and Nelson Mandela similar? How were they different? Copy this Venn diagram in your notebook. Write two sentences in each part of the diagram. Use the simple past form of the words and phrases in the box or your own ideas.

DR. MARTIN LUTHER KING, JR.
Dr. King . . .

Both men . . .

NELSON MANDELA
Mandela . . .

be born in/on	fight for equal rights
become	go to prison
boycott	grow up in
die	

[22] **civil rights:** things that every person should be allowed to do or have
[23] **segregation laws:** laws that separated people because of their race
[24] **boycott:** to stop using or buying something until changes happen

[25] **equal rights:** the same rights for all people (so everyone is allowed to do or have the same things)
[26] **vote:** to officially choose someone, such as a government leader (If you have the **right to vote**, you are allowed to vote by law.)

B | GRAMMAR IN SPEAKING Think of someone famous from the past. Go online and find answers to these questions. Then find two more facts. Tell your information to a partner, but don't say the person's name. Your partner will guess the person.

Where and when was the person born? _____

What did the person do? _____

Two more facts: _____

_____

8.8 Summary of the Simple Past

We use the simple past to talk about past events and situations.

POSITIVE STATEMENTS

I / You / We / He / She / It	arrived came	yesterday.

NEGATIVE STATEMENTS

I / You / We / He / She / It	did not didn't	arrive come	yesterday.

YES/NO QUESTIONS

Did	I / you / we / he / she / it	go	out?

SHORT ANSWERS

Yes,	you / I / we / he / she / it	did.
No,		didn't.

WH- QUESTIONS

When Where Why	did	I / you / we / he / she / it	leave?

WH- QUESTIONS ABOUT THE SUBJECT

Who	called?
What	happened?

THE SIMPLE PAST OF THE VERB *BE*

POSITIVE STATEMENTS

I / He / She / It	was	at home.
You / We / They	were	at home.

NEGATIVE STATEMENTS

I / He / She / It	was not wasn't	at work.
You / We / They	were not weren't	at work.

YES/NO QUESTIONS

Was	I / he / she / it	late?
Were	you / we / they	

WH- QUESTIONS

Where How	was	I / he / she / it?	
When Who	were	you / we / they	in class? with?

SHORT ANSWERS

Yes,	I he she it	was.
No,		wasn't.
Yes,	you we they	were.
No,		weren't.

WH- QUESTIONS ABOUT THE SUBJECT

Who	was	there?
What	was	on TV?

STATEMENTS WITH *THERE WAS / THERE WERE*

POSITIVE STATEMENTS

There	was	a band.
	were	a lot of people.

NEGATIVE STATEMENTS

There	wasn't	a cake.
	weren't	many seats.

9

Adjectives

WARM-UP 220

9.1 Placement of Adjectives 222

9.2 Adverbs of Degree 226

9.3 Questions with *How* + Adjective 231

9.4 Adjectives with *-er* and *More* 233

Spelling Note: Adjectives + *-er* 234

9.5 Using Adjectives to Compare 236

9.6 *Less* + Adjective 239

9.7 Adjectives with *-est* and *Most* 242

Spelling Note: Adjectives + *-est* 244

Usage Note: Prepositional Phrases after *-est*/Most Forms 246

WRAP-UP 248

Grammar in Reading 248

Grammar in Writing 249

9.8 Summary of Adjectives 249

IN THIS UNIT, WE USE adjectives to:

Describe nouns

1. My friend Kate is very **funny** and **friendly**.

2. That ride looks too **scary**!

3. Lake Hillier is a **pink** lake on an **Australian** island.

4. I love the ocean on **cold**, **windy** days!

Think about It Complete these sentences. You can circle more than one answer.

1. My friend _____ is (funny / friendly / interesting).

2. I like (funny / exciting / scary) movies.

3. I like (cold / snowy / warm / sunny) days.

4. I live in (a boring / an interesting) place.

GO ONLINE

For the Unit Vocabulary Check, go to the Online Practice.

Make comparisons

5. The Burj Khalifa is **taller** than the Empire State Building.

2,722 feet = 829.7 meters

1,250 feet = 381 meters

6. A peacock is **more colorful** than a pigeon.

7. Mount Everest is **the tallest** mountain in the world.

Think about It Do you agree with these statements? Check (✓) *True* or *False*.

		TRUE	FALSE
1.	Dubai is more interesting than New York.	☐	☐
2.	Paris is the most beautiful city in the world.	☐	☐
3.	Peacocks are more beautiful than pigeons.	☐	☐
4.	The beach is more relaxing than the mountains.	☐	☐

9.1 Placement of Adjectives

Adjectives describe and give more information about **nouns** (people, places, and things). We often place adjectives:

| before the **noun** they describe | after *be** |

A

1 The **new students** are from Dubai.
2 This **cheap phone** doesn't work well.
3 That was a **delicious dinner**!
4 Can I please have a **large coffee**?
5 I bought a **black wool coat**.

6 The **weather** today **is perfect**.
7 **Weekends are** too **short**!
8 I love your **boots**! **They**'re **awesome**!
9 **That test was** really **hard**!
10 Our **conversation was short** but **interesting**.

> Notice: We can use more than one adjective to describe a noun.

*In these sentences, **be** is a **linking verb**. A linking verb links, or joins, the subject noun (or pronoun) and the adjective(s).

Remember: We use **a** when the next word begins with a consonant sound. We use **an** when the next word begins with a vowel sound.

11 This is **an old car** with **a new engine**.

B

LINKING VERB + ADJECTIVE

We can use an adjective after a **linking verb**. **Be** is the most common linking verb. Here are some other common linking verbs:

seem	12 So far my new boss **seems nice**.	taste	19 The soup **tastes delicious**!
feel	13 Oof! Why does this box **feel** so **heavy**? 14 I **feel sorry** for Jason. He's having a hard time.	smell	20 Those roses **smell great**!
look	15 You **look** really **good** in that new dress. 16 Your book **looks interesting**. What is it about?	get*	21 The trip was long, and the children **got tired**.
sound	17 This music **sounds sad**. What is it? 18 The price **sounds good**. Let's buy it.		

*As a linking verb, *get* means "become."

For more linking verbs, see the Resources, page R-5.

1 | Noticing Adjectives and Nouns Look at the **bold** adjectives in these sentences. Underline the nouns that the adjectives describe. Then check (✓) the placement of the adjectives in each sentence. `9.1 A`

AMAZING ANIMALS	BEFORE THE NOUN	AFTER BE	
1. Aye-ayes live in the **tall** <u>trees</u> of Madagascar.	✓	☐	
2. Their <u>ears</u> are **big**.	☐	✓	
3. Their teeth are **sharp**.	☐	☐	
4. They have a very **long**, **thin** finger.	☐	☐	an aye-aye in a tree

5. Aye-ayes eat **small** insects in trees. ☐ ☐
6. They use their **big** ears to hear insects inside the trees. ☐ ☐
7. They use their **sharp** teeth to make a **small** hole in a tree. ☐ ☐
8. They use their **long**, **thin** finger to reach into the hole and get the insects. ☐ ☐

Now look at the <u>underlined</u> nouns. Circle the adjectives that describe these nouns. Then check (✓) the placement of the adjectives in each sentence.

BEFORE
THE NOUN   AFTER BE

9. Sand puppies live in the (hot) <u>deserts</u> of East Africa. They live under the ground. ☐ ☐

10. Sand puppies have no hair. They have short <u>legs</u> and tiny <u>eyes</u>. ☐ ☐

11. They have two very long, thin <u>teeth</u>. ☐ ☐

12. They dig long <u>tunnels</u> (sometimes over a kilometer long). ☐ ☐

13. Many people think <u>sand puppies</u> are ugly. ☐ ☐

14. <u>Axolotls</u> are often black or brown. ☐ ☐

15. Sometimes <u>they</u> are gold or pink. ☐ ☐

16. Axolotls have a special <u>ability</u>. Sometimes a leg falls off, and the axolotl grows a new <u>leg</u>! ☐ ☐

a sand puppy in a tunnel

an axolotl (pronounced "ax-o-lottle")

Write about It Look at these pictures of two more animals. Write two sentences about each animal: one with adjective + noun and one with *be* + adjective. Use the adjectives in the box below or your own ideas.

an alpaca

an Angora rabbit

| big | brown | cute | long | round | short | small | ugly |

The alpaca is brown. It has short legs.

2 | Identifying Linking Verbs + Adjectives Read the article below. Underline the uses of linking verb + adjective. Look for forms of the linking verbs in the box. **9.1 B**

| be | feel | get | look | seem | sound | taste |

CAN YOU *FEEL* THE MUSIC?

Synesthesia (pronounced "si-nəs-THEE-zhə") means "combined senses[1]." About 4 percent of people have synesthesia. There are many types of synesthesia. For example:

Letters and numbers → Color

Carol is an artist. For her, the letter *A* looks pink, *E* looks red, and *G* looks green. This type of synesthesia is common.

Letters and numbers → Personality

For a few people, letters and numbers have personalities. For example, one person says *J* always seems strong and *K* always seems quiet.

Sound → Feeling

Jennifer has this kind of synesthesia. For her, guitar music sounds beautiful. It also feels soft on her skin.

Taste → Color

For Sean, steak tastes delicious. It also tastes blue.

How does synesthesia feel? For some people, synesthesia gets tiring[2]. But for most people it feels normal and interesting.

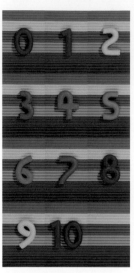

For some people with synesthesia, letters and numbers have colors.

Talk about It Do you think life is very different for people with synesthesia? Does synesthesia seem like a good or bad experience? Why?

3 | Using Linking Verbs + Adjectives Look at the pictures below. Write a sentence about each picture with a linking verb + adjective(s). Use the words in parentheses and adjectives from the box. **9.1 B**

| angry | beautiful | delicious | funny | interesting | sad |
| bad | dangerous | exciting | great | OK | scary |

1. (she/feel)

   She feels angry and sad.

   _____

2. (the food/taste)

   _____

   _____

3. (the music/sound)

   _____

   _____

---

[1] **senses:** the power to see, hear, smell, taste, and feel   [2] **tiring (adjective):** making you feel tired

4. (that/look)

5. (the movie/seem)

6. (the book/look)

_____

_____

_____

4 | Forming Sentences with Adjectives Complete these conversations with the words in parentheses. Put the words in order to form sentences with adjective + noun or linking verb + adjective. 9.1 A–B

ASKING FOR AN OPINION

1. A: Do you want to see that Korean movie?

   B: Yeah, _____*it sounds interesting*_____.
   (it / interesting / sounds)

2. A: _____?
   (this shirt / tight / does / look)

   B: Not at all. It looks great on you.

3. A: _____ in here?
   (does / it / hot / feel)

   B: Maybe a bit. _____ in the living room.
   (open / window / big / the)

4. A: Can you taste the soup for me? Is the seasoning³ OK? _____.
   (I / new / used / a / recipe)

   B: Yes, the seasoning is perfect. _____.
   (the / delicious / soup / tastes)

5. A: _____ near here?
   (is there / pizza place / a / good)

   B: Try Marino's. _____.
   (pizza / excellent / they / make)

6. A: Which set of plates do you like?

   B: I like both. _____. But the blue ones are pretty!
   (seem / white / the / plates / useful)

7. A: I think _____.
   (is / this class / confusing)

   B: Yeah, me too. _____.
   (hard / the material / is)

8. A: _____?
   (is / good / your / French teacher / new)

   B: Yeah, _____.
   (seems / she / great)

9. A: How was your winter vacation? _____?
   (did / good / time / you / have / a)

   B: _____! I worked at the store six days a week.
   (was / tiring / my vacation)

🔊 **Talk about It** Listen and check your answers above. Then practice the conversations with a partner.

Think about It Look at the sentences you wrote above. Answer these questions.

1. Which sentences have an adjective + noun?
2. Which sentences have a linking verb + adjective? (*be* or other linking verb)
3. Which sentences have an adjective + noun AND a linking verb + adjective?

³ **seasoning:** things we use to add flavor to food (salt, pepper, spices, etc.)

Talk about It Work with a partner. Ask your partner for an opinion. Ask about one of these topics or another idea.

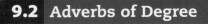

| a class | a movie | a product | a restaurant | a store |

A: *Are the stores on Fifth Avenue good?*
B: *They're nice, but they're expensive.*

9.2 Adverbs of Degree

A

We use **adverbs of degree** before **adjectives** to tell how strong or weak the adjective is.

(1)	(2)	(3)	(4)
not very	kind of	pretty	very
not really	fairly		really

low degree   high degree

1 This class is**n't very** hard.   **3** This class is **pretty** hard.

2 This class is **kind of** hard.   **4** This class is **really** hard!

For more adverbs of degree, see the Resources, page R-5.

B

TOO + ADJECTIVE

Too means "more than you want or need."

Notice: **Too** has a different meaning from **very** and **really**.

= a lot

6 This class is **really** hard. It's a good challenge for me!

7 This class is **too** hard. I need to change to a different class!

= a lot, and this is a problem

5 This shirt is **too** big.

C

(NOT +) ADJECTIVE + ENOUGH

enough = the necessary amount   **not . . . enough** = less than the necessary amount

8 This shirt is **big enough**.   **9** This shirt is**n't big enough**.

We put *enough* after the **adjective**.

Notice: We often use *enough* in questions.

10 A: Is the soup **hot enough**?
B: Yes, I think it's ready!

WARNING! Don't put *enough* before the adjective.

✓ The food is not **hot enough**.   ✗ The food is not **enough hot**.

5 | Understanding Adverbs of Degree Listen and write the adverbs you hear. Then underline the adjective that each adverb describes. `9.2 A`

CONVERSATIONS AT SCHOOL

1. A: I'm _____really_____ <u>nervous</u> about the exam. Are you?

   B: I'm actually _____ calm. I studied a lot. I know this stuff.

2. A: How late is the library open?

   B: I'm not sure. It's usually open _____ late.

3. A: I'm confused. Is the whole paper due on Monday or just

   the introduction?

   B: Hmm. It's _____ clear to me either.

4. A: I wanted to register for the child psychology class, but there's already

   a waiting list.

   B: I'm not surprised. That class is _____ popular.

5. A: Are we on time for the meeting?

   B: Actually, we're _____ early. No one's here yet.

6. A: It's lunchtime, but I'm _____ hungry. What about you?

   B: I'm not hungry either. Let's have lunch after class.

7. A: How's your economics class?

   B: It's _____ disappointing. We're just doing stuff from last

   semester again.

8. A: You look _____ tired today.

   B: I am! Some of my friends came over, and I stayed up _____ late.

9. A: Do you like your new adviser?

   B: I do! She's _____ helpful. She gave me some great advice

   about my class schedule.

10. A: Did you read the book for our English class?

    B: Not yet. Why?

    A: I don't understand it. It's _____ confusing!

> **RESEARCH SAYS...**
>
> The adverbs **pretty** and **kind of** are much more common in conversation than in writing. **Fairly** is more common in writing.
>
> CORPUS

> **FYI**
>
> Notice that the adverb **pretty** and the adjective **pretty** have different meanings.
>
> He's **pretty** smart.
> (adverb = softer than *really*)
>
> That's a **pretty** dress.
> (adjective = looks nice)

Talk about It Talk to a partner about the topics in this box. Use adverbs of degree and adjectives.

your breakfast/lunch today	your last exam
your classes this semester	your last vacation

"My lunch today was pretty good."
"My classes this semester are really interesting."

Think about It In conversation 7 above, there is one adjective that ends in -*ing* and one verb that ends in -*ing*. Label the adjective *A* and label the verb *V*.

6 | Using Adverbs of Degree Look at the personal qualities below. Do these qualities describe you? Write sentences about yourself with each adjective and an adverb of degree from the box. (Use a dictionary to look up any adjectives you don't know.) **9.2 A**

PERSONAL QUALITIES SURVEY

| not very   pretty   very |

I'm pretty calm.

1. calm _____
2. careful _____
3. confident _____
4. creative _____
5. curious[4] _____
6. helpful _____

7. honest _____
8. independent[5] _____
9. organized _____
10. outgoing[6] _____
11. polite _____
12. responsible _____

Talk about It Think about the qualities of a good manager. Which of the qualities above are the most important? Discuss your ideas as a class.

"Good managers are very confident. They are also very creative...."

7 | Using *Too* and *Really* Complete each conversation with *too* or *really*. Then listen and check your answers. **9.2 B**

AN EVENING AT HOME

1. A: Can we park there?

   B: I don't think so. That space is _____*too*_____ small for my car.

2. A: Did you finish your paper?

   B: Yes and no. I finished it, but it's _____ short. The assignment says 500 words, and I only have 400. I can't think of anything else to say.

3. A: Is the soup hot now? Does it seem ready?

   B: Yeah. It's _____ hot. And it smells delicious.

4. A: Where did you buy those new coffee cups? They're nice!

   B: At SaveCo. I liked them a lot, and they were _____ cheap.

5. A: What's wrong with the cake?

   B: I usually like sweet desserts, but this is _____ sweet. I can't eat it.

6. A: The hot water is working again. Is it OK now?

   B: Ouch! No, now it's _____ hot!

7. A: How are the new neighbors? Do they seem nice?

   B: Yeah, I like them. They're _____ friendly.

8. A: How was the movie?

   B: It was _____ interesting! I liked it a lot.

9. A: Did you find an apartment?

   B: Yes, I chose one yesterday! It's _____ big and sunny.

[4]**curious:** interested in learning about things
[5]**independent:** not needing help
[6]**outgoing:** friendly and interested in other people

8 | Using Enough Look at the pictures. Complete the sentences below with the words in parentheses. Use the verb *be* and *enough* or *not . . . enough*. `9.2 C`

1. <u>This office isn't big enough</u> _____ for all of us!
   (this office / big)

2. A: _____ now?
   (the ice cream / soft)

   B: Not yet! It needs a few more minutes!

3. A: _____?
   (that coat / warm)

   B: Not really. I'm pretty cold!

4. A: Do you need more sugar?

   B: No, thanks. _____.
   (the tea / sweet)

5. A: What do you think?

   B: _____!
   (the door / wide)

6. _____ now?
   (my room / clean)

7. _____ for your things.
   (this box / big)

8. A: Do you need help?

   B: Yes, please. Can you get me that box?

   _____.
   (I / tall)

9 | Using Adverbs of Degree Read these reviews. Complete the sentences with the phrases in each box. You will not use all of the phrases. `9.2 A–C`

Maria's Tacos

Reviews

Evan ★★★★★

The food at Maria's is _____*very good*_____. My wife and I love it! The portions[7] are

_____. You get a lot of food! And the owner and waiters make you

feel comfortable. It's a _____ place.

| really big |
| too friendly |
| too small |
| very friendly |
| very good |

Brad ★

The food is _____. Actually, it's terrible. And that's not the only

problem. The service[8] is _____. Last night my friends and I waited

almost an hour for our tacos! The tacos were probably in the kitchen all that time.

My tacos were _____, and my friends' tacos were cold.

| fast enough |
| hot enough |
| not hot enough |
| not very good |
| too slow |

Leonel ★★★

This is not a special restaurant, but everything is OK. Not great, not bad. The food is

_____. The service is _____. The waiter brought us

our food in about 15 minutes—not bad, but not great. Try the chicken and mushroom

tacos. The prices are OK.

| fast enough |
| good enough |
| really good |
| very fast |

---

[7] **portions:** amounts of food for each person

[8] **service:** the work people do for customers in a restaurant or other business

Tamara ★★

Where were the chilies? Mexican food is usually spicy. But at Maria's our food was

_____. We didn't finish our food because the portions were

_____. And Maria's is also _____—maybe because

you pay for all that extra food.

big enough
cheap enough
not very spicy
too big
too expensive

Rosa ★★★★

This restaurant has interesting and tasty food. There is only one problem: too

many people like Maria's! The restaurant is _____—there are

only about seven tables, so there's not a lot of space. For this reason, it is often

_____. I waited almost an hour for a seat! Don't go to Maria's for

an evening of quiet conversation—it's _____.

noisy enough
not very small
really small
too crowded
too noisy

Talk about It Work with a partner. Read the reviews in Activity 9 again. Do you want to eat at Maria's Tacos? Why or why not?

Write about It Write a short review (three to four sentences) of a restaurant you went to recently. Include answers to these questions. Use adjectives and adverbs of degree.

Is the food good?

Is the service fast?

Is the food expensive?

9.3 Questions with *How* + Adjective

We use **how** + an **adjective** to ask about the degree of the adjective:

	QUESTION	POSSIBLE ANSWERS
1	**How hot** is it today?	It's not very hot. It's about 80 degrees. (80°F = 27°C)
2	**How hungry** are you?	I'm starving! I'm not very hungry.
3	**How big** is your school?	It's pretty big. There are about 15,000 students.
4	**How far** is your house from here?	It's just a few blocks away. About 3 miles (4.8 km) from here.
5	**How tall** is your brother?	He's about 6 feet tall. He's 5'11". ("five-eleven" = 5 feet, 11 inches = 1.9 m)
6	**How high** is that hill?	It's pretty high! It's about 300 feet. (91 m)
7	**How long** is the trip?	Usually a couple of hours. It's not very long.
8	**How old** are your children?	They're 2 and 5 years old.

A

GO ONLINE

10 | Asking and Answering Questions with *How* + Adjective Complete the questions below. Use *how* + an adjective from the box. Then guess the answers to the questions. `9.3 A`

cold	deep	far	heavy	high	long	old	tall

Did You Know?

1. _How high_____ is Mount Everest?

   a. 26,105 feet   b. 29,029 feet   c. 30,230 feet
   (7,957 meters)   (8,848 meters)   (9,214 meters)

2. _____ is a flight from Auckland, New Zealand to New York City?

   a. 6 hours   b. 13 hours   c. 18 hours

3. _____ is the average[9] professional basketball player?

   a. about 6'3" (1.91 meters)   b. about 6'7" (2.01 meters)   c. about 6'11" (2.11 meters)

4. _____ are the Egyptian pyramids at Giza?

   a. about 2,500 years old   b. about 3,500 years old   c. about 4,500 years old

5. _____ is a new baby elephant?

   a. about 100 pounds   b. about 150 pounds   c. about 200 pounds
   (45 kilograms)   (68 kilograms)   (91 kilograms)

6. You see lightning. Five seconds later you hear thunder. _____ is the lightning from you?

   a. about 1 mile   b. about 5 miles   c. about 10 miles
   (1.6 kilometers)   (8 kilometers)   (16 kilometers)

7. _____ is the ocean on average?

   a. 5,500 feet (1,700 meters)   b. 9,000 feet (2,743 meters)   c. 14,000 feet (4,267 meters)

8. _____ is an average January day in New Delhi, India?

   a. about 55°F (13°C)   b. about 65°F (18°C)   c. about 70°F (21°C)

lightning

Answers: 1. b; 2. c; 3. b; 4. c; 5. c; 6. a; 7. c; 8. a

Talk about It Ask and answer these questions with a partner.

1. Do you have siblings? How old are they?
2. How big is your immediate family (mother, father, and siblings)?
   How big is your extended family (cousins, aunts, uncles, and grandparents)?
3. How far is your home from school? How long is your trip to school?
4. How big is your home? (How many rooms does it have?)
5. How tall are you?

[9] **average:** normal or usual

9.4 Adjectives with -er and More

A

We can use adjectives to **compare** (describe differences between) people or things. Adjectives that compare have two forms:

↓ ↓

With some adjectives, we use the **adjective** + **-er**.	With some adjectives, we use **more** + the **adjective**.

1 Tony's is **smaller** than Il Pranzo.

2 Il Pranzo is **more expensive**.

GRAMMAR TERM: These kinds of adjectives are also called **comparative forms**.

B

FORMING ADJECTIVES WITH -ER AND MORE

ONE-SYLLABLE ADJECTIVES	TWO-SYLLABLE ADJECTIVES ENDING IN Y*
cheap → **cheaper**	hap·py → **happier**
hard → **harder**	heav·y → **heavier**
strong → **stronger**	la·zy → **lazier**

TWO-SYLLABLE ADJECTIVES	THREE-SYLLABLE ADJECTIVES
bor·ing → **more boring**	ex·cit·ing → **more exciting**
care·ful → **more careful**	im·por·tant → **more important**
po·lite → **more polite**	prac·ti·cal → **more practical**

USE WITH -ER OR MORE

narrow → **narrower** OR more **narrow**
quiet → **quieter** OR more **quiet**

IRREGULAR FORMS

bad → **worse**	good → **better**	far → **farther**

*For more information on spelling -er adjectives, see the Spelling Note on page 234.

We usually use **-er** with:
- most one-syllable adjectives
- some two-syllable adjectives (for example, words that end in y)

We use **more** with:
- other two-syllable adjectives
- adjectives with more than two syllables

For some adjectives, we can use either **-er** or **more**.

Some adjectives like **bad**, **good**, and **far** have irregular comparative forms.

---

11 | Identifying Adjectives with -er and More Underline the adjectives with -er and *more* in these trivia questions. Then write the answers to the questions. `9.4 A`

World Trivia

GEOGRAPHY[10]

1. Which continent is <u>larger</u>, Europe or South America? _____

2. Which continent is <u>more populated</u>[11], Africa or Europe? _____

3. Which ocean is deeper, the Atlantic Ocean or the Pacific Ocean? _____

4. Which city is more expensive, London or Paris? _____

> **FYI**
>
> We can use the *wh-* word **which** to ask about a choice between things.
>
> Which color looks better, red or blue?

[10] **geography:** the study of the earth, including its land and people

[11] **more populated:** having more people

ANIMALS

5. Which animals are faster, lions or giraffes? _____

6. Which animals are bigger, lions or tigers? _____

7. Which whales are heavier, blue whales or gray whales? _____

8. Which insects are more dangerous to humans, mosquitoes or bees? _____

LANGUAGES

9. Which sound is more common in the world's languages, the /l/ sound or the /p/ sound? _____

10. Which alphabet is shorter, the English alphabet or the Russian alphabet? _____

11. Which English word is newer, *cell phone* or *blog*? _____

12. Which language is more similar to English, Russian or Swedish? _____

a giraffe

a mosquito

Look on page 249 for the answers.

Think about It For each adjective form you underlined in Activity 11, write the simple adjective (without *-er* or *more*). How many syllables does the simple adjective have?

1. <u>large</u> = 1 syllable
2. <u>populated</u> = 4 syllables

12 | Spelling Note: Adjectives + -er Read the note. Then do Activity 13.

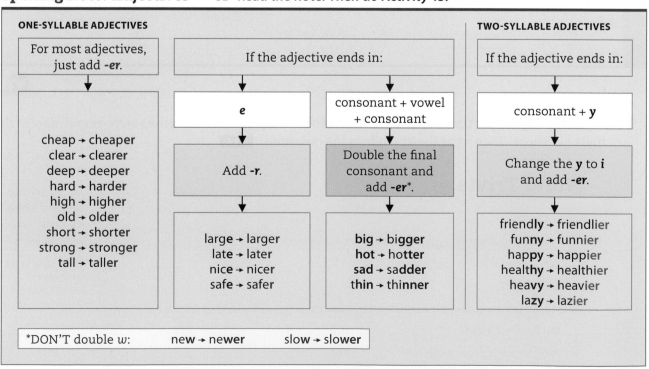

ONE-SYLLABLE ADJECTIVES			TWO-SYLLABLE ADJECTIVES
For most adjectives, just add *-er*.	If the adjective ends in:		If the adjective ends in:
	e	consonant + vowel + consonant	consonant + **y**
	Add *-r*.	Double the final consonant and add *-er**.	Change the **y** to **i** and add *-er*.
cheap → cheaper clear → clearer deep → deeper hard → harder high → higher old → older short → shorter strong → stronger tall → taller	large → larger late → later nice → nicer safe → safer	**big** → bi**gg**er **hot** → ho**tt**er **sad** → sa**dd**er **thin** → thi**nn**er	friend**ly** → friendlier fun**ny** → funnier hap**py** → happier health**y** → healthier heav**y** → heavier laz**y** → lazier

*DON'T double *w*:   new → ne**w**er   slow → slo**w**er

13 | Spelling *-er* Adjectives Write the *-er* form of each adjective in the box in the correct column of the chart below. `9.4 B`

big	close	early	hungry	loud	nice	sad	sunny
busy	cool	heavy	large	neat	noisy	safe	thin
cheap	deep	hot	late	new	old	slow	wet

ONE-SYLLABLE ADJECTIVES			TWO-SYLLABLE ADJECTIVES
Ending in *e*	**Ending in consonant + vowel + consonant (not *w*)**	**All other one-syllable adjectives**	**Ending in consonant + *y***
	bigger		

14 | Forming Adjectives with *-er* and *More* Complete these conversations with the correct form of the adjective(s) in parentheses. `9.4 B`

DECISIONS

1. A: Liam and Zach both seem good. Who do you want to hire?

   B: It's a difficult choice. . . . But maybe Liam. He seems
   _____*more outgoing*_____ (outgoing).

2. A: Are you taking Biology II?

   B: No, it was too hard for me. I switched to Environmental Science.
   It's a little _____ (easy).

3. A: Did you fly to Zurich?

   B: No, I took the train. It's a _____ (slow) trip, but it's
   _____ (cheap).

4. A: Which apartment did you choose?

   B: The apartment on the top floor. It's a little _____ (small)
   than the first-floor apartment, but it's a lot _____ (sunny).

5. A: Which supermarket do you go to—the ShopBest or the FoodPlace?

   B: I usually go to the ShopBest. It's a little _____ (far)
   for me, but the fruits and vegetables there are really good.

6. A: My friends want to go to an Ethiopian restaurant. Where can I take
   them? Maybe to Gojo?

   B: What about Kokeb? The food there is _____ (expensive),
   but it's also _____ (interesting).

7. A: We can take the red trail or the green trail. What do you think?

   B: Let's take the red trail. It's _____ (long), and it looks
   _____ (challenging).

> **FYI**
>
> We can use **much** and **a lot** before adjectives with *-er/more* to show a big difference between the two things in the comparison.
>
> My new apartment is **a lot** bigger than my old one. (My new apartment is very big, and my old apartment was very small.)
>
> We can use **a little** to show a small difference.
>
> The apartment is **a little** farther from school, but that's OK.

8. A: What schools did you get accepted to?

   B: Florida State University and the University of Chicago.

   A: Wow! The University of Chicago is a really good school!

   B: Yeah, but Florida State is a _____ (good) school for music.

Write about It Look again at the conversations in Activity 14. Complete the sentences below about the other thing or person in each conversation. Use an adjective from the box with *-er* or *more*.

bad	boring	dark	expensive	hard	quiet
big	cheap	easy	fast	near	short

1. Zach is _____*quieter*_____.

2. Biology II is _____.

3. The flight to Zurich is _____
   _____.

4. The first-floor apartment is _____.

5. The FoodPlace is _____.

6. The food at Gojo is _____.

7. The green trail is _____.

8. The music department at the University of
   Chicago is _____.

9.5 Using Adjectives to Compare

A

We can use an **adjective with *-er* or *more* + *than*** in sentences that compare two people or things.

		be	adjective + *-er* or *more*	than	
1	The bus	is	**cheaper**	**than**	the train.
2	Zack	is	**older**	**than**	his brother.
3	Tests	are	**more important**	**than**	quizzes.

We can also use the adjective alone (without *than*). We do this when the listener understands which nouns we mean.

4 A: Are the sandwiches here good?
   B: Yeah, but the hamburgers are **better**. (= The hamburgers are better than the sandwiches.)

B

USING PRONOUNS AFTER *THAN*

We can use a **subject pronoun** + *be* after *than*. This structure is common in writing.

↓

5a Sarah is older than **he is.**
   (= Sarah is older than John is.)

6a My roommate was neater than **I was.**

In speaking or very informal writing, we often use an **object pronoun*** after *than*.

↓

5b Sarah is older than **him.**

6b My roommate was neater than **me.**

7 The green dress is prettier than **the black one.** ←

8 Your phone is better than **mine.** ←

*For more information on object pronouns and possessive pronouns, see Unit 6, pages 153 and 157.

We can also use:
• a phrase with ***one***

• a **possessive pronoun*** or noun (*mine, yours, his, hers, ours, theirs, Karen's*)

These structures are common in both speaking and writing.

236

15 | Noticing Comparisons Read this online discussion. Circle the adjectives with *-er/more*. Underline *than* + the words after *than*. Then complete the instructions below. **9.5 A–B**

How are you different from your brother or sister?

Max: My brother and I look really similar, so people think we are similar in other ways. But we're actually very different. I am much (more athletic) than he is. In school I was better at sports. I was usually on the soccer and basketball teams. My brother was never on a team. But my brother is smarter than me. His grades in school were a lot better than mine. Our parents were always proud of his grades and angry about mine.

Karen: My sister is taller and thinner than I am. She's also a lot more energetic[12]. I like to sit in the park or in a café and read a book. My sister never sits still[13]. After two minutes, she jumps up and wants to go somewhere. We take a walk, and she talks to everyone! She is much more outgoing than I am. I love my sister, but after a visit from her, I'm happy to sit down and relax!

Diego: My brother is more practical[14] than me, and I'm more artistic[15] than him. He has a wife and child, and he spends most of his free time with them. I live alone, and I travel a lot. He's probably more responsible than me. We have very different ideas about the world, but that's OK. We just don't talk about politics!

Ahmed: My brother's handwriting is much worse than mine! No one can read his handwriting. But in many ways we are very similar. The differences between us are small. For example, I'm pretty funny, but my brother is even funnier. We're both friendly and happy people. We always have a great time together.

INSTRUCTIONS

1. Which sentences above have an *-er/more* adjective but DON'T have *than*? Write *X* above these adjectives.
2. Which sentences have *than* + **object pronoun** (*me, him, her*)? Write *O* above the object pronouns.
3. Which sentences have *than* + **possessive pronoun** (*mine, his, hers*)? Write *P* above the possessive pronouns.
4. Which sentences have *than* + **subject pronoun** + *am/is/are*? Write *S* above the subject pronouns.

---

[12]**energetic:** full of energy so you can do a lot of things
[13]**still:** without moving
[14]**practical:** good at dealing with problems and making decisions

[15]**artistic:** good at making things connected with art (such as painting or music)

Think about It Look at the sentences you labeled *O* (sentences with *than* + object pronoun) in Activity 15. Rewrite these sentences with *than* + subject pronoun + *am/is/are*.

But my brother is smarter than me. = But my brother is smarter than I am.

Talk about It Think of a family member or a friend. How are you different from him or her? Complete these sentences with *-er/more* adjectives. Discuss your answers with a partner.

1. I am _____ than my _____.
2. My _____ is _____ than me.

16 | Writing Comparisons Use each group of words to make a sentence. Use the **bold** adjective + *-er* or *more* + *than*. Keep the words in the same order. Do you agree with the sentence? Check (✓) *Agree* or *Disagree*. `9.5 A`

	AGREE	DISAGREE
COMPARING VACATIONS		
1. *The beach is more relaxing than the mountains.* (the beach / **relaxing** / the mountains)	☐	☐
2. _____ (a long vacation / **good** / a short vacation)	☐	☐
COMPARING AGES		
3. _____ (old people / **wise**[16]/ young people)	☐	☐
4. _____ (old people / **responsible** / young people)	☐	☐
COMPARING UNIVERSITY CHOICES		
5. _____ (a face-to-face[17] course / **good** / an online course)	☐	☐
6. _____ (small schools / **friendly** / large schools)	☐	☐
COMPARING PLACES TO LIVE		
7. _____ (life in a small town / **easy** / life in the city)	☐	☐
8. _____ (life in the country[18] / **healthy** / life in the city)	☐	☐
COMPARING ENTERTAINMENT		
9. _____ (basketball / **exciting** / soccer)	☐	☐
10. _____ (movies / **interesting** / TV shows)	☐	☐

Talk about It Discuss your ideas as a class. Which sentences above do most students agree with?

[16] **wise:** knowing and understanding a lot about many things
[17] **face-to-face:** in a classroom with other students and a teacher
[18] **the country:** land that is away from towns and cities

17 | Using Pronouns in Comparisons Complete these conversations with the words in parentheses. Use the adjective with *-er* or *more* + *than*. **9.5 B**

1. A: How is the new computer system?

   B: I'm not sure. In some ways, the old system was ___*easier than the new one*___ .
   (easy / the new one)

2. A: We can take my car.

   B: Let's go in my car. It's _____ .
   (big / yours)

3. A: Is your cousin Alfie our age?

   B: No, he's _____ .
   (young / us)

4. A: Can you help me with this paragraph in French?

   B: I can try. But your French is _____ .
   (good / mine)

5. A: Let's buy one of these photos. Which one do you like?

   B: Hmm. I think the little photo is _____ .
   (interesting / the big one)

6. A: Which math teacher is better, Ms. Alvarez or Mr. Tyson?

   B: They're both good. Ms. Alvarez's class is hard. Maybe Mr. Tyson's class is a little

   _____ .
   (easy / hers)

7. A: Do you need any help?

   B: Maybe you can open this jar. You're _____ .
   (strong / me)

8. A: Do you think we can win? Are we good enough?

   B: Sure. We're _____ .
   (good / them)

Talk about It Listen and check your answers above. Then practice the conversations with a partner.

9.6 *Less + Adjective*

We can use **less** with some adjectives. **Less** is the opposite of **more**.

A

$30 $85

1 The lamp on the left is **less expensive** than the one on the right.

2 I prefer this restaurant. It's **less noisy**.
3 My classes this semester seem **less interesting**.

4 In the United States, soccer is **less popular** than football.
5 Your phone is **less expensive** than mine.

Notice: We can use *less* in the same ways we use *more*. We can use:

• **less** + **adjective**

• **less** + **adjective** + *than* + noun phrase

18 | Using *Less* + Adjective Complete the blog entries below with *less* and an adjective from the box. `9.6 A`

difficult	expensive	fattening	hungry	interesting	lonely	worried

RESEARCH
SAYS...

Comparisons with *less* are less common than comparisons with *more*.

CORPUS

First Year, Second Semester

February 2

This semester I'm living on campus. I liked my apartment in town last semester. But I didn't meet many people at school. So over the vacation I moved to a dorm. This was the right decision! I feel a lot

_____*less lonely*_____. And the dorm is _____ than
    1   2

the apartment, so I'm also saving money.

February 8

The food in the cafeteria here is so fattening[19]. I gained 20 pounds last semester! But now I'm on a diet and it's really working. I cook all my meals and just make healthy stuff, so the food is _____.
                                                                          3

I'm eating less, but I actually feel _____.
                                       4

February 25

School is a lot better these days. I'm getting used to[20] the work, so my classes

seem _____. I'm feeling _____ about
        5   6

my grades.

Last semester I took an introduction to psychology class, but this semester I'm taking some advanced classes like child psychology. The introduction class was easier, but it was also _____.
                                                                  7

I love kids, so I'm really enjoying the child psychology class.

---

[19]**fattening:** likely to make you fat

[20]**get used to:** to become more familiar with something because you are doing it a lot

19 | Using *More/-er* and *Less* Complete the sentences below. Use the adjectives in each box + -er, more, or less. (See Chart 9.4 for help with -er/more.) **9.6 A**

WHICH IS BETTER—THE SUBURBS[21] OR THE CITY?

A. Advantages[22] of the suburbs:
People in the suburbs say . . .

B. Advantages of the city:
People in cities say . . .

> 1. interesting   safe

1a. People here don't worry about crime.
The neighborhoods seem _____*safer*_____.

1b. Streets in the suburbs all look the same. They're boring. City streets are _____.

> 2. friendly   similar

2a. People here are _____.
Everyone says hello.

2b. People in the suburbs all seem the same. In cities, people are much _____. You meet many different and interesting people!

> 3. interesting   quiet

3a. It's _____ here.
Some days I just hear the birds.

3b. Some people think city life is too stressful. But I disagree. Life in the city is fun, and fun activities make my life _____.

> 4. crowded   far

4a. It's much _____ here.
People have a lot of space. I have my own house and yard.

4b. I can walk everywhere, and there are lots of stores nearby. In the suburbs, the stores are _____ away, and you need a car.

> 5. exciting   expensive

5a. Homes are _____ here. For the same money, you can buy a tiny apartment in the city or a huge house in my neighborhood!

5b. Concerts, plays, movies, art—things are happening all the time. Life is _____ _____ here.

[21] **suburbs:** areas where people live that are outside the central part of a city

[22] **advantages:** things that are good or useful

6. difficult	healthy

6a. Our kids have clean, fresh air and lots of places for exercise. The suburbs are _____ places for kids.

6b. There are more jobs in the city. In the suburbs, good jobs are often _____ to find.

Write about It Look at the sentences in Activity 19 again. How can we use *too* and *not . . . enough* to talk about these ideas? Write two sentences about problems with life in the suburbs and two sentences about problems with life in cities. Use *too* and *not . . . enough* and the adjectives in Activity 19. (Review Chart 9.2 for help.)

Cities aren't safe enough.

Talk about It Where do you prefer to live: in a suburb or in a city? Why?

9.7 Adjectives with *-est* and Most

We can use adjectives to compare one member of a group to the rest of the group. We form these adjectives in two ways:

A

> With some adjectives, we use *the* + **adjective** + *-est*.

1 That's **the nicest** watch in the store.

> With some adjectives, we use *the most* + **adjective**.

2 It's also **the most expensive** one.

GRAMMAR TERM: These kinds of adjectives are also called **superlative forms**.

$500 $4000 $250

B

FORMING ADJECTIVES WITH *-EST* AND *MOST*

ONE-SYLLABLE ADJECTIVES	TWO-SYLLABLE ADJECTIVES ENDING IN Y*
cheap → **the cheapest** hard → **the hardest** strong → **the strongest** tall → **the tallest**	hap·py → **the happiest** heav·y → **the heaviest** la·zy → **the laziest**

TWO-SYLLABLE ADJECTIVES	THREE-SYLLABLE ADJECTIVES
bor·ing → **the most boring** care·ful → **the most careful** po·lite → **the most polite**	ex·cit·ing → **the most exciting** im·por·tant → **the most important** prac·ti·cal → **the most practical**

USE WITH *-EST* OR *MOST*

narrow → **the narrowest** OR **the most narrow** quiet → **the quietest** OR **the most quiet**

IRREGULAR FORMS

bad → **the worst**	good → **the best**	far → **the farthest**

*For more information on spelling *-est* adjectives, see the Spelling Note on page 244.

We usually use *the* + *-est* with:
- most one-syllable adjectives
- some two-syllable adjectives (for example, words that end in y)

We use *the most* with:
- other two-syllable adjectives
- adjectives with more than two syllables

For some adjectives, we can use either *-est* or *most*.

Some adjectives like *bad*, *good*, and *far* have irregular superlative forms.

20 | Identifying Adjectives with -est and Most Read this article. Underline the adjectives with -est and *most*. ▐9.7 A▐

Oldest Child and Youngest Child: Birth Order and Personality

Does birth order influence[23] personality? Many psychologists think so. Some personality qualities are more common in <u>the oldest</u> child in a family. Other qualities are more common in the youngest child. For example:

The oldest child in a family is often the most successful. In many families, this child is the smartest, the most confident, and the most responsible. As an adult, the oldest child often has a more important job than the other children.

The youngest child is often the most artistic and the most creative. This child is often the funniest and the most outgoing child in the family. He or she often has a bold[24] personality.

What explains these differences? Here are some possibilities:

The oldest child is often the only child for many years. Many parents pay a lot of attention[25] to their first child. This makes the child feel very confident. In many families, the oldest child also helps with younger siblings. This helps the child feel more responsible.

Many parents are less strict[26] with their youngest child. Maybe, with less strict parents, the child feels bolder.

Think about It Complete this chart with the forms from the article above.

ADJECTIVE + -EST		THE MOST + ADJECTIVE	
The + *-est* form	Adjective	*The most* form	Adjective
the oldest	old		

Talk about It Do you agree with the article above? Think about people you know who are the oldest or youngest in their family. Do these people have the qualities described above?

---

[23] **influence:** to change or shape in some way
[24] **bold:** brave and not afraid

[25] **pay a lot of attention:** to look or listen carefully very often
[26] **strict:** not allowing children to behave badly

21 | Spelling Note: Adjectives + -est Read the note. Then do Activity 22.

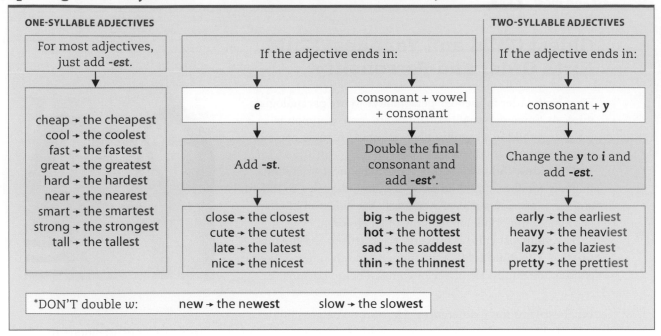

22 | Spelling -est Adjectives Write the -est form of each adjective in the box in the correct column of the chart below. Include *the*. **9.7 B**

big	fast	late	messy	rich	thin
brave	happy	lazy	near	rude	warm
cheap	healthy	loud	new	safe	wet
easy	hot	low	quick	scary	wide

ONE-SYLLABLE ADJECTIVES			TWO-SYLLABLE ADJECTIVES
Ending in *e*	Ending in consonant + vowel + consonant (not *w*)	All other one-syllable adjectives	Ending in consonant + *y*
	the biggest		

23 | Forming Adjectives with -est and Most Look at this chart that compares three tablets. Then complete the sentences below with the adjectives in parentheses and the information in the chart. Use *the* + adjective + *-est* or *the* + *most* + adjective. `9.7 B`

A COMPARISON OF THREE BEST-SELLING TABLETS			
Features	Tablet A	Tablet B	Tablet C
Overall[27] score (1–10)	9	8	5
Battery life (hours)	9 hours	11 hours	8 hours
Speed	2.5 GHz	1.8 GHz	1.5 GHz
Storage space[28]	32 GB	64 GB	16 GB
Screen size (inches)	7.87 inches (20 centimeters)	10 inches (25.4 centimeters)	13 inches (33 centimeters)
Weight (pounds)	0.73 pounds (331 grams)	1.6 pounds (726 grams)	2 pounds (907 grams)
Picture quality (1–10)	8	9	7
Ease of use (1–5 stars)	★★★★★	★★★★	★★★★
Quality of customer service (1–5 stars)	★★★★	★★★★★	★★★★
Cost	$399	$499	$219

1. Of the three tablets, Tablet _A_ gets _the best_ overall score.
   (good)

   Tablet ____ gets _____ overall score.
   (bad)

2. Tablet ____ has _____ battery life.
   (long)

3. Tablet ____ is _____. Tablet ____ has _____ price.
   (expensive)   (low)

4. Tablet ____ is _____ tablet. Tablet ____ is _____.
   (heavy)   (light)

5. The tablet with _____ speed is Tablet ____.
   (fast)

6. The tablet with _____ amount of storage space is Tablet ____.
   (large)

7. Tablet ____ is _____ tablet for people to use.
   (easy)

8. Tablet ____ has _____ screen.
   (big)

9. Tablet ____ has _____ picture quality.
   (good)

   Tablet ____ has _____ picture quality.
   (bad)

10. People with Tablet ____ can expect _____ customer service.
    (helpful)

[27] **overall:** including everything

[28] **storage space:** (electronics) space for information such as photos, music, videos, etc.

Write about It Choose a kind of product from this box or use your own idea. Think about some popular brands for the product. Write sentences with *-est/most* about the different brands.

| cars | makeup | shoes | smartphones | TVs |

24 | Usage Note: Prepositional Phrases after *-est/Most* Forms Read the note. Then do Activity 25.

Sometimes we include a **prepositional phrase** after adjectives with *-est* / *most*. This prepositional phrase describes the group.

1 Reina is the best runner **on the team**.
2 Breakfast is the most important meal **of the day**.
3 Mount Everest is the tallest mountain **in the world**.

We often don't use a prepositional phrase because the meaning is clear to the listener.

4 This store has **the lowest** prices.
5 He makes **the best** sandwiches.

25 | Writing Sentences with *-est* and *Most* Complete the questions with the words in parentheses. Use *the* + *-est* or *most* with the adjective. Then circle the correct answers. **9.7 B**

Geography Quiz

1. What is _____ *the longest river in Europe* _____?
   (long / river / in Europe)

   a. the Danube   b. the Dnieper   c. the Ural   d. the Volga

2. Which continent has _____?
   (tall / mountains)

   a. Africa   b. Asia   c. North America   d. South America

3. What is _____?
   (long / border / in the world)

   a. the border between   b. the border between   c. the border between   d. the border between
      China and India   China and   the United States   the United States
                                 Mongolia   and Canada   and Mexico

4. What is _____?
   (expensive / country / in the world)

   a. Japan   b. New Zealand   c. Norway   d. the United Kingdom

5. What is _____?
   (popular / country / for tourists)

   a. China   b. France   c. Spain   d. the United States

6. Which is _____?
   (large / island)

   a. Greenland   b. Iceland   c. Madagascar   d. New Guinea

7. What is _____?
   (large / country / in the world)

   a. Canada   b. China   c. Russia   d. the United States

8. What is _____?
   (populated / city / in the world)

   a. Buenos Aires   b. Moscow   c. Mumbai   d. Shanghai

9. What is _____?
   (small / country / in the world)

   a. San Marino   b. Vatican City   c. Monaco   d. Tuvalu

10. What is _____?
    (deep / ocean)

    a. the Arctic Ocean   b. the Atlantic Ocean   c. the Indian Ocean   d. the Pacific Ocean

Think about It Circle the prepositional phrases in the questions in Activity 25. Which questions DON'T have a prepositional phrase?

Write about It Work with a partner. Write three sentences with adjectives with -est or most about places you know. Use the phrases in this box or other adjectives.

the best	the biggest	the most beautiful	the most interesting	the worst

The University of Toronto is the biggest university in Ontario, Canada.

26 | Error Correction Find and correct the errors. (Some sentences might not have any errors.)

1. Languages are more harder for me than math or science.
2. In my opinion, Machu Picchu is the beautiful place in the world.
3. The suitcase isn't enough big for all those things.
4. The library is too quiet, so we study there.
5. Michael's new job is more bad than his last one.
6. All the children in the group are good, but Tanya is probably the most good child.
7. Jelani lives farther from school now.
8. This apartment is the larger one in the building.
9. Ayisha is the amazingest worker!
10. This apartment seems too small for us.
11. I live the most far from school, so I have the longest ride.
12. Lee is the tallest in his family.
13. Your smartphone is newer from mine.
14. My nephew is six years old.
15. This is the more large TV in the store.
16. Laurent is the most smartest person in the class.

A | GRAMMAR IN READING Read this article about two vacation spots. Underline the adjectives with -er, more, less, -est, or most. Circle the other adjectives.

Mexico's Best Resorts[29]

Acapulco: "The queen of Mexican beach resorts"

Acapulco is a city and resort on the Pacific Ocean. It is the largest

resort in Mexico, and it is probably also the most exciting resort. For many

tourists, Acapulco offers the perfect combination—amazing excitement

and natural beauty.

Acapulco

REVIEWS

"We come here every year and stay at the beach all day. The water is a beautiful blue color.

The sand on the beach looks gold. My children love Acapulco. It's a fun place for families!"—Sean H.

"Acapulco is a great place for shopping! The malls here are better and less expensive than the malls

at home. And the markets have interesting Mexican art."—Maria S.

"Evenings in Acapulco are special. The restaurants have excellent food. You can hear some great music.

The streets are full of people. Everyone's having a good time."—Katie R.

Tulum: Ancient, beautiful, and peaceful

Tulum is on the Caribbean. It is on top of a tall cliff[30] over the water.

The Mayas[31] lived at Tulum, and visitors today can see their buildings from

the years 1200 to 1500. They can see amazing Mayan art and learn about

Mayan life. Tulum is also a beach resort. Visitors can walk down the cliff to a

beautiful beach.

Tulum

REVIEWS

"Tulum is less crowded than other resorts. There aren't so many hotels or tourists. I come here

to relax!"—Tom D.

"My best photos are from Tulum. You see the tall cliff, the old buildings, and the bright blue sea.

It's amazing!"—Alexis G.

"Tulum is my favorite place for a vacation. The area has strange old buildings, interesting

plants and animals, quiet and beautiful beaches, and good yoga classes!"—Irina J.

[29] **resorts:** places where a lot of people go on vacation
[30] **cliff:** a high area of rock by the ocean, with a side that goes down very quickly

[31] **Mayas (noun), Mayan (adjective):** a group of Indian people, mainly from Mexico and Guatemala, that goes back several thousand years

Talk about It Where do you want to go on vacation: Acapulco or Tulum? Explain your reasons to a partner.

"I want to go to Tulum. It seems more relaxing. . . ."

B | GRAMMAR IN WRITING Write a short paragraph (about five to six sentences) about your favorite vacation place. Follow these guidelines:

1. In the first sentence, answer these questions:
   - What kind of place is it? (for example: a beach, a place in the mountains, a city, etc.)
   - Where is it?
2. In the other sentences, answer these questions:
   - Why is the place special? What do you and other visitors like about it?
   - What do visitors see and do there?
   - How is this place different from other vacation places?
3. Use adjectives in your paragraph. Use at least one adjective with *-er/more*, *less*, or *-est/most*. You can use some of these adjectives or your own ideas:

amazing	exciting	good	interesting	relaxing
beautiful	fun	great	popular	special

Bangkok is the capital of Thailand, and it is the biggest city in Thailand. It is a popular place for visitors because . . .

9.8 Summary of Adjectives

Adjectives describe or give more information about **nouns**. Adjectives can go:

Before the **noun** they describe	After *be* or another **linking verb**
I need some **large boxes**.	Your **friends** are really **nice**.
My **new apartment** is just a few blocks from school.	That **class** seems **interesting**.

COMPARISONS WITH ADJECTIVES

- We can use an **adjective** + *-er*, *more*, or *less* to describe differences between nouns.
- Sometimes we use a phrase with *than* after the adjective.

> Both restaurants are good, but I think Mitchell's pizza is **better**.
> My brother is much **taller than I am**. / My brother is much **taller than me**.
> Your apartment is **more expensive than mine**.
> This movie seems **more interesting**.
> New York is **less crowded than Beijing**.

- We can use *the* + **adjective** + *-est* or *the* + *most* + **adjective** to describe differences between one member of a group and the rest of the group.

> The python is **the longest** snake in the world.
> Mexico has **the most beautiful** beaches!
> Mitchell's pizza is **the best**.

Answers to Activity 11 on pages 233–234:

1. South America	3. Pacific Ocean	5. lions	7. blue whales	9. the /p/ sound	11. *blog*
2. Africa	4. London	6. tigers	8. mosquitoes	10. the English alphabet	12. Swedish

10

Future Forms

WARM-UP 250

10.1 Positive and Negative Statements with *Be Going To* 252

Pronunciation Note: *Gonna* 253

Usage Note: *There Is/There Are Going to Be* 255

10.2 Future Time Expressions 256

Usage Note: *I Think* and *Probably* 258

10.3 Yes/No Questions and Short Answers with *Be Going To* 259

10.4 *Wh-* Questions with *Be Going To* 261

10.5 Using the Present Progressive to Talk about Future Plans 263

10.6 *May* and *Might* for Future Possibility 266

10.7 Statements with *Will* 269

Pronunciation Note: *'ll* 271

10.8 Questions with *Will* 274

WRAP-UP 276

Grammar in Reading 276

Grammar in Writing 276

10.9 Summary of Future Forms 277

ONLINE

For the Unit Vocabulary Check, go to the Online Practice.

IN THIS UNIT, WE USE future forms to:

Talk about plans

1. I**'m going to travel** to London this summer.

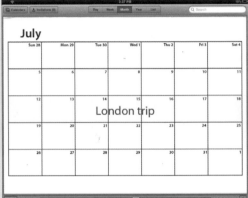

2. I **might go** to Dublin, too.

3. I**'m buying** my ticket this weekend.

Think about It Complete these sentences with your own information.

1. I'm going to travel to _____ this summer.
(place)

2. I might buy _____ next week.
(thing)

3. I'm going to see _____ this weekend.
(person)

Make predictions

4. It **might rain** later.

5. I**'m going to miss** my train!

6. In the future, people **will drive** flying cars.

7. A person **will land** on Mars.

Make offers and promises

8. I**'ll help** you with that.

9. Don't worry. I**'ll drive** carefully.

Think about It Think about your future. Check (✓) *Likely* (probably yes) or *Unlikely* (probably no).

	LIKELY	UNLIKELY
1. I'll eat a healthy dinner tonight.	☐	☐
2. I'll exercise two times this week.	☐	☐
3. I'm going to get a new job soon.	☐	☐
4. I might move to a different country someday.	☐	☐

10.1 Positive and Negative Statements with *Be Going To*

We can use **be going to** to talk about the future.

POSITIVE STATEMENTS

	subject	be	going to	base form verb	
1	I	am 'm		**stay.**	
2	We You They	are 're	**going to**	**be**	late.
3	He She It	is 's		**work**	this week.

A

Notice:
Be going to is a kind of **helping verb** in this form.
The base form verb is the **main verb**.

NEGATIVE STATEMENTS

	subject	be + not	going to	base form verb	
4	I	am not 'm not		**leave**	now.
5	We You They	are not 're not aren't	**going to**	**be**	here tomorrow.
6	He She It	is not 's not isn't		**work**	next week.

B

GO ONLINE

1 | Noticing *Be Going To* in Predictions Underline the forms of *be going to* + the main verb. Then check (✓) *Yes*, *No*, or *Maybe*. `10.1 A`

TEN YEARS FROM NOW . . .	YES	NO	MAYBE
1. I'm going to live in a different town or city.	☐	☐	☐
2. I'm going to have a job.	☐	☐	☐
3. I'm going to have a lot of money.	☐	☐	☐
4. I'm going to have the same friends.	☐	☐	☐
5. My parents are going to live near me.	☐	☐	☐
6. I'm going to speak English very well.	☐	☐	☐
7. I'm going to travel a lot.	☐	☐	☐
8. My personality is going to change.	☐	☐	☐
9. My appearance[1] is going to change.	☐	☐	☐
10. My life is going to be more fun.	☐	☐	☐

F Y I

Notice: We can use the main verb **go** after *am/is/are going to*.

We**'re going to go** to London next month.

When the main verb is *be*, we use the base form *be* after *am/is/are going to*.

I**'m going to be** at work at noon.

Talk about It Compare your answers above as a class.

[1] **appearance:** the way someone looks

2 | Pronunciation Note: *Gonna* Listen to the note. Then do Activity 3.

> We often pronounce *going to* as "gonna."
>
> **1** I'm **going to** go home soon.   *sounds like*   "I'm **gonna** go home soon."
>
> **2** She's **going to** call me back.   *sounds like*   "She's **gonna** call me back."
>
> **WARNING!** We don't usually use "gonna" in writing.

3 | Using *Be Going To* for Predictions Look at the television scenes below. Complete the sentence under each scene with the correct form of *be going to* and a verb from the box. Then listen and check your answers. `10.1 A`

drive	hit	make	trip²
get	jump	take	win

WHAT'S GOING TO HAPPEN NEXT?

1. That bike is _____ her!

2. They _____ lost.

3. He _____!

4. They _____ into the river!

5. He _____ the key!

6. She _____!

---

² **trip:** to hit your foot against something so that you fall

7. They _____!

8. She _____ an omelet.

Talk about It Take turns saying the sentences in Activity 3 to a partner. Pronounce *going to* as *gonna*. Your partner points to the correct photo.

Write about It Choose five of the scenes in Activity 3. Imagine what is going to happen next. Write a sentence about each scene.

1. *She's going to fall and break her phone.*

4 | Using *Be + Not + Going To* Complete each sentence below with the negative form of *be going to* and the verb in parentheses. Then match each picture with a sentence. **10.1 B**

a. ____

b. ____

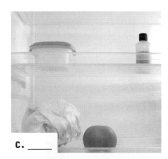
c. ____

d. ____

e. ____

f. _1_

g. ____

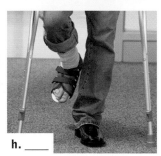
h. ____

CHANGE OF PLANS

1. I don't feel well. I _'m not going to go_ _____ to work today. (go)

2. Susanna has to study. She _____ with us. (come)

3. It's raining. We _____ soccer today. (play)

4. We _____ tonight. We don't have any food! (cook)

5. I _____ these boots. They're too expensive. (buy)

6. We _____ this exercise machine. Let's sell it. (use)

7. Jack _____ today. He hurt his foot. (run)

8. I _____ my sandwich. Do you want it? (eat)

5 | Usage Note: *There Is/There Are Going to Be* Read the note. Then do Activity 6.

We can make statements about the future with *there is* / *there are* (+ *not*) + *going to be*.

1 A: Do you want to go out later?
  B: I don't think so. **There's going to be** a storm tonight.

2 A: Are there any cookies in the kitchen?
  B: Yeah, there are a few. But go get one now. **There aren't going to be** any left later today.

There	is 's	going to	be	a storm	tonight.
	are			a lot of people	at the concert.

There	isn't 's not	going to	be	anyone*	at work tomorrow.
	aren't			a lot of people	next week.

For more information about *there is / there are*, see Unit 6.

Anyone is a singular pronoun. It means "a person."

---

6 | Using *There Is/There Are Going to Be* Complete conversations 1–5 with *there is/there are going to be*. Complete conversations 6–10 with *there is/there are not going to be*. Then listen and check your answers. `10.1 A–B`

1. A: The movie is at 7. What time do you want to leave?
   B: Let's leave early. _____ a lot of traffic.

2. A: _____ ten people here for dinner. Do we have enough food?
   B: Yeah, I went shopping this afternoon. We have a lot of food.

3. A: Do you want to play basketball tomorrow?
   B: Not tomorrow. _____ a big storm.

4. A: Why are you making cupcakes?
   B: I'm making them for school. _____ a study group after class.

5. A: Why is the break room³ closed?
   B: _____ a meeting in there at noon.

6. A: We can buy our tickets at the theater.
   B: No, let's buy them online. _____ any tickets left at 7:30.

7. A: Do you want to bring food to the park?
   B: Yeah, let's bring some sandwiches. _____ any food there.

8. A: These cookies are delicious.
   B: Don't eat them all. _____ any left for dessert!

9. A: Do you want to have lunch before the meeting?
   B: _____ time for lunch. Our appointment is at 12:30.

10. A: I want to return your sweater. Can I bring it over tonight?
    B: _____ anyone home tonight. How about tomorrow night?

> **F Y I**
>
> We can use *enough* before a noun.
>
> We're not going to have **enough food**.
> Do we have **enough money**?
>
> For more information about *enough*, see Unit 9, page 226.

cupcakes

³ **break room:** a room at a business that people use for coffee breaks, lunches, or other activities that are not work

10.2 Future Time Expressions

We use certain **time expressions** to refer to a specific time in the future.

TODAY

8:00 a.m.	9:00 a.m.	10:00 a.m.	11:00 a.m.	12:00 p.m.		4:00 p.m.		6:00 p.m.	8:00 p.m.
NOW	**in an hour**	**in a few hours**				**this** afternoon **later** today **at** 4:00		**tonight** **this** evening	
	soon					**later**			

today

THIS WEEK AND NEXT WEEK

MON	TUES	WED	THURS	FRI	SAT	SUN
12 TODAY	13 **tomorrow**	14	15 **this** Thursday **on** Thursday	16	17	18
					this weekend	

this week

A

MON	TUES	WED	THURS	FRI	SAT	SUN
19 **next** Monday **in** a week	20	21	22 **on** the 22nd	23	24	25

next week

1 I'm **going to finish** my paper **today**.

2 My friends **are going to come over** **tonight**.

3 I'm **going to start** my new job **next month**.

4 We're **going to go** to a concert **this weekend**.

5 I'm **going to see** Lisa **later tonight**.

6 I'm **going to call** you **around 7:00**.

7 Jim **is going to be** here **in a few minutes**.

8 We're **going to go** to Europe **in January**.

9 Our graduation **is going to be** **on May 28**.

today		
tonight		
next	+	week / month / year
this	+	afternoon / evening / weekend / week / month / fall / year
later	+	today / tonight / this afternoon / this evening / this month
at / around	+	8 a.m. / noon / 10:00
in	+	a second / a minute / a few minutes / a few hours / two weeks / the future
	+	January / March / 2030
on	+	Monday / Tuesday / the 15th / March 20

7 | Using *Be Going To* with Future Time Expressions Underline the time expressions in these sentences. Then complete the sentences with *be (not) going to* and the verbs in parentheses. Make true statements about your plans. **10.2 A**

MY PLANS

1. I _____ dinner with friends on Friday. (have)

2. I _____ a vacation next month. (take)

3. I _____ tonight. (study)

4. I _____ later today. (work out)

5. I _____ home in a few hours. (go)

6. I _____ late for class on Friday. (be)

7. My cousins _____ me next week. (visit)

8. My friends and I _____ tomorrow. (hang out⁴)

9. I _____ a new job soon. (get)

10. I _____ a new class in two months. (start)

11. I _____ to a new city in a few years. (move)

12. My friends and I _____ a movie this weekend. (see)

Talk about It Compare your answers in Activity 7 with a partner. Are your plans similar or different?

Write about It Change your negative sentences in Activity 7 to positive sentences. Use different time expressions. Share your answers with a partner.

1. *I'm going to have dinner with friends tonight.*

8 | Using Time Expressions to Talk about Future Plans
Alicia is a journalist for a magazine. Look at her calendar. Then check (✓) *True* or *False* for each statement on page 258. **10.2 A**

A JOURNALIST'S SCHEDULE

MON	TUES	WED	THURS	FRI	SAT	SUN
1	2 TODAY	3 have dinner with Mom	4	5 fly to Tokyo	6 go to the symphony with Akira	7 meet Japanese film directors
8 interview the prime minister⁵	9	10 return to LA from Tokyo	11 fly to New York	12 visit the *New York Times* office	13 have lunch with Mark and Lana	14 return to LA from New York
15 visit movie studio	16 interview Bradley Cooper	17	18 interview Jennifer Lawrence	19	20 fly to Buenos Aires	21
22 interview Spike Jonze	23	24 return to LA from Buenos Aires	25	26 start vacation: drive to Santa Barbara	27	28
29	30					

⁴**hang out:** (informal) to spend time with people

⁵**prime minister:** the leader of the government in some countries, for example, in Japan

	TRUE	FALSE
1. Alicia is going to fly to Tokyo next week.	☐	☐
2. Alicia and Akira are going to go to the symphony this Sunday.	☐	☐
3. Alicia is going to interview the prime minister next Monday.	☐	☐
4. She's going to have dinner with her mom tomorrow.	☐	☐
5. Later this week, she's going to meet some Japanese film directors.	☐	☐
6. Mark, Lana, and Alicia are going to have lunch this weekend.	☐	☐
7. Alicia is going to interview Jennifer Lawrence on the 21st.	☐	☐
8. She's going to visit a movie studio in two days.	☐	☐
9. In three weeks, she is going to interview Bradley Cooper.	☐	☐
10. Later this month, Alicia is going to take a vacation.	☐	☐

Write about It Correct the false statements in Activity 8. Use the correct time expressions.

1. Alicia is going to fly to Tokyo on Friday.

9 | Usage Note: *I Think* and *Probably* Read the note. Then do Activity 10.

When we're not sure about a plan or a prediction, we can use *probably* or *I think*.

1 It's **going to** rain all day tomorrow.

UNCERTAIN — CERTAIN

2 It's **probably going to** rain tomorrow.

3 **I think** it's **going to** rain tomorrow.

UNCERTAIN — CERTAIN

Use *probably* or *probably not* between *is / am / are* and *going to*.

4 I'm **probably** going to stay home tonight.

5 It's **probably** going to rain.

6 I'm **probably not** going to go out.

7 It's **probably not** going to snow.

Use *I think* or *I don't think* at the beginning of a sentence.

8 **I think** I'm going to stay home tonight.

9 **I think** it's going to rain.

10 **I don't think** I'm going to go out.

11 **I don't think** it's going to snow.

10 | Using *I Think* and *Probably* Write predictions about the weather in your area. Use *be going to* and *I think/I don't think* or *probably/probably not*. Use the time expressions in parentheses. Use the weather words and phrases in the box or your own ideas. ▮10.2 A▮

PREDICTING THE WEATHER

1. *I think it's going to rain tonight.* _____ (tonight)

2. _____ (tomorrow)

3. _____ (this weekend)

4. _____ (next week)

5. _____ (this summer)

6. _____ (this winter)

7. _____ (next month)

| be cloudy |
| be hot |
| be nice |
| be sunny |
| be windy |
| rain |
| snow |

Write about It Write predictions about the weather this weekend in these cities around the world. Use *be going to* and *I think* or *probably*. Then go online and check your predictions.

THIS WEEKEND . . .

1. In Seoul, South Korea: *It's probably going to be cold.* _____

2. In London, England: _____

3. In Santiago, Chile: _____

4. In Sydney, Australia: _____

5. In Riyadh, Saudi Arabia: _____

10.3 Yes/No Questions and Short Answers with *Be Going To*

A

YES/NO QUESTIONS

	be	subject	going to	base form verb	
1	Are	you we they		move	next month?
2	Am	I	going to	go	with you?
3	Is	he she it		be	there tonight?

SHORT ANSWERS

		subject	be
4	Yes,	I	am.
		you we they	are.
		he she it	is.

5	No,	I	am not. 'm not.
		you we they	are not. 're not. aren't.
		he she it	is not. 's not. isn't.

OTHER WAYS TO ANSWER *YES/NO* QUESTIONS

ANSWER *YES*	ANSWER *I DON'T KNOW*	ANSWER *NO*
Probably. I think so. I hope so. Yes, . . . (more information)	Maybe. I don't know. I'm not sure.	Probably not. I don't think so. I hope not. No, . . . (more information)

6 A: **Are** you **going to get** a new job?
   B: I hope so. I have an interview next week.

7 A: **Are** you **going to drive** to school?
   B: No, I'm going to take the subway.

8 A: **Are** you **going to be** here tomorrow?
   B: Probably.

9 A: **Am** I **going to be** late?
   B: I don't think so.

---

 11 | Asking *Yes/No* Questions with *Be Going To* Complete these conversations with the correct form of *be going to* and the verb in parentheses. Then listen and check your answers. **10.3 A**

ASKING ABOUT WEEKEND PLANS

1. A: _____ Carl _____ over tonight? (come)
   B: No, he's busy.

2. A: _____ you _____ shopping tomorrow? (go)
   B: No, why?
   A: I need to buy a gift for my mom.

3. A: _____ you and Karen _____ out this weekend? (go)
   B: Yeah, I think we're going to see a concert.

4. A: _____ you _____ your free movie ticket tonight? (use)

   B: No, do you want it?

5. A: _____ Elisa _____ with us this weekend? (stay)

   B: Probably not. I think she's going to stay with Sandra.

6. A: _____ we _____ anyone this weekend? (see)

   B: Yeah, we're going to have dinner with Joe and Mike.

7. A: Where's Jose?

   B: He went home.

   A: _____ he _____ back to the beach this weekend? (come)

   B: I don't think so. He's getting ready to start school next week.

8. A: How's Jackie?

   B: She's great. She and Elena are going to go to Portland this weekend.

   A: _____ they _____? (fly)

   B: No, they're going to drive.

9. A: _____ you _____ home this weekend? (be)

   B: Yeah, are you?

   A: Yeah, I am. Do you want to see a movie or something?

   B: Sure. That sounds great.

10. A: Who was that on the phone?

    B: It was Karen.

    A: _____ she _____ us at the restaurant? (meet)

    B: No, she wants us to pick her up.

Talk about It Work with a partner. Ask about your partner's plans. Use the phrases and time expressions in this box or your own ideas. Answer with short answers or with more information.

PHRASES				TIME EXPRESSIONS	
go out to dinner	go to a movie	read a book	study	on Saturday	tomorrow
go shopping	hang out with friends	stay home	watch TV	this weekend	tonight

A: Are you going to go out to dinner this weekend?
B: No, I'm not. / No, I'm going to stay home.

12 | Asking and Answering Questions about Future Plans Write *yes/no* questions with the words in parentheses and *be going to*. Then write two more questions. `10.3 A`

WHAT ARE YOU GOING TO DO THIS YEAR?

	Questions	Answered *yes*
1. (take music lessons)	*Are you going to take music lessons this year?*	
2. (move to a new city)		
3. (get a job)		

Questions	Answered *yes*
4. (get in shape[6])	
5. (learn a new sport)	
6. (go to a wedding)	
7. (leave the country)	
8. (learn a new language)	
9.	
10.	

Talk about It Ask your classmates your questions. Write the number of people who answer *yes* in the chart in Activity 12.

A: *Are you going to take music lessons this year?*
B: *No, I'm not.*

A: *Are you going to take music lessons this year?*
C: *Yes, I'm going to take guitar lessons.*

Talk about It Tell the class about the results of your survey.

"Two students are going to take music lessons this year: Eduardo and Maria."

10.4 Wh- Questions with *Be Going To*

A

	wh- word	be	subject	going to	base form verb
1	What	am	I	going to	do?
2	Where How long	are	you we they		stay?
3	When	is	he she it		leave?

4 A: **What are** you **going to do** this weekend?
   B: I'm going to visit my friend Paul.

5 A: **When is** Tina **going to be** here?
   B: Around noon, I think.

6 A: **How are** we **going to get** there?
   B: We can take the subway.

7 A: **Who are** you **going to stay** with?
   B: My aunt and uncle.

8 A **What is** the weather **going to be** like tomorrow?
   B: I think it's going to be sunny.

9 A: **How long is** the flight **going to take**?
   B: About five hours.

WH- QUESTIONS ABOUT THE SUBJECT

In these questions, *what* and *who* are the subjects.

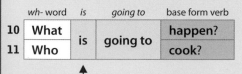

	wh- word	is	going to	base form verb
10	What	is	going to	happen?
11	Who			cook?

Notice: We usually use **is** when the subject is a *wh-* word.

[6] **get in shape:** to become healthy and physically fit (often by exercising and eating healthy food)

13 | Asking and Answering *Wh-* Questions with *Be Going To* Complete the conversations below with the correct form of *be going to*. Use the *wh-* words in the box and the verbs in parentheses. Then listen and check your answers. **10.4 A**

how long	what	when	where	who

1. A: Are you going to travel this summer?

   B: Yeah! I can't wait.

   A: _____*Where are*_____ you _____*going to go*_____? (go)

   B: Probably Los Angeles or San Diego.

2. A: Is everyone ready? Let's go.

   B: We're ready. _____ _____? (drive)

   A: Pam—she has the biggest car.

construction

3. A: Are you still watching that movie?

   B: Yeah, it's really long.

   A: _____ it _____? (end)

   B: Soon, I hope!

4. A: _____ the weather _____ like this weekend? (be)

   B: I think it _____ really hot. (be)

   A: Oh, let's go to the beach!

5. A: There's construction on my street. It wakes me up at 7 every morning!

   B: _____ the work _____? (last)

   A: Three more weeks!

6. A: _____ Marcie and Kim _____ for their vacation? (go)

   B: Mexico, I think.

   A: _____ they _____ stay? (stay)

   B: They want to find a hotel on the beach.

7. A: _____ Jose _____ his driver's license? (get)

   B: Next week! His driving test is on Friday.

8. A: _____ you _____ after class today? (do)

   B: I think I _____ home. Why? (go)

   A: Isabel and I want to go out for pizza. Do you want to come?

   B: Sure, thanks!

9. A: _____ you _____ this summer? (work)

   B: At my parents' restaurant. But in August, I _____ around Asia. (travel)

   A: That sounds great! _____ you _____ with? (go)

   B: My friend Carlos.

10. A: I think my job interview went really well!

    B: That's great! So, _____ _____ next? (happen)

    A: I have to meet the boss on Monday.

Think about It Which questions above are questions about the subject?

262

Talk about It Write questions with these words and *be going to*. Then ask and answer your questions with a partner.

YOUR NEXT VACATION

1. (where/you/go/on your next vacation) _____
2. (what/you/do/there) _____
3. (when/you/go) _____
4. (how/you/get there) _____
5. (who/go/with you) _____
6. (where/you/stay) _____
7. (who/make/the reservations) _____

1. A: *Where are you going to go on your next vacation?*
   B: *I think I'm going to go to Thailand.*

14 | Error Correction Find and correct the errors. (Some sentences may not have any errors.)

1. Where you going to go tonight?
2. I going to call Marisol later.
3. What she going to do?
4. You going to stay with Joanna?
5. Is Sonya going cook dinner tonight?
6. They no going be here tomorrow.
7. Sarah is going to come over tonight.
8. We're going to leaving in a few minutes.
9. When they're going to arrive?
10. Are we going have a test tomorrow?
11. They going to be here soon?
12. Who going to come with us?
13. Is she going to make a cake?
14. What's going be on TV tonight?

10.5 Using the Present Progressive to Talk about Future Plans

A

We sometimes use the **present progressive** to talk about future plans (when the plans are already decided). We often use **future time expressions** to show future meaning.

Remember: We form the present progressive with *be* (+ *not*) + the *-ing* **form of a verb**.

POSITIVE STATEMENTS

1 I'm leaving **tomorrow**.
2 She's starting school **next week**.

NEGATIVE STATEMENTS

3 Ken isn't coming **this weekend**.
4 We're not going out **tonight**.

YES/NO QUESTIONS

5 Are you cooking dinner **tonight**?
6 Is Gina staying with us **this weekend**?

WH- QUESTIONS

7 What are you doing **on Friday**?
8 Who's coming **tomorrow**?

PRESENT MEANING VS. FUTURE MEANING

Notice:

PRESENT MEANING

9 I can't talk now. I'm **working**.
10 What are you **doing** these days?

FUTURE MEANING

11 I'm working **this weekend**.
12 What are you **doing tomorrow**?

For more information about the present progressive, see Unit 7.

15 | Using the Present Progressive for Present and Future Meaning Complete these conversations with the present progressive form of the verbs in parentheses. Then check (✓) *Present Meaning* or *Future Meaning*. Practice the conversations with a partner. **10.5 A**

	PRESENT MEANING	FUTURE MEANING
1. A: Is Erica here? B: No, she __'s working__. (work)	✓	☐
2. A: _____ Alice and Jay _____ over for dinner tomorrow? (come) B: Yes, they are.	☐	☐
3. A: Hi, are you busy? B: No, I _____ anything right now. What's up? (not do)	☐	☐
4. A: What _____ Lucas _____? (do) B: I think he's writing an email.	☐	☐
5. A: _____ you _____ out tonight? (go) B: No, we can't. Ken has a really bad cold.	☐	☐
6. A: Katie _____ any classes next semester. (not take) B: Why not? A: She wants to work more hours.	☐	☐
7. A: Who _____ you _____ to? (talk) B: Stephen. He's in New York.	☐	☐
8. A: What _____ you _____ this weekend? (do) B: I'm not sure.	☐	☐
9. A: Can I ask you a question? B: I can't talk right now. I'm late. A: Where _____ you _____? (go) B: To class.	☐	☐
10. A: Do you want to see a movie on Friday? B: I can't. I _____ on Friday night. (work)	☐	☐
11. A: What time is your guitar lesson tonight? B: I _____ a lesson tonight. My teacher is sick. (not have)	☐	☐
12. A: _____ Sam _____ at the library? (study) B: No, he's at Ken's house.	☐	☐

Think about It Underline the future time expressions in the sentences above.

Talk about It Talk with a partner. Tell your partner your plans for this week. Use the present progressive.

> *"Tomorrow, I'm going to the movies with my friend Sarah. On Thursday, I'm working in the morning and going to class in the evening. . . ."*

◀))) 16 | Using the Present Progressive and *Be Going To* Listen and write the words you hear. Do the sentences use the present progressive or *be going to*? Write *PP* or *BGT* after the sentences. `10.5 A`

TALKING ABOUT PLANS

1. A: ____*Are*____ you ____*leaving*____ soon? __*PP*__

   B: No, we _____ for a while. _____

   How about you?

   A: We _____ around 8. _____

2. A: What _____ you _____ this summer? _____

   B: I _____ some classes. How about you? _____

   A: I _____ to Europe for the summer. _____

3. A: I _____ a new job next Monday. _____

   B: Congratulations! Where _____ you _____? _____

   A: At the new mall downtown.

4. A: _____ you _____ anything

   this weekend? _____

   B: Yeah, we _____ to the street fair

   on Saturday. _____

   A: Oh, I _____ to the fair, too! _____

5. A: What _____ you _____? _____

   B: I _____ a plane ticket online. _____

   A: Oh, where _____ you _____? _____

   B: To Mexico.

6. A. Hey, how are you?

   B: I'm great, but really busy.

   A: How many classes _____ you _____ this semester? _____

   B: Five! Next semester, I _____ three classes. _____

7. A: Is Misha home?

   B: No, she _____ at the library. _____

   A: OK. _____ she _____ home soon? _____

   B: I'm not sure. I can tell her to call you.

   A: Great. Thanks.

8. A: Do you have plans for this weekend?

   B: No, I think I _____ home. How about you? _____

   A: Sarah and I _____ to the beach on Saturday. Do you want to come? _____

   B: Hmm. OK. Thanks.

9. A: Can you email me your salmon recipe? I _____ dinner for my parents

   tonight. _____

   B: Of course. No problem.

a street fair

F Y I

When we use the present progressive for personal plans, it means our plans are already decided.

I'm taking a class this summer.
(= I already made plans to take a class this summer.)

Think about It Look at the present progressive sentences in the conversations above. Which sentences have a future meaning? Which have a present meaning?

10.6 May and Might for Future Possibility

We can use **may** or **might** + the **base form of a verb** to talk about possible future events.

A

POSITIVE STATEMENTS

	subject	*may / might*	base form verb	
1	I You We They He She It	**may** **might**	**be**	late tomorrow.

2 It **may rain** on Friday.
3 We **might go** out tonight.
4 They **might come** with us.

NEGATIVE STATEMENTS

	subject	*may / might + not*	base form verb	
5	I You We They He She It	**may not** **might not**	**be**	late tomorrow.

6 He **may not be** home tonight.
7 She **might not pass** the test.
8 I **may not play** tennis next year.

WARNING! Use the **base form of a verb** after *may* or *might*.

✓ We may **go** out tonight.
✓ I might not **take** this class next semester.

✗ We may **to go** out tonight.
✗ I might not **taking** this class next semester.

GRAMMAR TERM: *May* and *might* are **modals**. For more information about modals, see Units 11 and 12.

B

May and **might** show a weaker certainty than other future forms.

BE GOING TO	We're **going to go** out tonight.
PRESENT PROGRESSIVE	We're **going** out tonight.

MAY	We **may go** out tonight.
MIGHT	We **might go** out tonight.

GO ONLINE

---

17 | Using *Might* and *Might Not* Complete conversations 1–4 with *might* and a verb from the box. Then complete conversations 5–8 with *might not* and a verb from the box. `10.6 A–B`

MAKING, ACCEPTING, AND DECLINING[7] INVITATIONS

1. A: What are you doing tonight?
   B: I'm not sure. I _____*might see*_____ a movie later. How about you?
   A: I'm going to an art show. Do you want to come with me?
   B: Hmm. OK. Sure.

2. A: Do you want to do something this weekend?
   B: Thanks, but I can't. My brother is getting married this weekend.
   A: Oh, that's great! Have fun!
   B: What are you going to do this weekend?
   A: I don't know. I _____ skiing with my cousins.

go
see

RESEARCH SAYS...

Might is more common in conversation. *May* is more common in academic writing.

We **might** go out tonight.

The population **may** increase by 50 percent.

CORPU

[7] **declining:** saying no

3. A: Do you want to come to a concert in the park tonight?

   My friends have an extra ticket.

   B: I don't think so. Look at the sky. It _____.

   A: You're right.

like
rain

4. A: I'm going to a jazz show tonight. Do you want to come?

   B: Maybe. I don't really know jazz music.

   A: Just try it. You _____ it.

   B: OK.

5. A: I'm hungry! Do you want to go out for lunch after class?

   B: Yeah, but I _____ enough time.

   I have a meeting with my advisor at 1.

   A: Oh, OK. Maybe tomorrow!

go
have

6. A: Do you want a ride to school tomorrow?

   B: I don't know. I _____ to school tomorrow.

   I don't feel very well.

   A: Oh, no. There's a really bad cold going around right now.

7. A: Where are you going to go for vacation this summer?

   B: I _____ a vacation this summer.

   I don't think I have enough money.

   A: Kelly and I are going to go to my uncle's beach house in July.

   It's free. Do you want to come with us?

   B: Sure! Thanks!

be
take

8. A: Do you want to come over for dinner tonight? I'm making spaghetti with shrimp.

   B: That sounds delicious, but I _____ hungry for dinner.

   I ate a really big lunch.

   A: Come over anyway. Stacey is going to be there.

   B: OK.

Talk about It Listen and check your answers. Then practice the conversations in Activity 17 with a partner.

Think about It In the conversations in Activity 17, underline the forms of *be going to* and the present progressive with a future meaning. In each conversation, which speaker is talking about certain events? Which speaker is talking about possible events?

In conversation 1, Speaker A is talking about certain events.
Speaker B is talking about possible events.

18 | Writing Sentences with *May* and *Might* Look at these photos. For each photo, write one positive sentence and one negative sentence with *may* or *might*. Use verbs in the boxes below or your own ideas.

`10.6 A`

MAKING PREDICTIONS

1 | go   rain   stay | *It might rain later.*

2 | go   play   stay

3 | be   get   miss

4 | make   miss   score

19 | Writing Sentences with *Be Going To*, *May*, and *Might* Write sentences about your plans. Complete the sentences below with the ideas in the box or your own ideas. Use the forms in parentheses. (Look at Charts 10.1–10.2 for help with *be going to*.) `10.6 A–B`

DEFINITE PLANS AND POSSIBLE PLANS

be in school	buy a car	go on vacation	live in (city)	move
be in this city	get a pet	have my dream job	live in my dream house	take classes

1. (be going to) _____ next year.

2. (be not going to) _____ next year.

3. (might) _____ next year.

4. (might not) _____ next year.

5. (be going to) _____ in five years.

6. (be not going to) _____ in five years.

7. (may) _____ in five years.

8. (may not) _____ in five years.

9. (be going to) _____ in ten years.

10. (be not going to) _____ in ten years.

11. (might) _____ in ten years.

12. (may not) _____ in ten years.

10.7 Statements with *Will*

Another form we use to talk about the future is **will**. We use **will** + the **base form of a verb**.

POSITIVE STATEMENTS

A **1**

subject	will	base form verb	
I / You / We / They / He / She / It	**will** **'ll**	**be**	there in five minutes.

In speaking and informal writing, we usually use the contraction 'll.

2 I**'ll pick** you up after work.

3 Scientists **will discover** another planet soon.

4 The weather **will be** nice next week.

NEGATIVE STATEMENTS

B **5**

subject	will + not	base form verb	
I / You / We / They / He / She / It	**will not** **won't**	**leave**	without you.

In speaking and informal writing, we usually use the contraction won't.

6 We **won't stay** very long.

7 I promise I **won't leave**!

8 We **won't get** there on time.

 GO ONLINE

20 | Forming Statements with *Will* Complete these sentences with *will* and the verbs in parentheses. Do you think the predictions will happen? Check (✓) *Likely* or *Not Likely*. `10.7 A`

Predictions in Science and Technology

Here are some predictions from scientists and technology experts[8]:

	LIKELY	NOT LIKELY
1. Computers _____ a sense of smell. (have)	☐	☐
2. People _____ their thoughts into a computer. (upload[9])	☐	☐
3. People _____ all of their conversations. (record)	☐	☐
4. We _____ to computers directly from our brains. (connect)	☐	☐
5. People _____ on vacations in space. (go)	☐	☐
6. Cars _____ without human drivers. (drive)	☐	☐
7. Many people _____ for 150 years or more. (live)	☐	☐
8. Airplanes _____ without pilots. (fly)	☐	☐
9. Some buildings _____ ten kilometers high. (be)	☐	☐
10. An astronaut _____ on Mars. (land)	☐	☐

---

[8] **experts:** people who know a lot about something

[9] **upload:** to copy or transfer information from one computer to another

Talk about It Compare your answers in Activity 20 as a class. Which predictions do most students believe?

I can't reach that book.

🔊 **21 | Making Offers with *I'll*** Listen and complete these conversations with the words you hear (*I'll* + a main verb). Then practice the conversations with a partner. **10.7 A**

MAKING OFFERS

1. A: What's wrong?

   B: My taxi isn't here. I have to get to the airport soon.

   A: _I'll take_____ you.

   B: Really? Thanks so much!

2. A: Do you need some help?

   B: Yeah. I can't reach that book.

   A: _____ it for you.

3. A: Are you lost?

   B: Yeah, I'm looking for the museum. Is it near here?

   A: Yeah, let me see your map. _____ you.

   B: Thank you. I appreciate it.

4. A: What's wrong?

   B: I left my wallet at home.

   A: _____ this time. You can pay next time.

   B: It's a deal.

5. A: Did you do the math homework?

   B: Yeah, I did. Did you?

   A: Not yet. I don't understand it at all.

   B: _____ you with it.

6. A: Oh, are you baking cookies?

   B: Well, I wanted to, but I can't. We don't have any eggs.

   A: _____ some. I have to go to the store anyway.

   B: Great. Thanks.

7. A: Is Sarah here yet?

   B: No, she isn't. I don't know where she is.

   A: _____ her.

   B: Good idea.

8. A: Welcome! I'm so excited to see you!

   B: I'm excited to be here!

   A: Was it a long drive?

   B: Yeah, I'm really tired.

   A: Well, come in and sit down. _____ your suitcase

      in from the car.

22 | Pronunciation Note: 'll Listen to the note. Then do Activity 23.

> In conversation, we usually use the contraction **'ll** with pronouns. Sometimes the **'ll** is difficult to hear. Notice the difference between sentences with **'ll** and sentences with the simple present.
>
> | FUTURE WITH 'LL | SIMPLE PRESENT |
> |---|---|
> | **1** I'll call you tomorrow. | **3** I call my mother every weekend. |
> | **2** She'll make dinner tonight. | **4** She makes dinner on Tuesdays. |
>
> Time expressions and other clues can help you decide if the sentence describes the present or future.

23 | Listening for 'll Listen and write the words you hear. Check (✓) *Future with 'll* or *Simple Present*. Then practice the conversations with a partner. `10.7 A`

	FUTURE WITH 'LL	SIMPLE PRESENT
1. A: I'm going to be home late. Can you order a pizza for dinner? B: _____ dinner. I'm going to be home early.	☐	☐
2. A: Mom, I can't reach the cereal. B: _____ it for you.	☐	☐
3. A: The faucet is dripping again. B: The plumber[10] is coming tomorrow. _____ it.	☐	☐
4. A: Oh, no. We're out of milk. B: I'm going to the store today. _____ some.	☐	☐
5. A: Do your parents like this show? B: Yeah, they love it. _____ it every week.	☐	☐
6. A: Are you going to play tennis tonight? B: Yeah, _____ every Wednesday.	☐	☐
7. A: What do you do on the weekends? B: _____ at a sandwich shop.	☐	☐
8. A: These bags are so heavy. B: _____ one of them.	☐	☐
9. A: Oh, no! I'm late. I'm going to miss the bus. B: I'm not busy. _____ you a ride.	☐	☐
10. A: We need more towels. Also, there's no soap in the bathroom. B: _____ the front desk.	☐	☐

The faucet is dripping.

Think about It What words in the conversations above helped you choose *'ll* or the simple present?

[10] **plumber:** a person who repairs things like water pipes and toilets

24 | Using *Won't* Complete each sentence with *won't* and the verb in parentheses. When are these predictions going to happen? Check (✓) a time period for each statement. `10.7 B`

SOME PREDICTIONS ABOUT THE FUTURE

	10 **YEARS** FROM NOW	50 **YEARS** FROM NOW	100 **YEARS** FROM NOW
1. We _____ books on paper. (read)	☐	☐	☐
2. Cars _____ gasoline. (use)	☐	☐	☐
3. We _____ any gasoline left. (have)	☐	☐	☐
4. People _____ regular mail anymore. (send)	☐	☐	☐
5. Young children _____ handwriting. (learn)	☐	☐	☐
6. In big cities, the air _____ safe to breathe. (be)	☐	☐	☐
7. We _____ on paper anymore. (write)	☐	☐	☐
8. People _____ for things with cash anymore. (pay)	☐	☐	☐
9. In big cities, the tap water[11] _____ safe to drink. (be)	☐	☐	☐
10. People _____ a time without smartphones. (remember)	☐	☐	☐

Talk about It Compare your answers above as a class. Did you make the same predictions?

Write about It Write two more predictions about the future. Write one sentence with *will* and one sentence with *won't*. Share your predictions with a partner.

In the future, scientists will control the weather.
People won't worry about hurricanes or tsunamis.

25 | Using *'ll* and *Won't* Complete these conversations with *'ll* or *won't* and the verbs in parentheses. Then listen and check your answers. `10.7 A–B`

PROMISES AND REASSURANCES[12]

1. A: I need to pick up my car from the shop[13]. What bus is around here?

   B: I __'ll drive_____ you there. It's on my way.
   _(drive)

   A: Oh, thank you!

---

[11] **tap water:** water that comes from a faucet
[12] **reassurances:** things you say to make people feel better
[13] **the shop:** a place where cars get fixed

2. A: My taxi is going to be here in ten minutes and I'm not ready!

    B: Don't worry. The driver _____ without you.
                                        (leave)

    A: I don't want to miss my flight.

    B: You _____ your flight. You're probably going to get to the airport
              (miss)
       three hours early.

3. A: How's Karen doing?

    B: Not great. She's probably going to stay in the hospital for another week.

    A: Don't worry. She _____ OK.
                              (be)

4. A: What are you studying?

    B: Geometry. I can't understand anything! I think I'm going to fail the test.

    A: You _____. I _____ you study.
             (fail)   (help)

    B: Are you sure? You're so busy.

    A: Yeah, I don't mind at all. I really like geometry.

5. A: Are you excited about your interview tomorrow?

    B: No, I'm so nervous.

    A: Don't worry. You _____ fine. You're perfect for the job.
                              (be)

       They _____ you.
               (love)

    B: Thanks. I hope so!

6. A: Hi. Are you busy? I have a question for you.

    B: I'm cooking dinner. Can I call you back in half an hour?

    A: I _____ home in half an hour. I'm leaving in a few minutes.
            (be)

    B: OK. Then I _____ you later tonight.
                      (call)

    A: Don't forget, OK?

    B: I _____, I promise.
            (forget)

7. A: How do you like your new apartment?

    B: It's great! You're going to help me paint the living room this weekend, right? Don't forget!

    A: I _____, I promise. I _____ over at 10 on Saturday.
            (remember)   (come)

8. A: Hello?

    B: Hi, Mark. This is Sam. Sorry, but I _____ late for work this morning.
                                                   (be)
       My car isn't starting.

    A: OK. Are you going to miss the meeting?

    B: No, I _____ the meeting. I _____ there by 11.
                (miss)   (be)

10.8 Questions with Will

A

YES/NO QUESTIONS

	will	subject	base form verb	
1		I	**miss**	my flight?
2		you	**meet**	me tomorrow?
3		we	**get**	there on time?
4	**Will**	they	**help**	us?
5		he	**pass**	his class?
6		she	**be**	here tomorrow?
7		it	**leave**	on time?

SHORT ANSWERS

8	Yes,	you I we they he she it	**will.**
9	No,		**won't.**

OTHER WAYS TO ANSWER *YES/NO* QUESTIONS

ANSWER *YES*	ANSWER *I DON'T KNOW*	ANSWER *NO*
Probably. I think so. I hope so. Yes, . . . (more information)	Maybe. I don't know. I'm not sure.	Probably not. I don't think so. I hope not. No, . . . (more information)

10 A: Will you live in the city next year?
  B: **Yes,** I'm going to move in the fall.

11 A: Will you be here tomorrow?
  B: **No,** I'll be out of town.

B

WH- QUESTIONS

	wh- word	will	subject	base form verb	
12	**When**		I	**see**	you?
13	**Who**		you we	**hire?**	
14	**How**	**will**	they	**get**	here?
15	**How long**		he she	**stay**	with you?
16	**What time**		it	**start?**	

WH- QUESTIONS ABOUT THE SUBJECT

In these questions, *what* and *who* are the subjects.

	wh- word	will	base form verb	
17	**What**	**will**	**happen**	to Sandra?
18	**Who**		**be**	there tonight?

GO ONLINE

26 | Asking Questions with *Will* Put the words in the correct order to write *yes/no* and *wh-* questions with *will*. Circle the best answer for each question. `10.8 A–B`

1. (get/up tomorrow morning/when/you/will)

   When will you get up tomorrow morning?

   a. Yes, I will.   b. At 6.   c. I'll take the train.

2. (see/will/your friends tomorrow/you)

   _____

   a. No, I won't.   b. In the morning.   c. At school.

3. (you/get/home today/when/will)

   _____

   a. Yes, I will.   b. At 5:30.   c. I think so.

4. (you/be/tomorrow/will/in class)

   _____

   a. In Mexico.   b. Next month.   c. Probably.

5. (do/what/on your next vacation/will/you)

_____

    a. Go to San Diego.   b. Probably.   c. No, I won't.

6. (have/more information/when/will/you)

_____

    a. Next week.   b. I don't think so.   c. Probably not.

7. (will/what/your next job/be)

_____

    a. In the summer.   b. Yes, I will.   c. I don't know.

8. (be/who/will/at your house tonight)

_____

    a. No, I won't.   b. My roommate Jane.   c. I don't think so.

Talk about It Work with a partner. Ask the questions in Activity 26. Answer with your own ideas.

A: When will you get up tomorrow morning?
B: At 8.

27 | Asking and Answering Questions with *Will* Use the words in parentheses to write *yes/no* and *wh-* questions with *will*. `10.8 A–B`

What will your life be like in the future?

Imagine your life in 5 years and in 20 years. Think about these questions.

1. (you/own a house)
   Will you own a house?

2. (where/you/live)

   _____

3. (who/you/live/with)

   _____

4. (what/job/you/have)

   _____

5. (you/have/children)

   _____

6. (how many/children/you/have)

   _____

7. (what/you/do/for fun)

   _____

8. (you/have/a pet)

   _____

9. (you/be/in school)

   _____

10. (what/you/look like)

    _____

Talk about It Ask and answer the questions above with a partner. Ask each question twice. Add "in 5 years" and "in 20 years."

A: Will you own a house in 5 years?   *A: Will you own a house in 20 years?*
B: Probably not.   *B: I hope so!*

Write about It Write predictions about your life in 60 years.

In 60 years, I will live with my grandchildren.

WRAP-UP

A | GRAMMAR IN READING Read this article. Underline the verbs that refer to future time. Then check (✓) *True* or *False* for each statement below.

Is the World's Population Growing or Shrinking?

There are now more than 7 billion people on Earth. The population grew from 6 billion to 7 billion in only 12 years (from 1999 to 2011). In comparison, the population grew from 1 billion to 2 billion from 1804 to 1927—that's 123 years. The recent growth rate[14] is almost ten times faster.

Today the growth rate is a little slower than it was in the 1990s. In the past, people had a lot of children. Now, couples in many countries have just one or two children. But the growth rate may rise again. The United Nations estimates[15] that we will reach 8 billion people by 2024 and 10 billion people by 2064. Some environmentalists[16] are worried about faster population growth. They say we are going to run out of[17] clean water and oil.

Some experts disagree about the problem. Warren Sanderson is an expert on population growth. He's a professor of economics, and he does research at Austria's International Institute for Applied Systems Analysis (IIASA). He believes the world's population may never reach 10 billion. He says the population will reach 9 billion in 2050—then it will get smaller: "After 2050, we're going to reach a state of . . . zero population growth." That means the population won't get bigger or smaller. Then the growth rate will go down. The IIASA believes the population will fall to 3.5 billion by 2200. By 2300, there may be only 1 billion people on Earth.

THE UNITED NATIONS AND ENVIRONMENTALISTS SAY . . .	TRUE	FALSE
1. The world's population won't reach 10 billion by 2064.	☐	☐
2. The growth rate will continue to fall.	☐	☐
3. We're going to run out of oil.	☐	☐

WARREN SANDERSON AND THE IIASA SAY . . .	TRUE	FALSE
4. The population will reach 10 billion.	☐	☐
5. The population is going to grow after 2050.	☐	☐
6. There will be 3.5 billion people on Earth in 2200.	☐	☐
7. There may be only 1 billion people on Earth in 2300.	☐	☐

Write about It Correct the false statements above.

B | GRAMMAR IN WRITING According to the reading above, environmentalists predict that we will run out of clean water or oil. Predict more possible problems. Write six sentences with *will*, *won't*, *may*, and *may not*. Use the ideas in the box or your own ideas.

apartments/be smaller	have enough food	there/be enough houses
food/be more expensive	have enough water	there/be too many cars

We may have more violent weather in the future.   *The sea level will rise a lot more in the next 20 years.*

[14] **growth rate:** the measurement of how fast something grows
[15] **estimate:** to guess or predict the size of something
[16] **environmentalists:** people who try to protect the environment
[17] **run out of:** to not have any left

Talk about It Imagine that it's the year 2050 and your predictions happened. What are you going to do? Write four ideas with *be going to*. Compare your ideas with a partner.

I'm not going to build a house near the ocean!
I'm going to plant a big garden and share the food with other people.

10.9 Summary of Future Forms

BE GOING TO

POSITIVE STATEMENTS

I	am		
You / We / They	are	going to	leave.
He / She / It	is		

NEGATIVE STATEMENTS

I	am not 'm not		
You / We / They	are not 're not aren't	going to	stay.
He / She / It	is not 's not isn't		

YES/NO QUESTIONS

Am	I		
Are	you / we / they	going to	come?
Is	he / she / it		

SHORT ANSWERS

	you / we / they	are.
Yes,	I	am.
	he / she / it	is.

	you / we / they	are not. 're not. aren't.
No,	I	am not. 'm not.
	he / she / it	is not. 's not. isn't.

WH- QUESTIONS

What	am	I		do?
Where	are	you / we / they	going to	go?
When	is	he / she / it		arrive?

QUESTIONS ABOUT THE SUBJECT

Who	is	going to	drive?
What			happen?

MAY, MIGHT, AND WILL

POSITIVE STATEMENTS

I / You / We / They / He / She / It	may might will 'll	arrive	on Friday.

NEGATIVE STATEMENTS

I / You / We / They / He / She / It	may not might not will not won't	be	here tomorrow.

QUESTIONS WITH *WILL*

YES/NO QUESTIONS

Will	I / you / we / they / he / she / it	be	at the office on Monday?

SHORT ANSWERS

Yes,	you / I / we / they / he / she / it	will.
No,		won't.

WH- QUESTIONS

What		I / you / we / they / he / she / it	do?
Where	will		go?
When			arrive?

WH- QUESTIONS ABOUT THE SUBJECT

Who	will	be there?
What		happen?

11

Modals I

WARM-UP 278

11.1 Can for Ability and Possibility 280

Usage Note: *Very Well, Pretty Well, and Not at All* 281

Pronunciation Note: *Can vs. Can't* 282

11.2 Questions with *Can* 283

11.3 *Could* for Past Ability 286

11.4 *Be Able To* 290

11.5 Permission with *Can, Could, and May + I/We* 293

11.6 Requests with *Can, Could, and Would + You* 295

Usage Note: *Borrow, Have, Lend, and Give* 298

11.7 *Would Like* for Desires, Offers, and Invitations 299

Pronunciation Note: *Would You* 300

Usage Note: *Would Like vs. Want* 302

Pronunciation Note: *D'you Wanna* 302

WRAP-UP 304

Grammar in Reading 304

Grammar in Speaking 304

11.8 Summary of Modals I 305

GO ONLINE

For the Unit Vocabulary Check, go to the Online Practice.

IN THIS UNIT, WE USE modals to talk about:

Ability and possibility

1. I **can** play the piano.

2. My great-grandfather **could** fix cars.

3. We **won't be able to** go swimming today.

4. She **can't** see the board.

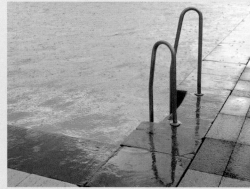

Think about It Read these sentences. Check (✓) *True* or *False*.

	TRUE	FALSE
1. I can play the piano.	☐	☐
2. I can fix cars.	☐	☐
3. I'll be able to go swimming tomorrow.	☐	☐
4. I can see the board right now.	☐	☐
5. I will be able to come to class tomorrow.	☐	☐
6. I was able to finish my homework last night.	☐	☐

Requests and permission

5. A: **Can** you call back later?
    B: Sure.

6. A: **Could** I use your computer for a minute?
    B: Sorry. I need it right now.

Offers and invitations

7. A: **May** I help you?
    B: I'm looking for a formal shirt.

8. A: **Would you like to** sit down?
    B: Thank you.

Think about It Read the conversations above. Underline the word before the subject in each question. Does each question ask about the past, the present, or the future?

11.1 Can for Ability and Possibility

We can use **can** to talk about ability and possibility in the present.

A

POSITIVE STATEMENTS

	subject	*can*	base form verb	
1	I He She We You They	**can**	**work**	today.

NEGATIVE STATEMENTS

	subject	*can + not*	base form verb	
2	I He She We You They	**cannot*** **can't**	**work**	today.

> The modal **can** (+ **not**) is a **helping verb**. The **base form verb** is the **main verb**.

*The full negative form is **cannot**. In speaking and informal writing, we usually use the contraction **can't**.

Notice: Sometimes **can** has a future meaning.

3 I **can call** you after 3:00.

4 She **can come** to work early tomorrow.

5 I'm sorry I **can't come** to dinner tonight.

6 We **can't get** to the airport on time.

1 | Using *Can* Complete the sentences below with *can* + a base form verb from the box. `11.1 A`

OLYMPIC ATHLETES

a ski jumper

a weightlifter

a shot putter

a downhill skier

a speed skater

an archer

a luge racer

a figure skater

1. Olympic runners _____*can run*_____ a marathon[1] in 2 hours and 18 minutes.

2. Olympic swimmers _____ 100 meters (109.4 yards) in 48.82 seconds.

3. Olympic ski jumpers _____ over 200 meters (218.7 yards).

4. Some Olympic weightlifters _____ over 200 kilograms (440 pounds).

jump lift run swim

[1] **marathon:** a long-distance race of about 26 miles

5. Olympic shot putters _____ a shot put over 20 meters (65.6 feet).

6. Downhill skiers _____ down a mountain at over 120 kilometers (74.6 miles) per hour.

7. Speed skaters _____ 1000 meters (1093.6 yards) in just over a minute.

| skate |
| ski |
| throw |

8. Archers _____ a 12.2-centimeter (4.8-inch) bull's-eye[2] from 70 meters (76.6 yards) away.

9. Luge racers _____ 140 kilometers (87 miles) an hour.

10. A figure skater _____ 30 or 40 times without falling down.

| go |
| hit |
| spin[3] |

Talk about It Go online and look up information about Olympic athletes. Take notes. Then tell a partner what three different athletes can do.

"Apolo Ohno can skate 40 miles an hour!"

2 | Usage Note: *Very Well*, *Pretty Well*, and *Not at All* Read the note. Then do Activity 3.

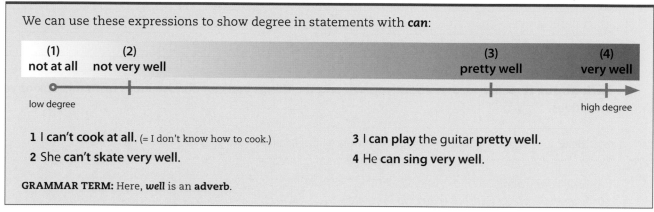

We can use these expressions to show degree in statements with **can**:

(1) not at all   (2) not very well   (3) pretty well   (4) very well

low degree ————————————————————————→ high degree

1 I **can't cook at all.** (= I don't know how to cook.)

2 She **can't skate very well.**

3 I **can play** the guitar **pretty well.**

4 He **can sing very well.**

GRAMMAR TERM: Here, *well* is an **adverb**.

3 | Using *Can* and *Can't* How well can you do the things in this chart? Check (✓) the box that describes your ability. Then write a sentence on page 282 for each item. **11.1 A**

JOB SKILLS SURVEY

	VERY WELL	PRETTY WELL	NOT VERY WELL	NOT AT ALL
1. work with others				
2. work independently				
3. learn new things				
4. solve problems				
5. accept criticism[4]				
6. lead others				
7. speak English				

[2] **bull's-eye:** the center of a target
[3] **spin:** to turn around quickly

[4] **criticism:** a description of someone's bad points

	VERY WELL	PRETTY WELL	NOT VERY WELL	NOT AT ALL
8. do basic math				
9. use common software programs				
10. use tools and building equipment[5]				
11. drive				
12. cook				

I can work with others very well.

1. _____
2. _____
3. _____
4. _____
5. _____
6. _____
7. _____

8. _____
9. _____
10. _____
11. _____
12. _____

Talk about It Tell a partner about yourself and the things you can do. Use ideas from this box or your own ideas.

draw	speak in public[6]	type	work with children

A: *I can't draw at all.*
B: *I can draw pretty well, but I can't type very well.*

Write about It Choose three of the jobs from this box. Write about what people with those jobs can do well.

astronomer	counselor	engineer	manager	server
cashier	designer	journalist	nurse	teacher

A nurse can read a medical chart.

4 | Pronunciation Note: *Can* vs. *Can't* Listen to the note. Then do Activity 5.

We usually do not stress *can*. We stress the **main verb**, and we pronounce *can* as /kn/.

1 I can **WORK** tomorrow.   2 We can **HELP** you with that.

In sentences with *can't*, we often stress both **can't** and the **main verb**. We pronounce *can't* with a clear "a" sound (/æ/), as in *man*.

3 I **CAN'T WORK** tomorrow.   4 We **CAN'T HELP** you with that.

Sometimes we stress the word *can* to disagree or show a contrast.

5 A: Did you say you **CAN** or you **CAN'T** help me?
   B: I **CAN** help you. I'm happy to do that.

[5] **equipment:** things that are needed for a particular activity   [6] **in public:** when other people are there

5 | Listening for *Can* and *Can't* Listen to these sentences. Circle the word you hear. Then listen again and repeat the sentences. `11.1 A`

SCHEDULES

1. I (can / can't) get to school early tomorrow.
2. I (can / can't) go out to dinner tonight.
3. I (can / can't) meet at lunchtime tomorrow.
4. I (can / can't) pick you up from the airport on Wednesday.
5. I (can / can't) go home before 4:00.
6. I (can / can't) call you in the morning.
7. I (can / can't) come to class next week.

8. I (can / can't) study over the weekend.
9. I (can / can't) stay late today.
10. I (can / can't) watch TV tonight.
11. I (can / can't) study in the library tonight.
12. I (can / can't) take some time off this week.
13. I (can / can't) go to a movie tomorrow night.
14. I (can /can't) sleep late tomorrow morning.

Talk about It Read the sentences above to a partner. Use *can* or *can't* to make each sentence true for you. Your partner listens for the correct form.

1. A: *I can't get to school early tomorrow.*
   B: *You said* can't.

Talk about It Make a lunch date with your partner. Talk about when you can and can't go to lunch. Your partner listens for *can* or *can't*. Check your understanding.

A: *I can't meet you tomorrow.*
B: *Did you say* can't?
A: *That's right. I can't meet you tomorrow. I can meet you on Tuesday.*

11.2 Questions with *Can*

A

YES/NO QUESTIONS

	can	subject	base form verb	
1	Can	I you he she it we they	finish	today?

SHORT ANSWERS

		subject	can / can't
2	Yes,	you I he she it we they	can.
3	No,		can't.

B

WH- QUESTIONS

	wh- word	can	subject	base form verb	
4	What		I	eat?	
5	Where		he	meet	us?
6	When		she	get	here?
7	How fast	can	it	go?	
8	Why		we	hear	your neighbor?
9	Who		you	ask	about the schedule?
10	How		they	swim	so fast?

ANSWERS

There's some leftover pizza.
At the station.
In a couple of hours.
About 50 miles per hour.
He speaks very loudly.
I'm not sure. Maybe Mr. Potter?
They practice every day.

GO ONLINE

6 | Asking *Yes/No* Questions with *Can* Write *yes/no* questions with *can you* and the phrases in this chart. Add two questions of your own. Then ask and answer the questions with a partner. **11.2 A**

Abilities	
1. ride a motorcycle	*Can you ride a motorcycle?*
2. make a cake	
3. say a poem from memory	
4. wiggle[7] your ears	
5. raise one eyebrow	
6. remember your first teacher's name	
7. run 12 miles	
8. sing well	
9. count to ten in French	
10. play a musical instrument	
11. add two-digit numbers in your head[8]	
12. name the seven continents in English	
13. [your own question]	
14. [your own question]	

raise one eyebrow

$$\begin{array}{r} 83 \\ + 54 \\ \hline 137 \end{array}$$

add two-digit numbers in your head

F Y I

In short answers, we stress *can*. We pronounce it /kæn/, not /kn/.

Yes, I **CAN**.

Yes, she **CAN**.

1. A: *Can you ride a motorcycle?*
   B: *Yes, I can. / No, I can't.*

7 | Understanding Questions and Statements with *Can* Look at these photos and captions. Then listen and complete the statements and *yes/no* questions on page 285. Add punctuation. **11.2 A**

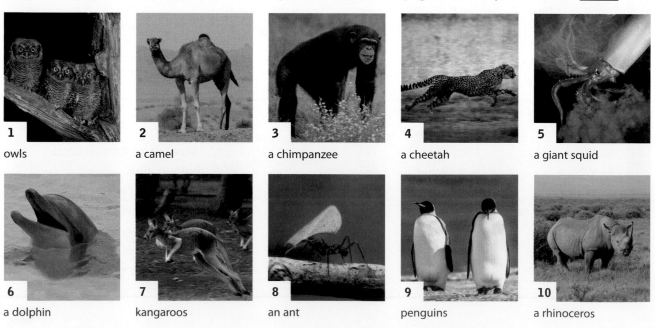

1 owls

2 a camel

3 a chimpanzee

4 a cheetah

5 a giant squid

6 a dolphin

7 kangaroos

8 an ant

9 penguins

10 a rhinoceros

[7] **wiggle:** to move back and forth   [8] **in [your] head:** without writing

1. _Can owls see_ _____ in the dark?
2. _____ for more than a week without water
3. _____ swim
4. _____ over 60 miles per hour
5. _____ to over 40 feet long
6. _____ underwater
7. _____ 30 feet
8. _____ more than three times its own weight
9. _____ fly
10. _____ jump

Talk about It Ask a partner the questions in Activity 7. Go online to find any answers that you and your partner don't know.

1. A: *Can owls see in the dark?*
   B: *Yes, they can.*

Write about It Write three more questions with *can* about animals. If you don't know the answers, look them up online.

8 | Asking and Answering Questions with *Can* Complete these questions using the words in parentheses and *can*. 11.2 A–B

MAKING PLANS

1. A: _____ after class today?
      (how long / you / stay)
   B: I can stay until 1. I have to work at 1:30.

2. A: _____?
      (when / we / meet)
   B: I'm not sure. Maybe next week.

3. A: _____ to lunch with us?
      (your brother / come)
   B: I don't know. I'll ask him.

4. A: _____ you?
      (when / I / call)
   B: After 6 tonight.

5. A: _____ together?
      (when / we / get)
   B: Hmm. I'm busy this week. How about next weekend?

6. A: _____ here at 3?
      (you / be)
   B: I think so. I'll hurry.

7. A: _____ batteries?
      (where / I / find)
   B: They're next to the cash register.

8. A: _____ the doctor?
      (when / I / see)
   B: Are you free this afternoon? The doctor is available around 3.

9. A: _____ a good meal around here?
    (where / I / get)
    B: Smythe's. The food is good and it's cheap.

10. A: _____ me with my computer?
    (who / help)
    B: Ask Barry.

11. A: _____ more days this week?
    (I / work)
    B: Maybe, but I'm not sure yet.

12. A: _____ to about my class schedule?
    (who / I / talk)
    B: Dr. Andrews can help you with that.

Talk about It Choose three of the questions in Activity 8. Ask a partner the questions. Give your own answers.

11.3 *Could* for Past Ability

We sometimes use **could** and **could not** to talk about past ability.

A

POSITIVE STATEMENTS

	subject	*could*	base form verb	
1	I / You He / She / It / We / They	**could**	**run**	very well.

NEGATIVE STATEMENTS

	subject	*could + not*	base form verb
2	I / You He / She / It / We / They	**could not** **couldn't**	**swim.**

In speaking, we usually use the contraction **couldn't**.

Notice: When we talk about ability, **could** refers to past time. **Can** refers to present or future time.

PAST ABILITY (*COULD*)	PRESENT OR FUTURE ABILITY (*CAN*)
3a My grandmother **could sew** beautiful clothing.	**3b** I **can sew** pretty well. I learned from my grandmother.
4a As a young girl, I **could run** really fast.	**4b** I **can run** short distances.
5a My parents **couldn't speak** English.	**5b** I **can't speak** Spanish well, but I'm taking classes.

B

We can use **can**, **can't**, and **couldn't** to talk about specific actions and possibilities.

	PAST MEANING (*COULD*)	PRESENT OR FUTURE MEANING (*CAN*)
POSITIVE	–	**6** I **can study** with you next week. **7** I **can hear** you now.
NEGATIVE	**8a** I **couldn't study** in the library yesterday. It was closed. **9a** We called them, but they **couldn't hear** us. **10a** I tried to talk to her last night, but I **couldn't find** her.	**8b** Sorry, I **can't study** with you tomorrow. **9b** I **can't hear** you. Can you speak louder? **10b** I **can't find** my keys. Do you have them?

WARNING! We don't usually use the positive form *could* for specific past actions.

✗ I **could** study in the library yesterday.

9 | Using *Could* and *Couldn't* for Past Ability Think about your life at age seven. Complete these sentences with *could* or *couldn't*. Underline the main verb in each sentence. Then compare your sentences with a partner. **11.3 A**

WHEN I WAS SEVEN YEARS OLD . . .

1. I _____ <u>stand</u> on my head.
2. I _____ do a cartwheel.
3. I _____ swim across a pool.
4. I _____ run a mile.
5. I _____ draw well.
6. I _____ multiply large numbers.
7. I _____ speak two languages.
8. I _____ ride a bicycle.
9. I _____ make my own dinner.
10. I _____ tie my own shoes.

stand on my head   do a cartwheel

$$987 \times 652 \over 643{,}524$$

multiply large numbers

Talk about It Talk to a partner. Compare the past with the present. Which of the things above can you do now? Which things *can't* you do now?

"When I was seven years old, I could do a cartwheel. I can't do a cartwheel now."

10 | Writing Sentences with *Could* and *Couldn't* Complete the sentences below. Use *could* or *couldn't* and the verbs in parentheses. **11.3 A**

THE OLD DAYS

1. In the 1600s, people _____ *could eat* _____ (eat) fresh vegetables only in the summer. They _____ (freeze) their food for later.

2. In the 1700s, many people _____ (ride) horses, but they _____ (travel) very fast.

3. In the 1800s, most people

_____ (buy) new

clothing very often, but many women

_____ (sew) their

own clothes.

4. In the 1950s, some people

_____ (watch) TV

in their living room, but most people

_____ (afford[9]) a television.

5. In the 1960s, people _____
(talk) to each other on the phone, but they

_____ (text) their friends.

6. In the 1980s, people _____
(type) on a computer, but they

_____ (search) for

information on the Internet.

Write about It Choose one of the time periods from Activity 10. Write two more sentences about what people could or couldn't do at that time. Use the verbs in this box or your own ideas.

buy	drive	make	travel
call	fly	see	work

In the 1700s, people could see a lot of stars at night.
They couldn't make telephone calls.

[9] **afford:** to have enough money to pay for something

11 | Using *Couldn't* and *Can't* Complete these sentences with *couldn't* or *can't*. Then listen and check your answers. `11.3 B`

EXPLANATIONS AND EXCUSES

1. A: Where's your book?

   B: I don't know. I looked for it last night,

   but I _____ find it.

2. A: Did you ask your brother about the car?

   B: He wasn't home, so I _____

   ask him.

3. A: What did she say?

   B: I don't know. I _____ hear her.

4. A: Did you like the dinner?

   B: It was good, but I _____ finish

   my food. I wasn't very hungry.

5. A: Do you want to come to dinner tonight?

   B: I really want to, but I _____.

   I have to work.

6. A: I _____ hear the radio. Can you

   turn it up a little?

   B: Sure.

7. A: How was the movie last night?

   B: I'm not sure. I didn't see the end.

   I _____ stay awake.

8. A: Do you know him?

   B: I know his face, but I _____

   remember his name.

9. A: You look bored.

   B: I'm not bored; I'm frustrated[10].

   I _____ understand

   this article.

10. A: Where were you last week?

    B: I was home sick. I _____

    get out of bed.

11. A: I want to visit my family, but I

    _____ afford it.

    B: Yeah, flights are really expensive now.

12. A: What did you do last summer?

    B: I wanted to take a vacation, but I

    _____ take time off work.

Think about It How did you choose *can't* or *couldn't* above? What other words in the conversations helped you decide?

Write about It Complete these sentences. Use *can't* or *couldn't* and your own ideas.

1. I wanted to _____, but I _____.

2. I want to _____, but I _____.

12 | Error Correction Find and correct the errors. (Some sentences may not have any errors.)

1. We can to leave at 6 p.m.

2. Do you can come over next week?

3. My brother can't swim very well.

4. I looked for you at school, but I can't find you.

5. When I can call you?

6. She can't decided where to go.

7. I couldn't hear you. The children were very noisy.

8. He can very well play the piano.

9. I asked him, but he couldn't to answer my question.

10. Where I can get a good deal[11]?

[10] **frustrated:** angry or not satisfied
[11] **a good deal:** a good price on something

11.4 Be Able To

Sometimes we use **be able to** to talk about ability in the present, past, and future.

POSITIVE STATEMENTS

A

		subject	be	able to	base form verb	
PRESENT	1	I	am 'm	able to	spend	more time at home now.
	2	He / She / It	is 's		add	numbers quickly.
	3	We / You / They	are 're		see	the stars at night.

		subject	be	able to	base form verb	
PAST*	4	I / He / She / It	was	able to	fly.	
	5	We / You / They	were		attend	the meeting.

		subject	*will + be*	able to	base form verb	
FUTURE	6	I / He / She / It / We / You / They	will be 'll be	able to	complete	the task.

↑
The **base form verb** is the **main verb**.

Notice: *Be able* to often has a meaning similar to *can / could*.

*We can use *was / were able* to to talk about specific abilities in the past. We don't use *could* in these situations.

✓ I **was able to** finish the project yesterday.   ✗ I **could** finish the project yesterday.

GRAMMAR TERM: *Be able* to is a **phrasal modal**. Phrasal modals are different from simple modals (like *can* and *could*) because they must agree with the subject.

NEGATIVE STATEMENTS

B

		subject	be + not	able to	base form verb	
PRESENT	7	I	am not 'm not	able to	come	home now.
	8	He / She / It	is not 's not isn't		add	numbers quickly.
	9	We / You / They	are not 're not aren't		see	the stars at night.

		subject	be + not	able to	base form verb	
PAST	10	I / He / She / It	was not wasn't	able to	fly.	
	11	We / You / They	were not weren't		attend	the meeting.

		subject	*will + not + be*	able to	base form verb	
FUTURE	12	I / He / She / It / We / You / They	will not be won't be	able to	complete	the task.

WARNING!

✓ We **will not be able** to go.   ✗ We will be not able to go.

13 | Noticing Forms of *Be Able To* Read these texts. Underline *be* (*not*) *able to* + the main verb. Label the forms *PA* (past), *PR* (present), or *F* (future). `11.4 A–B`

Is there a black rose?

Roses grow all around the world—from China to Egypt, and from Australia to

Alaska. People <u>are able to grow</u> roses in hundreds of colors. There is no black
_{PR}

rose, but growers keep trying to make one. They can grow very dark purple

and red roses. Maybe someday they will be able to grow a black rose.

a dark purple rose

Who is Stephen Hawking?

Stephen Hawking is a famous physicist[12]. He is not able to walk or speak.

He uses a wheelchair and communicates through a computer. He first

became ill when he was 21 years old. Doctors said he might only live for

two more years. But Hawking was able to finish graduate school, and he

became a university professor. He gives lectures[13] and writes popular books

about science.

Stephen Hawking

What is Halley's Comet?

Most comets pass by Earth very rarely—for example, every 200 years or every

1,000 years. You usually need a telescope[14] to see most comets. But every

75–76 years, people are able to look up at the sky and see Halley's Comet.

People described the comet thousands of years ago. In 1705, the astronomer

Edmond Halley studied the comet. Now we have more information about it.

People were able to see Halley's Comet in February 1986. We will be able to

see it again in 2061.

a comet

14 | Using *Be Able To* for Past, Present, and Future Ability Read these conversations. Look at the bold words. Check (✓) *Past*, *Present*, or *Future* for each conversation. Then complete the conversations with the correct form of *be able to*. Use positive forms for 1–5. Use negative forms for 6–10. `11.4 A–B`

COMPUTER PROBLEMS

Use *be able to*

	PAST	PRESENT	FUTURE
1. A: What's the problem?	☐	✓	☐
B: I <u>'m able to</u> log in, but I **can't see** my information.			
2. A: Is there a problem with the file?	☐	☐	☐
B: Yes. I _____ open it, but it **doesn't look** right.			

---

[12]**physicist:** a person who studies or knows a lot about physics (the scientific study of things like heat, light, and sound)
[13]**lectures:** talks to groups of people to teach them about something

[14]**telescope:** a long tool that you look through to make things that are far away look bigger

	PAST	PRESENT	FUTURE

3. A: Is your computer working?

   B: Yeah. The tech[15] _____ fix it **yesterday**. ☐ ☐ ☐

4. A: I don't know what to do!

   B: I'm busy right now. I _____ help you

   in a few minutes. ☐ ☐ ☐

5. A: What happened?

   B: My computer **crashed**[16], but the tech _____

   save my files. ☐ ☐ ☐

Use *be not able to*

6. A: What's the problem? ☐ ☐ ☐

   B: I _____ hear anything through the headset.

7. A: I need my computer back tomorrow! ☐ ☐ ☐

   B: I'm sorry. I _____ return it **tomorrow**.

   It will be ready next week.

8. A: Did the tech look at your computer? ☐ ☐ ☐

   B: Yeah, he **came yesterday**. But he _____ fix it.

9. A: Sorry for the mistakes. My "e" key **is** broken, so ☐ ☐ ☐

   I _____ type very well.

   B: That's OK. Do you need to buy a new keyboard?

10. A: What's wrong with your mother's computer? ☐ ☐ ☐

    B: I don't know. We _____ start it up.

    A: Is it plugged in[17]?

Talk about It Practice conversations 6–10 above with a partner. Use *can't* or *couldn't* instead of *be (not) able to.*

6. A: *What's the problem?*
   B: *I can't hear anything through the headset.*

15 | Using *Be Able To + Not* Rewrite these sentences with a negative form of *be able to.* 11.4 B

APOLOGIES

1. I'm sorry I can't come to your dinner next week.

   I'm sorry I won't be able to come to your dinner next week.

2. I'm sorry I couldn't help with the cooking last night.

3. He's very sorry, but he can't help you right now.

4. We apologize. We couldn't respond to your email yesterday. Our office was very busy.

5. I'm sorry, but Mr. Wong can't come to the phone right now.

6. I'm sorry I can't come to class tomorrow.

7. I'm sorry I couldn't call you last night.

8. We're sorry we cannot complete your order at this time.

9. John is sorry, but he can't come to the office this morning.

10. Gina sends her apologies, but she can't attend the meeting next month.

[15]**tech (technician):** a person who helps fix computer problems
[16]**crash:** to stop working (computer)

[17]**plugged in:** connected to the electrical supply with a plug

Think about It How did you know which form of *be able to* to use in Activity 15? Underline the words that tell you the sentence is past, present, or future.

Talk about It Work with a partner. Your partner reads a question or statement from this box. You respond with an apology. Use a form of *be not able to* in your apology.

1. Can you come over to our place tomorrow evening?	4. Did you call Mr. Thompson?
2. You missed the meeting yesterday!	5. Can you work on Tuesday?
3. Can you pay me back now?	6. Can you help me with this?

A: *Can you come over to our place tomorrow evening?*
B: *Sorry, but we won't be able to. We'll be out of town.*

11.5 Permission with *Can, Could,* and *May* + *I / We*

A

We often use **can** and **could** to ask for permission.

1 A: **Can we have** dessert now?
B: Finish your dinner first.

2 A: **Could I use** your pencil?
B: Sorry. I need it.

> **Could** usually sounds a little more formal and polite than **can**.
>
> Notice: **Could** describes the present or future in these questions. It does NOT describe the past.

B

Sometimes we use **may** to ask for permission. **May** is more formal. It is much less common than *can* or *could*.

3 A: **May I ask** you a question?
B: Of course.

4 A: **May we sit** down?
B: Yes, of course.

---

16 | Asking for Permission with *Can* and *Could* Complete these questions. Put the words in parentheses in the correct order. Then match each question with the speaker. Compare your answers with a partner. `11.5 A`

WHO'S TALKING?

1. A: _Could I sit_____ near the board, please? (could/sit/I) __b__

   B: Sure. There's an empty seat right here.

2. A: _____ with you for a minute about my work schedule?

   (I/could/speak) ____

   B: Of course.

3. A: _____ dinner at Tim's house? (can/eat/we) ____

   B: No. I want you both home tonight.

a. child to parent
b. student to teacher
c. employee to employer
d. classmate to classmate
e. customer to store clerk

4. A: _____ your dictionary for a minute? (use/I/can) ___

   B: Sure.

5. A: _____ TV now? (we/can/watch) ___

   B: Did you clean your rooms?

6. A: _____ yesterday's homework back? (have/could/I) ___

   B: Of course. And please look at my comments about your writing.

7. A: _____ your notes? (can/copy/we) ___

   B: Yeah, sure.

8. A: _____ a different color? (see/we/can) ___

   B: Yes. We have it in blue and brown.

9. A: _____ your office for the sales meeting tomorrow morning? (could/use/we) ___

   B: Good idea. There's lots of space.

10. A: _____ these shoes? (I/can/try on[18]) ___

   B: Of course. What size do you need?

a. child to parent
b. student to teacher
c. employee to employer
d. classmate to classmate
e. customer to store clerk

Write about It Choose three of the speakers in Activity 16. Write a different request for permission for each one.

Child: Can I go outside?   *Parent: OK. But don't play in the street.*

17 | Using *May I* Look at the pictures below. Complete each question with *may I* + a verb from the box. `11.5 B`

ask	buy	come	take

1. A: _____ in?

   B: Of course. And please sit down.

2. A: _____ this chair?

   B: Go ahead. I'm not using it.

3. A: _____ a question?

   B: Of course.

4. A: _____ that cake?

   B: Certainly.

[18] **try on:** to put on clothes to see if they fit

| help | look at | sit | speak |

5. A: Excuse me. _____ to you for a minute?

   B: OK, just a second.

6. A: _____ that?

   B: Sure!

7. A: _____ you?

   B: No, thanks. I'm just looking.

8. A: _____ here?

   B: Yeah, sure.

11.6 Requests with *Can*, *Could*, and *Would* + *You*

We can use **can**, **could**, and **would** with the subject **you** to ask someone to do something.

A

1 A: **Can you call** back later?
  B: Sure.

2 A: **Can you hand** me that glass?
  B: I can't reach it.

3 A: **Could you hold** this for a minute?
  B: Of course.

4 A: **Would you save** my seat?
  B: Sure. No problem.

> **Could** and **would** are a little more formal and polite than *can*.

B

We can make requests more polite with **please**. We can put **please** between the subject and the main verb.

	modal	subject	*please*	main verb	
5	Can			speak	a little louder?
6	Could	**you**	**please**	repeat	the question?
7	Would			sit	in the front?

We can also put *please* at the end of the question:

8 Could you wait a moment, **please**?

9 Can you pick up the kids today, **please**?

WARNING! Don't put *please* before *can*, *could*, or *would*.

✓ Can you **please** speak a little louder? ✗ **Please can** you speak a little louder?

18 | Making Requests with *Can*, *Could*, and *Would* Listen and complete these requests with the words you hear. `11.6 A–B`

1. A: _Could you clean_____ your room? It looks terrible.

   B: Now?

2. A: _____ your chair a little? I can't see the board.

   B: Sure.

3. A: _____ dinner? I'm tired.

   B: Of course.

4. A: _____ that book? I can't reach up there.

   B: No problem.

5. A: _____ the homework? I don't understand it.

   B: Yeah, sure.

6. A: _____ this box into my office? It's too heavy for me.

   B: Of course.

7. A: _____ a message?

   B: Sure. Let me get my pencil.

8. A: _____ that? I didn't hear you.

   B: No problem.

9. A: _____ the door? It's cold in here!

   B: OK.

10. A: _____ back tomorrow? I can't talk right now.

    B: OK.

11. A: _____ a few more minutes? I'm almost ready.

    B: No problem.

12. A: _____ over? I want to sit down.

    B: Uh-huh.

13. A: _____ a picture of us? Here's my camera.

    B: Sure. No problem.

14. A: _____ off the light? I have a headache.

    B: Oh, of course. I'm sorry.

Think about It Listen to the requests above again. Which people do you think are talking to a friend or family member? Why?

Talk about It Practice the conversations above with a partner. Use *please*.

> *1. A: Could you please clean your room? It looks terrible.*
> *B: Now?*

Talk about It Write four new requests. Use *can*, *would*, *could*, and four of the verbs from the activity above. Ask and answer your requests with a partner. Use *please*.

> *A: Could you please move your backpack?*
> *B: OK.*

19 | Making Requests and Asking for Permission

Complete these conversations. Use the verb in parentheses and *you* or *I* as the subject. Then practice the conversations with a partner. (See Chart 11.5 for help with permission with *I*.) **11.6 A**

ON AN AIRPLANE

1. A: _____ me another blanket? (could/bring)

   B: Of course. I'll be right back.

2. A: _____ some water? (can/have)

   B: Sure!

3. A: _____ me a new pair of headphones? (would/get)

   B: OK. I'll be right back.

AT A BANK

4. A: _____ four twenties and two tens? (could/have)

   B: Yes, of course.

5. A: _____ my balance[19], please? (would/check)

   B: Can I see your ID?

6. A: _____ my sister's check? (can/deposit[20])

   B: I'm sorry. Your sister needs to sign it.

AT A CLOTHING STORE

7. A: _____ this in a larger size? (could/see)

   B: I'll check.

8. A: _____ this for me until tomorrow? (would/hold)

   B: I'm sorry. I can't do that.

9. A: _____ this shirt? (can/try on)

   B: Of course. The fitting room[21] is over there.

AT A CAFETERIA

10. A: _____ a table? (could/look for)

    B: Uh-huh.

11. A: _____ in front of you? (could/go) I'm in a hurry.

    B: No problem.

12. A: _____ some more sugar? (could/have)

    B: Sure. How many packets?

Think about It In the questions above, which speakers are asking for permission? Which speakers are making a request (asking someone else to do something)?

Talk about It Work with a partner. Write another question and answer for each location above. Use *can*, *could*, and *would*. Use the ideas in this box or your own ideas.

bring me a pillow	have some salad dressing	open a new account
get a fork	help me find . . .	speak to a manager

A: Can I open a new account, please?
B: Of course. Let me help you with that.

---

[19] **balance:** the amount of money in someone's bank account
[20] **deposit:** to put money in the bank
[21] **fitting room:** a room in a store where people try on clothes

20 | Usage Note: *Borrow, Have, Lend,* and *Give* Read the note. Then do Activity 21.

We often make requests with **borrow**, **have**, **lend**, and **give**.

We can use **borrow*** or **have** in questions with **I** (permission questions).

1	Can / Could	I	borrow	your eraser?
			have	a glass of water?

We can use **lend**** or **give** in questions with **you** (requests).

2	Can / Could / Would	you	lend	me	your book?
			give		a glass of water?

Notice: We use an **object** after **lend** and **give**. This is often an object pronoun (*me, you, him, her, us,* or *them*).

*When you **borrow** something, you do not keep it. You return it.
When someone **lends you something, you do not keep it. You return it.

WARNING! Do not confuse *borrow* and *lend*.

✓ Could you **lend** me a pen?   ✗ Could you **borrow** me a pen?

21 | Using *Borrow, Have, Lend,* and *Give* for Permission and Requests Complete the questions with *can, could,* or *would* + *I* or *you.*

LENDING AND BORROWING

1. A: _Could I_____ have that eraser?

   B: Sure.

2. A: _____ give me a ride to school?

   B: Sure.

3. A: _____ lend me some money for lunch? I'll pay you back.

   B: Sorry. I'm broke.[22]

4. A: _____ give me some paper? I forgot my notebook.

   B: No problem.

5. A: _____ borrow your phone? Mine is dead.

   B: I'm sorry. I left mine in the car.

6. A: _____ give me a different laptop? This one doesn't work.

   B: I'm sorry. We don't have any extras.

7. A: _____ borrow your keys?

   B: Why?

8. A: _____ have your phone number?

   B: Sure. Give me your phone. I'll add my number.

9. A: _____ have the scissors?

   B: Sure. Don't forget to put them back.

10. A: _____ borrow your calculator tonight?

    B: Sorry. I need it for my homework.

> F Y I
>
> Remember:
>
> ✗ ~~Would I~~ . . .

[22] **broke:** having no money

Talk about It Work with a partner. Ask and answer the questions below. Use the items in this box or your own ideas. Use the subjects *I* or *you*.

some money	some paper	your car	your laptop	your notes	your phone

1. Can ___ borrow ___?
2. Would ___ lend me ___?

3. Could ___ have ___?
4. Would ___ give me ___?

A: Can I borrow your car?   *B: Sorry. I don't have a car!*

22 | Error Correction Find and correct the errors. (Some sentences may not have any errors.)

1. May you ask a question?
2. Could I can use the computer?
3. Would you borrow me your dictionary?
4. Can I call you tomorrow?
5. Please can you repeat that?
6. Could you take a number.

7. You could wait here a minute?
8. Can I have a cup of coffee?
9. Can I lend me a few dollars?
10. Would I please have another sandwich?
11. Would you can answer a question for me?
12. Could I have another cup of coffee.

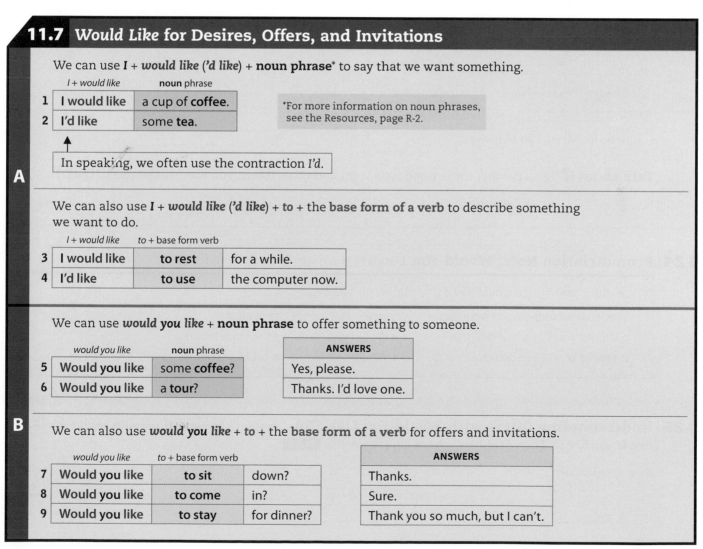

11.7 *Would Like* for Desires, Offers, and Invitations

A

We can use **I** + ***would like*** (***'d like***) + **noun phrase*** to say that we want something.

	I + would like	**noun** phrase
1	I would like	a cup of **coffee**.
2	I'd like	some **tea**.

*For more information on noun phrases, see the Resources, page R-2.

In speaking, we often use the contraction *I'd*.

We can also use **I** + ***would like*** (***'d like***) + **to** + the **base form of a verb** to describe something we want to do.

	I + would like	*to* + base form verb	
3	I would like	**to rest**	for a while.
4	I'd like	**to use**	the computer now.

B

We can use ***would you like*** + **noun phrase** to offer something to someone.

	would you like	**noun** phrase	**ANSWERS**
5	Would you like	some **coffee**?	Yes, please.
6	Would you like	a **tour**?	Thanks. I'd love one.

We can also use ***would you like*** + **to** + the **base form of a verb** for offers and invitations.

	would you like	*to* + base form verb		**ANSWERS**
7	Would you like	**to sit**	down?	Thanks.
8	Would you like	**to come**	in?	Sure.
9	Would you like	**to stay**	for dinner?	Thank you so much, but I can't.

23 | Using *I'd Like* (*To*) Complete the statements with *I'd like* or *I'd like to*. Then listen and check your answers. `11.7 A`

AT WORK

1. A: _____ go home early today.

   B: OK.

2. A: _____ some more time to finish this project.

   B: OK. You can have another day.

3. A: _____ work some overtime this week.

   B: That might be possible. I'll check the schedule.

4. A: _____ take Thursday off.

   B: That's fine.

5. A: _____ get a new chair. Mine is broken.

   B: No problem. Talk to Alan about that.

6. A: _____ the morning shift²³.

   B: I'm sorry. The morning shift is full.

7. A: My computer isn't working very well. _____ get a new one.

   B: Let's try to fix it first.

8. A: _____ some help with this project.

   B: OK. Could you ask Celine?

9. A: _____ ask you a question.

   B: Sure. What is it?

10. A: _____ some information about my benefits²⁴.

    B: Sure. Maria can help you.

Talk about It Tell a partner three things you want and three things you want to do. Use *I'd like* (*to*).

"*I'd like . . .*"   "*I'd like to . . .*"

24 | Pronunciation Note: *Would You* Listen to the note. Then do Activity 25.

We often pronounce **would you** as "wouldju" or "wouldja."

WOULD YOU SOUNDS LIKE "WOULDJU"

1 **Would you** like a free calendar?

2 **Would you** like to come in?

WOULD YOU SOUNDS LIKE "WOULDJA"

3 **Would you** like to try the strawberries?

4 **Would you** like some cake?

25 | Understanding Offers with *Would You Like* (*To*) Complete the questions with *would you like* or *would you like to*. Then listen and check your answers. `11.7 B`

AT A RESTAURANT

1. A: _____ sit near the window?

   B: That would be great.

2. A: _____ some more water?

   B: Yes, please.

---

²³**shift:** a group of workers who work together during a specific period of time

²⁴**benefits:** money or other advantages that you get from your job (for example, health care)

3. A: _____ something to drink?

   B: I'll have some tea.

4. A: _____ see the

   dessert menu?

   B: No, I think we're finished. Thanks.

5. A: _____ hear about

   our specials?

   B: Sure.

6. A: _____ a few more minutes?

   B: That's OK. We're ready.

7. A: _____ another soda?

   B: No, that's OK.

8. A: _____ order now?

   B: Yes, we're ready.

9. A: _____ a box for

   your leftovers[25]?

   B: No, thanks.

10. A: _____ your check now?

    B: Yes, please.

11. A: _____ join our

    diners' club?

    B: Not today, thanks.

12. A: _____ anything else?

    B: No, we're good. Thanks.

Talk about It Practice the conversations in Activity 25 with a partner. Pronounce *would you* as *wouldju* or *wouldja*.

Think about It In the questions in Activity 25, underline the noun or pronoun after *would you like*. Circle the verb after *would you like to*.

1. *Would you like to (sit) near the window?*
2. *Would you like some more water?*

Talk about It Add two more items to each list. Ask and answer the questions with a partner.

WOULD YOU LIKE . . .	WOULD YOU LIKE TO . . .
a salad?	get some dessert?
dessert?	have lunch now?
some coffee?	order anything else?
_____	_____
_____	_____

26 | Using *Would You Like* and *Would You Like To* Complete these conversations with *would you like* or *would you like to*. Then read the questions and answers with a partner. `11.7 B`

TALKING TO GUESTS

1. A: _____ come over for dinner?

   B: I'd love to.

2. A: _____ sit down?

   B: Thanks.

3. A: _____ give me your coat?

   B: Sure. Thanks.

4. A: _____ see the house?

   B: Yes, please.

5. A: _____ a pillow?

   B: That's OK.

> **F Y I**
>
> We often use these words and phrases to say yes to offers and invitations:
>
> | Sure. | That sounds great. |
> |---|---|
> | Yes, please. | I'd love to. |
> | Thanks. | |
>
> We often use these phrases to say no:
>
> | No, thank you. | It's all right. |
> |---|---|
> | That's OK. | I'm sorry. I can't. |
> | Not right now. | |

[25]**leftovers:** food that is left after the meal

6. A: _____ cream or sugar?

   B: No, thank you.

7. A: _____ play a game?

   B: That sounds great.

8. A: _____ watch a movie?

   B: Sure.

9. A: _____ another cookie?

   B: Yes, thank you.

10. A: _____ a ride home?

   B: That's OK. Thanks. I enjoy taking the bus.

11. A: _____ some ice?

   B: No, thank you.

12. A: _____ sit outside
   on the patio?

   B: That sounds great.

13. A: _____ come back
   next week?

   B: I'm sorry. I can't.

14. A: _____ something to eat?

   B: That's OK. Thank you.

Talk about It Write four more offers or invitations for a guest in your home. Practice asking and answering the questions with a partner.

Would you like to _____?

Would you like _____?

Would you like to _____?

Would you like _____?

A: Would you like to take a walk?
B: That sounds great.

27 | Usage Note: *Would Like* vs. *Want* **Read this note and the Pronunciation Note below. Then do Activity 29.**

We can use **would like** or **want** to make offers and invitations. *Would like* is more formal and polite than *want*.

WANT + **NOUN PHRASE**

1 Do you **want** some coffee?

WANT + **TO** + **VERB**

2 Do you **want** to have lunch?

WOULD YOU LIKE + **NOUN PHRASE**

3 **Would** you **like** some coffee?

WOULD YOU LIKE + **TO** + **VERB**

4 **Would** you **like** to see a menu?

28 | Pronunciation Note: *D'you Wanna* **Read the note. Then do Activity 29.**

We often pronounce **do you** as "d'you" or "do ya" and **want to** as "wanna."

1 Do you want to go?	*sounds like*	"**D'you wanna** go?"
2 Do you want to try again?	*sounds like*	"**D'you wanna** try again?"
3 Do you want to come over?	*sounds like*	"**Do ya wanna** come over?"
4 Do you want to watch TV?	*sounds like*	"**Do ya wanna** watch TV?"

In informal speaking, we sometimes omit *do you*.

5 Want to come over after class? (= <u>Do you</u> want to come over after class?)

6 Want to get some coffee? (= <u>Do you</u> want to get some coffee?)

29 | Using _Would Like_ and _Want_ Listen and complete these conversations. Are the speakers using formal or informal language? Check (✓) the correct column.

OFFERS AND INVITATIONS	FORMAL	INFORMAL
1. A: _____ sleep for a little while? B: No, I'm OK.	☐	☐
2. A: _____ a cough drop? B: Thanks.	☐	☐
3. A: _____ wait for Mr. Burns in his office? B: Yes, please.	☐	☐
4. A: _____ hear my poem? B: Yeah, sure.	☐	☐
5. A: _____ see the red one? B: Please.	☐	☐
6. A: _____ work some extra hours next week? B: Yes, please.	☐	☐
7. A: _____ meet at the library? B: Can't today. Maybe tomorrow.	☐	☐
8. A: _____ a bag for that? B: Yes, thank you.	☐	☐
9. A: _____ call Tony? B: Mm. Not really.	☐	☐
10. A: _____ take a walk? B: Yeah, sure.	☐	☐
11. A: _____ speak to the secretary? B: Yes, please.	☐	☐
12: A: _____ go out tonight? B: Maybe. I'll call you.	☐	☐

Talk about It Practice the conversations above with a partner. Pronounce _want to_ as _wanna_ and _would you_ as _wouldju_ or _wouldja_.

Talk about It Talk to a partner. Use the words in this box to make offers and invitations. Use _do you want_ and _would you like_.

a piece of candy	have lunch together	study with me
an eraser	some help	use my phone

A: _Do you want to have lunch together?_
B: _Sorry, I can't today. How about tomorrow?_

WRAP-UP

A | GRAMMAR IN READING Read this article. Underline the forms of *can*, *could*, *would like*, and *be able to*.

LA's Favorite Food Truck

<u>Would you like</u> to eat food from a truck? Go to downtown Los Angeles at lunchtime, and you will see food trucks everywhere. You can get Mexican food, Chinese food, Indian food, or Korean food. You can get gourmet[26] food or hamburgers and hot dogs. Nowadays, food trucks sell just about everything. Can't find your favorite truck? Just check online! Many trucks post their locations on blogs or other websites.

Korean tacos from the Kogi food truck

In 2008, food trucks were not so popular in Los Angeles. Many trucks sold tacos or sandwiches, but there wasn't much variety[27]. You couldn't find gourmet or unusual food at a truck. Then a man named Roy Choi helped to change that. Choi could cook Korean food and Mexican food, so he decided to put them together. He made Mexican tacos and quesadillas with Korean ingredients and spices. He started a food truck company called Kogi. Soon his food trucks became very popular.

People loved Choi's food, but they often weren't able to find the Kogi trucks. So Choi started to use social media (websites like Facebook) to communicate with customers. He had thousands of followers online. Sometimes more than 600 people came to his truck and waited in line for an hour.

Choi became famous. He was able to open two restaurants, and now he is writing a book about his life. These days, there are gourmet food trucks all over the U.S. Thousands of people follow food trucks on social media. Go to any big American city, and you will be able to buy interesting food from a truck!

Think about It Which modals above describe the past? Which describe the present? Which describes the future? Write *PA* above the past forms, *PR* above the present forms, and *F* above the future form.

B | GRAMMAR IN SPEAKING Interview a classmate. Use these questions and two questions of your own.

NOW

1. Can you find food trucks in your city? Where?
2. What kinds of food can you get near here?
3. Would you like to try Roy Choi's Mexican-Korean food?
4. Would you like to have lunch from a food truck?
5. Can you cook well?
6. What is one thing you can't cook?

WHEN YOU WERE 12 YEARS OLD

7. Could you cook your own dinner?
8. What kinds of food were you able to prepare?
9. Were there any foods you couldn't eat?

Write about It Write your partner's answers to questions 5–9 above.

5. Suma can cook very well.

---

[26] **gourmet food:** very good or special food   [27] **variety:** different kinds

11.8 Summary of Modals I

OVERVIEW OF MODAL USES

		CAN	COULD	BE ABLE TO	MAY	WOULD	WOULD LIKE
ABILITY / POSSIBILITY	PAST	—	✓	✓	—	—	—
	PRESENT	✓	—	✓	—	—	—
	FUTURE	✓	—	✓	—	—	—
ASKING PERMISSION		✓	✓	—	✓	—	—
REQUESTS		✓	✓	—	—	✓	—
DESIRES, OFFERS, AND INVITATIONS		—	—	—	—	—	✓

You will learn more uses of modals in Unit 12.

MODALS	USES	EXAMPLES
CAN	Ability / Possibility	**Can** you **swim**? I **can't see** you. She **can visit** tomorrow.
	Asking Permission	**Can** I **sit** here?
	Requests	**Can** you **call** me later? **Can** they **take** me home? **Can** she **bring** her parents?
COULD	Past Ability	My grandfather **could play** the piano. **Could** you **hear** him? I **couldn't come** to class yesterday.
	Asking Permission	**Could** I **have** the car keys?
	Requests	**Could** you **help** me with this?
MAY	Asking Permission	**May** I **ask** a question?
WOULD	Requests	**Would** you **say** that again?
WOULD YOU LIKE (TO)	Offers and Invitations	**Would** you **like** a cup of tea? **Would** you **like to call** back later?
BE ABLE TO	Present Ability	I'm **able to open** my files. She's **able to understand** me. They're **able to attend** the meetings. He **isn't able to be** here. We **aren't able to help** you.
	Past Ability	He **was able to fix** my car. They **were able to finish** on time. I **wasn't able to call** you. We **weren't able to start**.
	Future Ability	I'll **be able to do** this later. He'll **be able to talk** to you. They **won't be able to work** on Tuesday.

12

Modals II

WARM-UP 306

12.1 Advice and Opinions with *Should* and *Shouldn't* 308

Pronunciation Note: Stress with *Should* and *Shouldn't* 308

Usage Note: *I (Don't) Think* and *Maybe* in Statements with *Should* 310

12.2 Questions with *Should* 311

12.3 Suggestions with *Why Don't You/We* 314

12.4 Necessity with *Have To* and *Need To* 318

Pronunciation Note: *Have To* and *Need To* 319

12.5 Questions with *Have To* and *Need To* 321

12.6 Necessity and Prohibition with *Must* 323

Usage Note: *Must Not* vs. *Not Have To* 324

12.7 Comparing Modals: *Can* vs. *Should* vs. *Have To* 326

WRAP-UP 329

Grammar in Reading 329

Grammar in Speaking 330

12.8 Summary of Modals II 331

GO ONLINE

For the Unit Vocabulary Check, go to the Online Practice.

IN THIS UNIT, WE USE modals to:

Give our opinion

1. He **should** go to bed.

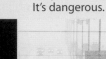

2. They **shouldn't** drive now. It's dangerous.

Give advice and make suggestions

3. You **should** call the IT department.

4. **Why don't you** rest for a few minutes?

Think about It Read these sentences. Check (✓) *True* or *False*.

TODAY . . .	TRUE	FALSE
1. I should go to bed early.	☐	☐
2. I shouldn't go outside.	☐	☐
3. I should rest for a while before dinner.	☐	☐
4. I should do the laundry.	☐	☐
5. I should finish my homework.	☐	☐

Talk about necessity and prohibition

5. The students here **have to** wear uniforms.

6. He **has to** study for the exam.

7. Employees **must** wear safety glasses.

8. Visitors **must not** touch the art.

Think about It Read these sentences. Check (✓) *True* or *False*.

	TRUE	FALSE
1. I have to study for a test tonight.	☐	☐
2. I need to bring a laptop to class.	☐	☐
3. Students at my school have to do a lot of homework.	☐	☐
4. I need to take a math class next semester.	☐	☐

Check (✓) the rules that are true at your school.

5. ☐ Students must not chew gum.

6. ☐ Students must not use cell phones during class.

7. ☐ Students must not eat or drink in class.

8. ☐ Visitors must report to the office.

12.1 Advice and Opinions with *Should* and *Shouldn't*

We can use **should** or **shouldn't** to give advice or to give our opinion about the right or wrong thing to do.

1 It's late. You **should** go to bed soon. (The speaker is giving advice TO someone.)

2 Children **should respect** their parents. (The speaker is giving an opinion ABOUT someone or something.)

A

POSITIVE STATEMENTS

	subject	*should*	base form verb	
3	I / You / He / She / We / They / Teenagers	should	study	for the test.
4			see	a doctor once a year.
5			exercise	more.

NEGATIVE STATEMENTS

	subject	*should + not*	base form verb	
6	I / You / He / She / Bob / We / They	should not shouldn't	leave	too late.
7			worry	about it.

GO ONLINE

🔊 **1 | Pronunciation Note: Stress with *Should* and *Shouldn't*** Listen to the note. Then do Activity 2.

We do not usually stress **should**. We stress the main verb.

1 Students should **BRING** a pen and a notebook.   **2** You should **CALL** him.

In sentences with **shouldn't**, we often stress both *shouldn't* and the main verb.

3 We **SHOULDN'T PAY** for this.

4 Teenagers **SHOULDN'T SPEND** too much time online.

🔊 **2 | Noticing *Should* and *Shouldn't*** Listen and complete these statements with *should* or *shouldn't* + the main verb. Then check (✓) *Always Agree, Sometimes Agree,* or *Disagree.* **12.1 A**

OPINIONS	ALWAYS AGREE	SOMETIMES AGREE	DISAGREE
1. Rich people _____ money to charity[1].	☐	☐	☐
2. Everyone _____ children.	☐	☐	☐
3. Students _____ each other with homework.	☐	☐	☐
4. People _____ kind to animals.	☐	☐	☐
5. Parents _____ their children.	☐	☐	☐
6. Stores _____ on holidays.	☐	☐	☐
7. Everyone _____ married.	☐	☐	☐
8. Children _____ to their parents.	☐	☐	☐
9. The government _____ health care[2].	☐	☐	☐
10. Employees _____ six weeks of paid vacation every year.	☐	☐	☐
11. Teenagers _____ violent[3] video games.	☐	☐	☐

[1] **charity:** organizations that collect money to help people who need it

[2] **health care:** medical care
[3] **violent:** showing harm and destruction

	ALWAYS AGREE	SOMETIMES AGREE	DISAGREE
12. Universities _____ free.	☐	☐	☐
13. A ten-year-old child _____ a cell phone.	☐	☐	☐
14. Governments _____ money to the arts.	☐	☐	☐

🔊 **Talk about It** Listen again and repeat the sentences in Activity 2. Pay attention to the stressed words.

Talk about It Discuss your answers for Activity 2 as a class. Which statements do most students agree with?

3 | Using *Should* and *Shouldn't* Read these sentences about the average American. Then complete the advice with *should* or *shouldn't* and a main verb. **12.1 A**

ADVICE FOR AMERICANS

1. Americans spend 34 hours a week watching television.

   They _____*should watch*_____ less television.

2. Twenty percent of Americans sleep less than 6 hours a night.

   They _____ for 8 hours a night.

3. Americans use credit cards very often. Many families have over $15,000 in credit card debt[4].

   They _____ credit cards so often.

4. About 48 percent of Americans drink soda every day.

   They _____ soda every day.

5. Many American children play video games for over 13 hours a week.

   They _____ video games so much.

6. Eighty percent of Americans don't exercise enough.

   They _____ more.

7. Most American high school students do not study calculus.

   More students _____ calculus.

8. Many Americans don't save money. Half of Americans don't have enough savings to pay their bills for three months.

   They _____ more money.

9. Many Americans do not learn a second language.

   More people _____ a second language.

10. Most Americans eat too many calories every day.

    They _____ so many calories.

calculus

Talk about It Tell a partner about your habits. Explain which things you should or shouldn't do, and which are OK.

"I watch television for about five hours a week. I think that's OK."
"I only study two hours a day. I should study for four or five hours a day."

---

[4] **debt:** money that you need to pay

4 | Usage Note: *I (Don't) Think* and *Maybe* in Statements with *Should* Read the note. Then do Activity 5.

We can use **I think** or **maybe** in sentences with **should** to make our opinions softer (less strong).

I THINK ... SHOULD
1 **I think** you **should talk** to your teacher.

MAYBE ... SHOULD
2 **Maybe** he **should wait** for a couple of days.

I DON'T THINK ... SHOULD
3 **I don't think** you **should give** him the answers.
4 **I don't think** she **should come** in tomorrow.

MAYBE ... SHOULDN'T
5 **Maybe** we **shouldn't eat** here.
6 **Maybe** we **shouldn't leave** now.

Sometimes we use **I think** and **maybe** together.
7 **I think maybe** we **should leave**.

5 | Using *I (Don't) Think* or *Maybe* + *Should* Read each situation. Choose two of the phrases in the box. Write advice with *I (don't) think* or *maybe*. `12.1 A`

WHAT SHOULD THEY DO?

1. John's co-worker steals office supplies.

   I think John should tell his boss.
   Maybe he shouldn't tell his other co-workers.

tell his boss	talk to his co-worker
tell his other co-workers	ignore[5] it

2. Someone hit a parked car and drove away. Marta saw him.

call the police	ignore it
chase the car	

3. Sara's classmate cheated[6] on a test.

tell the teacher	talk to the classmate
tell other students	ignore it

4. An old woman stole fruit from the grocery store. Tom saw her.

call the police	tell the store owner
talk to the woman	ignore it

5. Ana found $100 cash in the street.

keep it	tell people nearby
take it to the police	

6. Rita is driving at night. She sees a car broken down[7] by the side of the road.

call the police	stop and help
keep driving	

7. There is a suspicious-looking person[8] in front of Sean's neighbor's house. His neighbor isn't home.

call the police	keep watching
go talk to the person	

[5] **ignore:** to not pay attention to
[6] **cheat:** to do something that is not honest (for example, copy another student's answers)

[7] **broken down:** not working
[8] **suspicious-looking person:** a person who looks like they might commit a crime

8. The teacher missed some of Teruko's mistakes on the test and gave her a high score.

tell her friends	ignore it
tell the teacher	

9. The cashier at the grocery store gave George too much change. George is already home.

go back to the store and return the money	
call the store	keep the money
go back the next day	

10. Anita's friend has bad breath[9].

give her friend some mouthwash	ignore it
tell her friend	

Write about It Write a new piece of advice for each of these situations. Use your own ideas.

1. Ann's sister has a new dress. Ann thinks it's ugly.
2. There's an important football game on TV. Jim doesn't want to go to work.
3. Carol has a new employee. He's very nice, but he's not very good at his job.

1. I think Ann should tell her sister the truth.

Talk about It Work with a partner. Write two more problems. Give each other advice with *should* or *shouldn't*.

A: I'm angry at my best friend.
B: I think you should talk to her.

12.2 Questions with *Should*

A

YES/NO QUESTIONS

	should	subject	base form verb	
1	**Should**	I / you / he / she / we / they	**buy**	this?
2			**take**	the job?

SHORT ANSWERS

	yes / no	subject	*should (+ not)*
3	Yes,	you / I / he / she / we / they	**should.**
4	No,		**shouldn't.**

OTHER WAYS TO ANSWER *YES/NO* QUESTIONS

ANSWER *YES*	ANSWER *NO*
5 A: **Should** I **take** the job? B: **Definitely!** It sounds great.	7 A: **Should** we **wait** for you? B: **No**, you can start eating. We'll be there later.
6 A: **Should** I **buy** this watch? B: **Why not?**	8 A: **Should** I **call** Robert? B: **I don't think so.** He's really busy.

B

WH- QUESTIONS

	wh- word	*should*	subject	base form verb	
9	**Where**	**should**	I / you / he / she / we / they / Aunt Karen	**have**	dinner?
10	**When**			**arrive?**	
11	**How long**			**wait?**	

---

[9] **bad breath:** when the air that comes out of your mouth has a bad smell

6 | Asking and Answering *Yes/No* Questions with *Should* Write each question for Speaker A under the correct picture. Then practice the conversations with a partner. `12.2 A`

Should I bring an umbrella?	Should I invite Karen?	Should we get dessert?
Should I buy this?	Should I throw it away?	Should we go to Tahiti?
Should I call the doctor?	Should we call the police?	

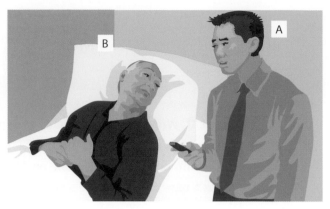

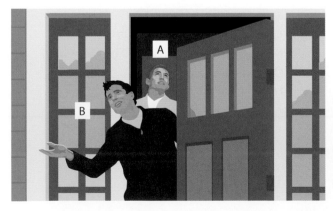

1. A: _____

   B: I don't think so.

2. A: _____

   B: No, I'll be fine.

3. A: _____

   B: Oh, yes. She's really fun.

4. A: _____

   B: Oh, I don't think so. I'm too full!

5. A: _____

   B: Good idea. It's pretty cloudy out there.

6. A: _____

   B: Yes, I think we should.

7. A: _____

B: Maybe. Or maybe we should go to Hawaii!

8. A: _____

B: Nah. I can fix that for you.

Talk about It Choose three of the pictures in Activity 6 and write a new question with *should* for each. Then ask and answer your questions with a partner.

Picture 1
A: *Should I try a different size?*
B: *Yes—and maybe a different color, too.*

7 | Asking for and Giving Advice with *Should* Complete these questions and answers. Use the words in parentheses and *should* or *shouldn't*. `12.2 A–B`

Making a Good Impression[10]: FAQ

I have a job interview tomorrow.

1. Q: _____?
     (what / I / wear)
   A: Wear professional clothes. It's OK to be a little too formal, but it's not OK to be too casual.

2. Q: _____ about the salary[11]?
     (when / I / ask)
   A: Don't ask at the interview. Ask when they offer you the job.

3. Q: _____ after the interview?
     (what / I / do)
   A: Send a thank-you note right away, but don't call about the job right away.

   _____ them time to interview other people and make a decision.
     (you / give)

I'm having dinner with my boss tomorrow.

4. Q: My boss invited me to a restaurant. _____ for dinner?
                                              (I / pay)
   A: Your boss won't expect you to pay for dinner. He or she will pay.

5. Q: _____?
     (what / I / order)
   A: Order something you like, but _____ the most expensive thing
                                        (you / not get)
   on the menu.

---

[10]**making a good impression:** making other people have positive thoughts or feelings about you

[11]**salary:** money that you receive for the work you do

My co-worker is having a potluck dinner[12].

6. Q: How much food _____ (I / bring) ?

   A: Bring a small serving for everyone.

7. Q: _____ (I / arrive) right on time?

   A: It's OK to be 10 or 15 minutes late, but not much later than that.

   And _____ (you / not arrive) early!

8. Q: _____ (I / bring) my wife/husband?

   A: _____ (you / ask) the host. At casual events, people sometimes bring their spouses.

My co-workers are exchanging gifts.

9. Q: _____ (when / I / open) my presents?

   A: This can be different for different people. Thank them for the gift.

   Then ask, "_____ (I / open) it now?"

10. Q: _____ (I / send) a thank-you card to everyone?

    A: Everyone likes a thank-you card. For a small group of co-workers, _____ (you / send)

    one to each person. For a large group, you can post one thank-you note for the whole group.

Talk about It Write two questions with *should* for each of these situations. Write one *yes/no* question and one *wh-* question. Ask and answer the questions with a partner.

1. You are attending a friend's wedding.

   What should I wear?

2. You are attending an important meeting at your new job.

12.3 Suggestions with *Why Don't You / We*

A

We can use **why don't you** or **why don't we** to make a suggestion.

	base form verb	
1	**Why don't you**	**sit**	down?
2	**Why don't we**	**go**	somewhere?

3 A: You look tired. **Why don't you** sit down?
   B: Good idea. I think I will.

4 A: I'm bored. **Why don't we** go somewhere?
   B: Sure. Where should we go?

Notice: The meaning of *why don't we* is similar to *let's*. For more information on *let's*, see Unit 1, page 19.

B

Why don't you has a softer meaning than **should**.

STRONGER, MORE DIRECT MEANING

5 A: I want to go out, but I have a test tomorrow.
   B: You **should stay** home and study. You can go out tomorrow.

SOFTER, LESS DIRECT MEANING

6 A: **Why don't you get** some rest? You'll feel better.
   B: Thanks. That's a good idea.

[12] **potluck dinner:** a dinner where each guest brings some of the food

8 | Making Suggestions with *Why Don't You* and *Why Don't We* Complete these conversations with the suggestions in the box. Then listen and check your answers. Practice the conversations with a partner. `12.3 A`

GOING OUT

1. A: Well, we can't go to the zoo now. It's raining.

   B: _____

   A: That's a good idea. I think there's a Picasso exhibit

   this month. And it's free today.

2. A: I need to get some exercise.

   B: Me too. _____

   A: OK. I'll change my shoes.

3. A: I'm bored.

   B: _____

   A: He's working today.

4. A: Oh, no! The show is sold out[13] this weekend.

   B: _____

   A: OK. I'm free next Saturday. I'll get the tickets now.

5. A: What should we do today?

   B: _____

   A: No, it's not hot enough. And the water is too cold.

6. A: _____ There are a lot of good sales.

   B: I can't. I'm broke[14].

7. A: Ugh. I'm so tired of pizza.

   B: _____

   A: That's a good idea. Want to come?

8. A: _____ You're really good.

   B: I want to, but I don't have time to play every weekend.

> Why don't we go next weekend?
> Why don't we go shopping tomorrow?
> Why don't we go to a museum?
> Why don't we go to the beach?
> Why don't we take a walk?
> Why don't you call Tomas?
> Why don't you join the baseball team?
> Why don't you try the new Chinese place?

Talk about It Choose three of the conversations above. Write a different suggestion with *why don't you* or *why don't we*. Practice the new conversations with a partner.

A: I'm bored.
B: Why don't we go to a movie?
A: OK. What's playing?

9 | Using *Why Don't You* and *Why Don't We* Write a suggestion for each problem. Use *why don't you* or *why don't we*. Use the phrases in each box. `12.3 A`

SCHOOL PROBLEMS

1. A: You look tired.

   B: I am. I can't finish this homework tonight.

   A: *Why don't you sleep for a while?* _____

> get a tutor
> go to the library
> sleep for a while

---

[13] **sold out:** there are no more tickets   [14] **broke:** having no money

2. A: Should we study in your room?

   B: We can't. My roommate makes too much noise.

   A: _____

3. A: What's wrong?

   B: My chemistry class is really difficult.

   A: _____

get a tutor
go to the library
sleep for a while

4. A: I'm hungry.

   B: Me too, but the cafeteria is closed.

   A: _____

5. A: I didn't understand the class today. Did you?

   B: No, I didn't. _____

6. A: I'm thinking about changing my major.

   B: _____

go off-campus today
go see the teacher
talk to your adviser first

7. A: Oh, no! I lost my homework.

   B: _____

8. A: I have three tests next week.

   B: Me too. _____

9. A: I'm tired of eating the same food.

   B: _____

ask for some extra time
study together
try something new

10. A: Want to study with me?

    B: Sure, but I think the library is closed.

    A: _____

11. A: I really want to take that class, but it's full.

    B: _____

12. A: The textbook is really expensive.

    B: _____

buy a used one
email the professor
go to a café

Talk about It Continue the conversations in Activity 9 with a partner. Respond to each suggestion with one of the answers from this box. If your partner gives a negative answer, make another suggestion.

OK.	I want to, but I can't.
Good idea.	I don't have enough money.
Sure.	I don't have time.

A: *You look tired.*
B: *I am. I can't finish this homework tonight.*
A: *Why don't you sleep for a while?*
B: *I want to, but I can't. I'm too worried about my homework!*
A: *OK. Why don't you watch TV for a while? Then maybe you'll be able to sleep.*

10 | Using *Why Don't You* or *You Should* Listen and complete the suggestions with the words you hear. **12.3 B**

AT HOME

1. A: _You should leave_____ soon. You'll be late for the bus.

   B: Oh, you're right! I didn't notice the time! Thanks.

2. A: Ugh. I feel horrible.

   B: You look really sick. _____ home?

   A: I want to, but I can't. I have a meeting with my boss this morning.

   B: She'll understand. Just call her.

3. A: Can I borrow the car?

   B: I'm not sure. _____ your dad. He might need it.

AT A RESTAURANT

4. A: I can't eat spicy food.

   B: Well, _____ the noodles? They're not spicy.

   A: OK. I'll have those.

5. A: What do you recommend?

   B: _____ the hot and sour soup. It's delicious.

   A: OK. I'll try it.

AT A POST OFFICE

6. A: This needs to get to Seoul by tomorrow.

   B: _____ it Overnight Express.

7. A: I need to send this bracelet to Buenos Aires.

   B: _____ insurance[15] for that.

8. A: The line is so long! I just need to buy some stamps.

   B: _____ them from the machine?

AT A LIBRARY

9. A: Can you recommend a book for me? I like mysteries[16].

   B: _____ Agatha Christie? She's a very famous English mystery writer.

10. A: I'd like to reserve a study room for Wednesday.

    B: How many people are in your group?

    A: Eight.

    B: _____ Room C. It's the biggest one.

Talk about It Write a new conversation for each location above: home, a restaurant, a post office, and a library. Practice your conversations with a partner. Include suggestions with *why don't you* and *you should*.

---

[15] **insurance:** an agreement where you pay money to a company so that it will give you money if something bad happens

[16] **mysteries:** (literature) stories about something strange that you cannot understand or explain (for example, a strange crime)

12.4 Necessity with *Have To* and *Need To*

A

POSITIVE STATEMENTS

We can use **have to** or **need to** to say that something is necessary or required.

1 There's no food in the house.
I **have to** go shopping.

2 School is starting next month.
Julie **needs to register** for classes.

3

subject	*have to / need to*		base form verb	
I You We They	**have to** **need to**		**do**	the laundry.

4

subject	*has to / needs to*		base form verb	
He She Julie	**has to** **needs to**		**buy**	the course book.

Notice: *Have to* is a **phrasal modal**. It must agree with the subject. We often use *need to* like we use *have to*.

B

NEGATIVE STATEMENTS

We can use **do / does** + **not** + **have to / need to** to say that something is NOT necessary or required.

5 There's a lot of food in the house.
We **don't have to** go shopping.

6 Paul **doesn't need to work** today.
It's his day off.

7

subject	*do + not*	*have to / need to*	base form verb	
I You We They	**do not** **don't**	**have to** **need to**	**leave.**	

8

subject	*does + not*	*has to / needs to*	base form verb	
He She Julie	**does not** **doesn't**	**have to** **need to**	**work**	today.

We usually use the contractions **don't** and **doesn't** in conversation.

Notice:

✓ We **don't have** to come today.

✓ He **doesn't have** to come today.

✗ We **no have** to come today.

✗ He **don't** have to come today.

✗ He **doesn't has** to come today.

---

11 | Using *Have To* and *Need To* Complete excerpts 1–3 with *have to/has to* and excerpts 4–5 with *need to/needs to*. Underline the main verb.   **12.4 A**

PREPARING FOR CAREERS

Medical doctor

1. Medical doctors go to school for a long time. Medical students ____*have to*____ take

    a lot of biology courses. They also _____ get a medical license[17].

Commercial pilot

2. Some pilots get a private license first. Other pilots start in the military[18].

    A commercial pilot _____ complete many hours of flying time.

    Many pilots also _____ pass a medical exam every year.

a commercial pilot

---

[17] **license:** an official piece of paper that shows you are allowed to do or have something

[18] **military:** a country's soldiers who fight on land, in the air, or on water

Police officer

3. In many places, police officers _____ have a high school diploma. They usually also _____ take written tests and physical tests.

Lawyer

4. Lawyers _____ attend law school. Then they _____ get a license to practice law. In some places, it's very hard to get the license. They _____ take a very long, difficult test.

Teacher

5. A teacher _____ have a college degree and take special courses in education. Student teachers[19] usually _____ practice in a classroom.

F Y I	

Notice: We can use the main verb **have** after **have to**.

A truck driver **has to have** a special license.

Nurses **have to have** a license.

Talk about It Think of another career. Talk with a partner about things that people have to do to prepare for the career. Use the ideas in this box or your own ideas.

> be a good speaker
> be a good writer
> be in good physical health
> get a college degree
> get a license
> take a difficult exam
> take a lot of science courses

12 | Pronunciation Note: *Have To* and *Need To* Listen to the note. Then do Activity 13.

Notice how we usually pronounce **have to** and **need to**. The **to** sounds like /tə/.

1 have to	*sounds like*	"hafta"	I **have to** go.
2 has to	*sounds like*	"hasta"	He **has to** try again.
3 need to	*sounds like*	"need-ta"	I **need to** get up early.
4 needs to	*sounds like*	"needs-ta"	She **needs to** come back tomorrow.

Notice: We also use **have/need** + **noun phrase***. There is no *to* before the noun phrase.

5 I have a class today.

6 A: Do you **need the car** today?
B: No, I **need it** tomorrow.

*For more information on noun phrases, see the Resources, page R-2.

---

[19] **student teachers:** people who are studying to become teachers

13 | Listening for *Have To* and *Need To* Listen and complete these conversations. Are the speakers saying *have to/need to* + verb or *have/need* + noun phrase? Check (✓) the correct column. Then practice the conversations with a partner. `12.4 A`

	HAVE TO / NEED TO + VERB	HAVE / NEED + NOUN PHRASE
EXCUSES		
1. A: Why don't we go out tonight?		
B: I can't. I _____.	☐	☐
2. A: Do you want to have breakfast tomorrow?		
B: I can't. I _____ in the morning.	☐	☐
3. A: Do you want to come over?		
B: Thanks, but I _____ home. My father	☐	☐
_____ with something.	☐	☐
4. A: Can you stay a little longer today?		
B: I'm sorry. I can't. I _____ in about ten minutes.	☐	☐
5. A: Did you get my message?		
B: No, I didn't, sorry. I _____.	☐	☐
6. A: Where is Karla?		
B: She _____ late on Tuesdays. She'll be here later.	☐	☐
7. A: Can we talk at 12?		
B: Not today. I _____ Brad a ride home after class.	☐	☐
8. A: Did you just wake up?		
B: Yeah, sorry. I _____.	☐	☐
9. A: Can you help me move this weekend?		
B: Sorry. I _____ a paper.	☐	☐
10. A: Call me tomorrow!		
B: I _____ all day. I'll call you on Saturday.	☐	☐
11. A: Want to go to the movie?		
B: I can't. I _____ early tomorrow.	☐	☐
12. A: Can I borrow your book?		
B: Sorry. I _____ tonight.	☐	☐

14 | Using *Not Have To* and *Not Need To* Complete conversations 1–5 with a form of *not have to* and conversations 6–10 with a form of *not need to*. Use the verbs in parentheses. Then listen and check your answers. `12.4 B`

GETTING READY FOR GUESTS

1. A: I ordered pizza tonight, so we _____. (cook)

   B: Oh, good. I'm exhausted[20].

2. A: Ana will bring coffee and soda.

   B: She _____ coffee. Max is bringing some. (bring)

> **RESEARCH SAYS...**
>
> We use *have to* more often in conversation than in writing.

[20]**exhausted:** very tired

3. A: I'll call you before we come.

   B: You _____. Just come! (call)

4. A: I hope you can come to the city with us.

   B: Oh, I can. I just talked to my boss. I _____ that day. (work)

5. A: Mick wants to help us get ready.

   B: He _____. But that's nice of him. (help)

6. A: I'll order some flowers.

   B Thanks, but you _____ that. My uncle is a florist. He'll bring some flowers. (do)

7. A: The dinner might get pretty loud. Should we tell the neighbors?

   B: No, we _____ them anything. They'll be out of town. (tell)

8. A: My oven isn't very big.

   B: Why don't you barbecue[21]? Then you _____ the oven. (use)

9. A: Ana wants to make dessert.

   B: She _____ dessert! She made it last time. (make)

10. A: How much is the salad dressing?

    B: You _____ for it. It comes with the salad. (pay)

Talk about It Imagine ten people are coming to your home for dinner. What do you have to do? What do you not have to do? Use the ideas in this box or your own ideas. Tell a partner.

| borrow furniture | buy paper plates | cook | order food | warn your neighbors |

"I have to cook all the food."
"I don't have to make dessert. My friend is making a cake."

Talk about It Compare your answers in Activity 14 as a class. How are your ideas different?

12.5 Questions with *Have To* and *Need To*

YES/NO QUESTIONS

		do / does	subject	*have to / need to*	base form verb	
A	1	Do	I / you / we / they	**have to**	**leave**	now?
	2	Does	he / she / Maria	**need to**	**work**	today?

SHORT ANSWERS

Yes,	you / I / we / they	**do.**
No,		**don't.**
Yes,	he / she	**does.**
No,		**doesn't.**

WH- QUESTIONS

		wh- word	*do / does*	subject	*have to / need to*	base form verb	
B	3	What time / When	do	we	**need to**	**get**	there?
	4	How long / Why / Where	does	he	**have to**	**wait?**	

[21] **barbecue:** to cook food on a fire outside

15 | Asking Questions with *Have To* or *Need To* Complete these questions with *have to* or *need to* and the words in parentheses. Use the subject *you*. `12.5 A–B`

CHORES

1. *What do you have to do* _____ next weekend? (what/do)
2. _____ tonight? (study)
3. _____ today? (when/leave)
4. _____ the floors today? (clean)
5. _____ tomorrow morning? (what time/get up)
6. _____ any emails tonight? (send)
7. _____ your rent? (when/pay)
8. _____ the dishes every day? (wash)
9. _____ to class? (what time/get)
10. _____ grocery shopping tomorrow? (go)
11. _____ today? (how long/work)
12. _____ dinner tonight? (cook)

Talk about It Ask and answer the questions above with a partner.

A: *What do you have to do next weekend?*
B: *I have to do laundry and clean my apartment.*

Talk about It Work with a new partner. What do you remember about your classmates? Quiz your partner. Use *does . . . have to/need to.*

"What does Jin have to do next weekend?"

Write about It Write about three differences between yourself and your partner.

Jamal has to study tonight, but I don't. I don't have any homework.
I have to pay my rent on the first of the month. Jamal doesn't need to pay rent. He lives at home with his parents.

16 | Error Correction Find and correct the errors. (Some sentences may not have any errors.)

1. He don't have to wear a uniform.
2. She need to come on time every day.
3. What time does he should call you?
4. I'm not have to study for this test.
5. What time are you have to be at work?
6. When he has to finish the essay?
7. I think I should to study a little more.
8. I don't need get up early tomorrow.
9. How long do we have to wait?
10. When do he have to arrive?
11. I have to homework tonight.
12. Does she has to pay for the tickets?

12.6 Necessity and Prohibition with *Must*

A

POSITIVE STATEMENTS

We can use **must** to talk about things that are necessary.

1 All students **must take** an English exam at the beginning of the semester.

subject	*must*	base form verb	
2	I / You / He / She / Carlos / We / They	**must**	**follow**	the directions.

Must is similar in meaning to **have to** and **need to**, but it is more formal. We don't usually use *must* to express necessity in conversation.

WARNING! Don't add *to* after *must*.

✓ Employees **must arrive** on time.   ✗ Employees **must to arrive** on time.

B

NEGATIVE STATEMENTS

We use **must not** to express **prohibition**: to say that something is forbidden (not permitted).

3 Students **must not smoke** on campus. (= Smoking is not permitted on campus.)

subject	*must + not*	base form verb	
4	I / You / He / She / Lisa / We / They	**must not**	**enter**	the construction area.

17 | Noticing *Must* and *Must Not* Complete these signs with *must* or *must not*. Underline the main verb.

`12.6 A–B`

1.

2.

3.

4.

5.

6.

7.

All players _____ register
and pay at the office

8.

Talk about It Where might you see each of the signs in Activity 17?

Write about It Choose two locations from this box. Write two rules with *must* and *must not*. Write complete sentences.

an apartment building	a library
a beach	a park
a gym	a public swimming pool

A public swimming pool
Swimmers must not run near the pool.
You must bring your own towel.

18 | Usage Note: *Must Not* vs. *Not Have To* Read the note. Then do Activity 19.

The negative forms **not have to** and **must not** have very different meanings.

NOT HAVE TO = NOT NECESSARY; NOT REQUIRED

1 Students **don't have to bring** a laptop to school.
(It's not required.)

2 Maria **doesn't have to wake** up early today.
It's a holiday. (It's not necessary.)

MUST NOT = FORBIDDEN; NOT PERMITTED

3 Students **must not smoke** on campus.
(It's not permitted.)

19 | Using *Not Have To* and *Must Not* Complete these sentences with *must not* or *don't/doesn't have to.*

12.6 B

STATEMENTS FROM A HOTEL MANAGER

To guests

a hotel guest

1. Welcome to the Oaks Hotel! We provide daily housekeeping, so you ___*don't have to*___ clean up.

2. You _____ leave your room for meals. We have a full room service[22] menu.

3. This is a smoke-free hotel. You _____ smoke in the rooms, bathrooms, or lobby.

4. Checkout time is 12:00. You _____ notify[23] the front desk if you leave on time.

5. We offer automatic checkout. You _____ check out at the front desk. Just leave the key in your room.

To housekeepers

a housekeeper

6. Your job is to keep the rooms clean for our guests. You will make the beds, vacuum, pick up trash, and clean the bathrooms every day. Usually, you _____ change the sheets every day for the same guest. You can change them every other day.

7. Guests _____ take towels or pillows from the room. Please notify the front desk if items are missing.

8. You _____ look through the guests' suitcases or personal items.

9. You _____ provide extra services to guests, like carrying suitcases. Guests should contact the front desk for extra help.

To desk clerks

a desk clerk

10. You _____ wear a uniform, but please wear a black or gray jacket.

11. The privacy of our guests is very important. You _____ give guests' names or room numbers to other people.

Write about It Work with a partner. Write six sentences with *don't have to* and *must not* about people at a restaurant. You can write about customers, servers, cooks, or hosts.

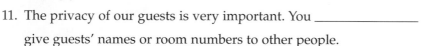

1. Customers don't have to clean the tables.

---

[22]**room service:** food that comes to your hotel room   [23]**notify:** to tell

12.7 Comparing Modals: *Can* vs. *Should* vs. *Have To*

A

STATEMENTS

We use **can** for ability, possibility, and permission*.	We use **should** for advice, opinions, and suggestions.	We use **have to** for necessity.
1 She **can type** 90 words per minute. **2** You **can't use** your phone here. **3** We **can be** there at 5:00.	**4** He looks cold. He **should go** inside. **5** You **shouldn't bother** her. She's busy.	**6** You **have to throw** away old food. It can make you sick. **7** You **don't have to wear** a suit. This is an informal meeting.

QUESTIONS

We use **can** for permission*.	We use **should** to ask for advice or an opinion.	We use **do / does . . . have to** to ask if something is necessary.
8 Can I have a glass of water?	**9** Should I call him?	**10** Does he **have to stay** home from school?

*For more information on *can*, see Unit 11, pages 280 and 283.

🔊 **20 | Noticing *Can*, *Should*, and *Have To*** Listen and complete these conversations with the words you hear. Then match each conversation with a place in the box. Practice the conversations with a partner. `12.7 A`

___c___ 1. A: My son wants to study engineering.

        B: That's a difficult major. He _____ *has to* _____ get very high scores in math.

        A: Oh, he does.

_____ 2. A: What time is my appointment?

        B: It's at 3:00, but you _____ try to get here at 2:45.

        A: Why?

        B: You _____ complete some paperwork[24] before your appointment.

_____ 3. A: First, you _____ take the written test. Then you can take the driving test.

        B: OK. _____ I make an appointment for the driving test?

        A: Of course.

_____ 4. A: Oh, it's too crowded here. We _____ go somewhere else.

        B: But I really want fried chicken!

        A: Well, we _____ find another place.

a. at a doctor's office
b. at a restaurant
c. at a school counselor's office
d. at an amusement park
e. at the Department of Motor Vehicles (DMV)

Department of Motor Vehicles (DMV)

[24] **paperwork:** written work that you have to do, such as completing forms

_____ 5. A: You _____ go on the

Scream Machine! It's so much fun!

B: No, thanks. I don't like scary rides.

A: Really? Oh, that's too bad. . . . But you

_____ try it anyway! It's fun.

B: Nope.

_____ 6. A: Do I _____ take any medication?

B: No, you don't. But you _____

change your diet.

A: I know, I know.

_____ 7. A: You _____ take a history class

next semester.

B: Next semester? Why?

A: It's a graduation requirement.

_____ 8. A: Where _____ I go now?

B: Stand in that line over there. We _____ take your picture.

A: OK.

_____ 9. A: I'm sorry. Your son _____ go on this ride.

B: But he's nine years old.

A: Passengers _____ be five feet tall.

B: Oh, I didn't see that.

_____ 10. A: I _____ eat any of this food! I _____ watch my diet.

B: You _____ order a salad.

A: I guess.

an amusement park

Think about It Look at each example of *have to* in Activity 20. Why do you think the speaker chose *have to* instead of *should*?

Write about It Choose two places from Activity 20. Write new conversations with *can*, *should*, or *have to*. Practice your conversations with a partner.

Doctor's office
A: When should I come back?
B: Sometime next week. We have to do a few more tests.

21 | Using Can, Should, and Have To Complete these conversations with the correct modal in parentheses. Then practice the conversations with a partner. 12.7 A

1. A: Do you want to see a movie or go dancing?

B: Hmm. I think we _____*should*_____ go dancing.
   (should / have to)

2. A: Can you come over tomorrow?

B: I can't. I _____ go to work.
   (should / have to)

3. A: Ron is applying for a job in Mexico.

B: _____ he speak Spanish?
        (can / should)

A: Yes, he speaks it very well.

4. A: I have a headache.

B: You _____ drink some tea.
          (should / have to)

A: Good idea.

5. A: Do you want some peanuts?

B: No, thanks. I _____ eat nuts. I'm allergic[25] to them.
                  (don't have to / can't)

6. A: Why is Tina wearing that cap?

B: It's part of her uniform. She _____ wear it.
                                  (has to / can)

7. A: Can I buy one of these?

B: You _____ buy them. They're free.
          (don't have to / shouldn't)

8. A: Are you coming to the show?

B: No, I'm not. Sorry. I _____ work from 9 a.m. to 9 p.m. that day.
                          (have to / can)

9. A: I can't go out tonight.

B: _____ study?
     (should you / do you have to)

A: Yep. Big test tomorrow.

10. A: I don't think I like this color.

B: _____ show you a different color?
     (do I have to / should I)

A: Yes, please.

Write about It Write a response for each of these statements and questions. Use *can*, *should*, or *have to*.

1. A: Why are you working so late?

   B: *I have to make some extra money.* _____

2. A: The store is closed.

   B: _____

3. A: My phone isn't working.

   B: _____

4. A: What's the matter?

   B: _____

5. A: Uh-oh. My car won't start.

   B: _____

[25]**allergic:** having a medical condition that makes you sick when you eat something

WRAP-UP

A | GRAMMAR IN READING Read this article. Underline the forms of *should*, *have to*, *need to*, *can*, and *must*.

Tips for Travelers

1. Packing

Are you traveling to several places? You don't want to carry a heavy suitcase around, so you should plan your trip carefully. Maybe you don't really have to take that winter coat. Sometimes it's better to take two sweaters. Do you really need that fancy dress? Maybe you can just bring a simple dress and a nice piece of jewelry. And you definitely don't have to carry your heavy guidebook[26]. Read it *before* you go. Then photocopy the important pages.

2. Airplane comfort

Airplanes are noisy, crowded, and uncomfortable, but you don't have to suffer[27] on your trip. A pair of good headphones will reduce the noise so you can enjoy your music and videos.

You don't have to eat the terrible airplane food. Bring your own food. Or order the vegetarian choice. It won't be as heavy, and you'll feel better. You should wear comfortable shoes, but don't wear sandals on the plane. They won't protect your feet.

3. Travel apps

Do you need to take public transportation[28] in a strange city? There are apps to help you plan routes in most major cities. Apps can also give you information about interesting places to visit. Most of the apps are very cheap. But on some phone plans, customers must pay high fees for international Internet service. You should download the apps before you leave. Use free Wi-Fi as much as possible.

4. Making friends

You don't have to speak the language in a foreign country. You can still make friends. Smile, be polite, and communicate with your hands—people will be happy to help you! You should try to learn a few words in the local language. People love that. And you shouldn't shout[29] at them in English. That doesn't help.

Maybe you want to travel, but you don't have anyone to go with. Don't worry—you don't have to travel alone. You can join a tour group and make new friends!

Have a nice trip!

---

[26]**guidebook:** a book that tells you about a place you are visiting
[27]**suffer:** to feel pain, sadness, or another unpleasant feeling

[28]**public transportation:** buses, trains, subways, etc.
[29]**shout:** to speak very loudly

Write about It Complete these statements about the article on page 329. There are many possible answers. Compare your sentences with a partner.

ACCORDING TO THE WRITER . . .

1. Sometimes travelers have to *take public transportation in a strange city* _____.

2. Travelers shouldn't _____.

3. Travelers don't have to _____.

4. Travelers should _____.

B | GRAMMAR IN SPEAKING Work with a partner. Complete this chart with your partner's responses.

TRAVEL ADVICE	
When I travel . . .	**My partner's name:** _____
1. What should I bring on the airplane?	
2. What should I always pack?	
3. What shouldn't I bring?	
4. What should I do in a new city?	
Complete these sentences about your native country.	**Native country:** _____
5. Visitors should . . .	
6. Foreign visitors have to . . .	
7. Visitors don't have to . . .	
8. I don't think visitors should . . .	
9. Visitors can . . .	
10. Visitors shouldn't . . .	
11. Foreign visitors must not . . .	
12. Visitors must . . .	

Write about It Write a list of tips for travelers. Use your partner's ideas and/or your own ideas. Write about traveling in general, visiting your own country, or visiting another country.

You should bring a tablet on the plane.

12.8 Summary of Modals II

USES		EXAMPLES
Advice / Suggestions / Opinions	should should not	You **should do** your homework.
		He **should study** more.
		Should we **take** the bus?
		Jack **shouldn't stay** up so late.
Suggestions	why don't you / we	**Why don't we have** a salad?
		Why don't you take a break?
Necessity	have to	I **have to clean** the house.
		She **has to pay** her bills.
		Do you **have to work** tomorrow?
		Does he **have to take** this class?
	need to	You **need to call** the doctor.
		He **needs to go** home.
		Do you **need to borrow** a pen?
		Does she **need to work** late?
	must	Everyone **must report** to the manager.
No Necessity	not have to	We **don't have to go** to school on Saturday.
		He **doesn't have to buy** a new book.
	not need to	We **don't need to read** page 43.
		She **doesn't need to call** me.
Prohibition (something forbidden; not permitted)	must not	Children **must not play** in this area.

For more modals, see Chart 11.8 on page 305.

13

Types of Verbs

WARM-UP 332

13.1 Overview of Past, Present, and Future Verb Forms 334

Usage Note: Action Verbs and Non-Action Verbs with Present Forms 336

13.2 Verb + Object 340

Usage Note: Common Phrases with *Make* and *Take* 341

13.3 Verbs with No Object 343

Usage Note: Verb + Object vs. No Object 344

13.4 *Be* and Other Linking Verbs 345

13.5 Comparing Different Types of Verbs 346

13.6 *Be* + Adjective Phrase + Preposition 348

13.7 Multi-Word Verbs (Part 1) 351

13.8 Multi-Word Verbs (Part 2) 353

WRAP-UP 355

Grammar in Reading 355

Grammar in Writing 357

13.9 Summary of Types of Verbs 357

ONLINE

For the Unit Vocabulary Check, go to the Online Practice.

IN THIS UNIT, WE STUDY verbs.

Past, present, and future verb forms

1. In the 1800s, people **rode** in carriages. (past)

2. Today many people **drive** cars. (present)

3. In many cities, bicycles **are becoming** popular. (present)

4. In the future, there **will be** new kinds of transportation. (future)

Think about It Read these sentences. Check (✓) *True* or *False*.

	TRUE	FALSE
1. In my childhood, I traveled a lot.	☐	☐
2. Most years I go somewhere on vacation.	☐	☐
3. I usually fly one or more times a year.	☐	☐
4. I'm planning a vacation this year.	☐	☐
5. In the future, I'll probably travel a lot.	☐	☐

WE USE different types of verbs in different ways.

5. I **bought some vegetables** for dinner.
   (verb + object)

6. I **slept** a lot last night.
   (verb with no object)

7. I**'m sick** today. I **feel terrible**.
   (linking verb + adjective)

8. My sister **is** in Colorado. She**'s** a ski instructor.
   (*be*)

9. My friend Gina and I **talk about** everything.
   (multi-word verb)

10. I'll **pick** you **up** at 6:00.
    (multi-word verb)

Think about It Choose all the answers that are correct for you.

1. I bought ____ last weekend.

   ☐ food   ☐ clothes   ☐ music   ☐ other: _____

2. I ____ a lot yesterday.

   ☐ worked   ☐ slept   ☐ laughed   ☐ walked   ☐ studied   ☐ other: _____

3. Today I feel ____.

   ☐ sick   ☐ relaxed   ☐ excited   ☐ bored   ☐ happy   ☐ tired   ☐ other: _____

4. My friends and I often talk about ____.

   ☐ movies   ☐ books   ☐ sports   ☐ politics   ☐ other: _____

13.1 Overview of Past, Present, and Future Verb Forms

We studied these **past**, **present**, and **future** verb forms in this book.

Notice that some verb forms have **helping verbs** and **main verbs**.

STATEMENTS

A

		POSITIVE STATEMENTS	NEGATIVE STATEMENTS	COMMON TIME EXPRESSIONS
PAST	**SIMPLE PAST***	We **worked** last week. I **came** to class yesterday.	They **didn't work** yesterday. You **didn't come** to class.	yesterday last week five years ago in 2010
	BE	She **was** angry. We **were** here yesterday.	He **wasn't** angry. Our friends **weren't** here.	
PRESENT	**SIMPLE PRESENT**	We often **work** there. He **works** twice a week.	They **don't work** there. She **doesn't work** with me.	always, usually every day twice a week
	BE	I'm a student. We're never late for class. She's here today.	I'm not the teacher. They're not late. He's not here.	
	PRESENT PROGRESSIVE	I'm **working** on my paper. We're **working** together. It's **working** now.	I'm not **working** right now. We're not **working** now. This isn't **working**.	(right) now these days this semester
FUTURE	**FUTURE WITH BE GOING TO**	I'm **going to go** soon. They're **going to go** later. She's **going to go** at 6:00.	I'm not **going to go** to class. We're not **going to go**. He's not **going to go** tomorrow.	soon, later tomorrow next week in two weeks
	FUTURE WITH WILL	I'll **go** with you.	They **won't go** next week.	
	FUTURE WITH PRESENT PROGRESSIVE	We're **leaving** tomorrow.	We're not **leaving** tomorrow.	
IMPERATIVE		**Do** your homework now. **Call** me tonight!	**Don't forget** your keys!	

*For a list of irregular simple past verbs, see the Resources, page R-4.

QUESTIONS

B

		YES/NO QUESTIONS AND SHORT ANSWERS		WH- QUESTIONS AND WH- QUESTIONS ABOUT THE SUBJECT
PAST	**SIMPLE PAST**	Did he **fall**?	Yes, he **did**. No, he **didn't**.	**When** did he **fall**? **What fell**?
	BE	**Was** he angry? **Were** they angry?	Yes, he **was**. No, they **weren't**.	**Why** was he angry? **Who** was angry?
PRESENT	**SIMPLE PRESENT**	Do you **work**? Does she **work**?	Yes, I **do**. No, she **doesn't**.	**Where** do they **work**? **Who works** here?
	BE	**Is** he a student? **Are** you hungry?	Yes, he **is**. No, I'm not.	**Where** is it? **Who** is at the door?
	PRESENT PROGRESSIVE	Am I **working**? Are they **working**? Is it **working**?	Yes, you **are**. No, they **aren't**. No, it **isn't**.	**Why** are you **working**? **What's happening**?
FUTURE	**FUTURE WITH BE GOING TO**	Am I **going to drive**? Is she **going to drive**? Are they **going to drive**?	Yes, you **are**. No, she **isn't**. No, they **aren't**.	**Where** are you **going to go**? **Who's going to drive**?
	FUTURE WITH WILL	**Will** you **stay** here?	Yes, I **will**. No, I **won't**.	**Where** will you **stay**? **Who** will **stay** here?
	FUTURE WITH PRESENT PROGRESSIVE	Are you **working** this weekend?	No, I'm not.	**Why** are you **working** tomorrow? **Who** is **coming** this weekend?

🔊 **1 | Identifying Past, Present, and Future Verb Forms** Listen and write the words you hear.
Are the verbs past, present, or future forms? Label the verbs *PA* (past), *PR* (present), or *F* (future).
(For present progressive verbs with future meaning, write *F*.) **13.1 A–B**

TALKING ABOUT PLANS

1. A: What _____*are you doing*_____ these days? Are you still in school?

   B: No, _____ last semester. A friend and I started a business.

   A: What kind of business is it?

   B: We design and _____ jewelry. Next month

   _____ a little store.

2. A: _____ yet?

   B: No, _____ so. But it's going to start soon.

   _____ almost two feet of snow!

   A: We'll be OK. _____ lots of groceries this morning.

3. A: Sure, _____ your cats next week. No problem.

   B: Thanks. I really appreciate it. _____ for Kenya on Monday.

   A: That _____ exciting! _____ on a safari?

   B: No, _____ for my friend Danielle's wedding. Danielle _____ my first

   roommate in college. She's from Nairobi.

4. A: Where _____ for graduate school?

   B: I don't know. MIT was my first choice. But _____ in[1].

   A: That's too bad!

   B: Yeah. So right now _____ for decisions from the other schools. _____

   probably _____ from them this week.

5. A: How was your weekend?

   B: Crazy! My friend Erin _____ over with all her stuff around midnight on Friday.

   She and her roommates _____ a huge fight.

   A: What's she going to do now?

   B: _____ back. She's going to look for a new place.

6. A: _____ cream and sugar in your coffee?

   B: No, thanks. I usually _____ lots of cream and three spoons of sugar. But these days

   _____ on a strict diet. So now _____ my coffee black.

   A: A strict diet—that's great!

   B: Yeah. My goal[2] is to lose 20 pounds by summer.

---

[1] **get in:** to be accepted

[2] **goal:** something you want to do very much

FYI

We can use some **time expressions** with **present**, **past**, or **future** forms.

I'm working at the office **this morning.** (I'm at the office, and it's before noon.)

I saw Jim **this morning.** (I saw Jim today before noon.)

I'm going to see Jim **this morning.** (I'm going to see Jim today before noon.)

These time expressions include *today*, *tonight*, and *this + morning/afternoon/week.*

TYPES OF VERBS   **335**

Think about It Circle the time expressions in Activity 1. Which verb forms are used with each time expression?

Think about It Which sentences in Activity 1 use the present progressive? Which sentences use the present progressive to talk about the future?

2 | Usage Note: Action Verbs and Non-Action Verbs with Present Forms Read the note. Then do the tasks below.

Remember: We often use verbs like *be, feel, have, like, need, own, seem, think,* and *want* as **non-action verbs**.

With **non-action verbs** in present time, we usually use the **simple present**, even if the action is happening now.

With **action verbs**, we often use the **simple present** or the **present progressive**.

	FACTS, HABITS, AND ROUTINES Use the **simple present** for all verbs.	THINGS HAPPENING NOW Use the **present progressive** for action verbs. Use the **simple present** for non-action verbs.
ACTION VERBS	The kids often **drink** hot chocolate.	The kids **are drinking** hot chocolate now.
NON-ACTION VERBS	The kids often **want** hot chocolate.	The kids **want** hot chocolate now.

For more information about action verbs and non-action verbs, see Unit 7, pages 185 and 188.
For a list of non-action verbs, see the Resources, page R-5.

Think about It Look at conversation 6 in Activity 1. Which verbs are action verbs and which are non-action verbs? Do they use the simple present or the present progressive? Why?

Talk about It What is your life like these days? Tell a partner. Use some of the verbs from each box.

ACTION VERBS				NON-ACTION VERBS			
drink	go	study	wear	be	have	need	seem
eat	sleep	take	work	feel	like	own	want

"These days I'm not sleeping enough. I often feel tired. I need to sleep more."
"This semester I really like school. My classes all seem interesting."

3 | Forming Statements with Past, Present, and Future Forms Underline the time expressions in these sentences. Then complete the sentences with the correct form of the verbs in parentheses. (More than one verb form may be possible.) `13.1 A`

BICYCLES: PAST, PRESENT, AND FUTURE

1. In 1817, Baron von Drais ___*invented*___ (invent) a bicycle.

    The bicycle _____ (not/be) very useful.

    It _____ (not/have) any pedals. People used their

    feet to push the bicycle.

2. The French _____ (introduce) the word *bicycle*

    (*bicyclette*, or "two wheel") in the 1860s.

the first "bicycle" from 1817

3. By 1865, bicycles had pedals on the front wheel. In the 1870s and 1880s, the front wheel _____ (become) larger and larger. Bicycles _____ (be) more useful and more popular. But they were expensive, and they _____ (not/be) very safe. Many riders got hurt.

4. By the 1890s, new designs _____ (make) bicycles cheaper and more useful. Workers _____ (buy) bicycles and _____ (ride) their bikes to work. After the 1890s, bicycles _____ (not/change) very much.

5. Today there _____ (be) more than 1 billion bicycles in the world! Every year factories _____ (make) more than 100 million new bicycles.

6. People in China _____ (own) more than half of the bicycles in the world.

7. These days, even in China, people _____ (drive) cars more than before, and they _____ (not/use) bicycles as much.

8. Will bicycles have a place in our future? According to some experts, bicycles _____ (become) even more important in the future, for several reasons.

9. These days more people _____ (move) to cities. Bicycles are very useful in cities.

10. Bicycles are better for the environment than cars. These days many cities _____ (build) more bicycle paths. Amsterdam and Copenhagen are two examples.

11. In Amsterdam and Copenhagen, many people _____ (ride) their bicycles to work every day. In these cities, many people _____ (not/own) cars.

12. New designs may make bicycles even more popular in the future. In a few years, your new bicycle _____ probably _____ (have) a special design. For example, maybe you _____ (not/need) a lock for your bike. Your bike _____ (fold) into a backpack!

a bicycle from 1875

a bicycle of the future

Think about It Look at the verb forms you added to the sentences in Activity 3. Which of these forms use the helping verbs *be*, *do*, or *will*? Circle the helping verbs.

Talk about It Ask a partner these questions. Share your partner's answers with the class.

BICYCLE SURVEY

1. Can you ride a bicycle? (If YES, go to #2. If NO, go to #5.)
2. When did you learn to ride a bicycle? How old were you?
3. Do you own a bicycle now?
4. Do you ride a bicycle to school and/or work? Do you ride a bicycle for fun?

5. In your opinion, does your city/town have enough bicycle paths?

6. In the future, will you own and ride a bicycle?

7. In your opinion, will bicycles become more important in the future? Why or why not?

4 | Understanding Questions with Past, Present, and Future Forms Listen and write the questions you hear. Circle the best response to each question. 13.1 B

1. _Did the 12:00 bus come?_

   (a. No, it didn't.)   b. No, it doesn't.   c. No, it won't.

2. _____

   a. No, I didn't. Sorry!   b. No, I don't. Sorry!   c. No, I won't. Sorry!

3. _____

   a. No, I probably didn't.   b. No, I probably don't.   c. No, I probably won't.

4. _____ We need a ride home.

   a. Yes, I was.   b. Yes, I am.   c. Yes, I will.

5. Excuse me. _____

   a. Yes, it did.   b. Yes, it does.   c. Yes, it will.

6. _____

   a. Yes, I did.   b. Yes, I do.   c. Yes, I will.

7. _____

   a. Yes, you were.   b. Yes, you do.   c. Yes, you are.

8. _____

   a. No, there probably weren't.   b. No, there aren't any now.   c. No, there probably won't.

9. _____

   a. Yes, earlier today.   b. Yes, I'm on the last paragraph.   c. Yes, maybe next week.

10. _____

    a. He graduated from UCLA.   b. He's studying at UCLA.   c. He'll go to UCLA.

11. _____

    a. A few days ago.   b. These days.   c. Next week.

12. _____

    a. I enjoyed it.   b. I enjoy it.   c. I'll enjoy it.

13. _____

    a. I didn't do much,   b. I'm not doing much,   c. I probably won't do
       but I relaxed a lot!   but I'm relaxing a lot!   much, but I'll relax a lot!

14. _____

    a. Last Saturday.   b. On Saturdays.   c. Next Saturday.

Talk about It Practice the conversations above with a partner. Give your own answers.

1. A: _Did the 12:00 bus come?_
   B: _Yes, it came five minutes ago._

5 | Forming Questions with Past, Present, and Future Forms Use the words in parentheses to write *yes/no* and *wh-* questions. Put the **bold** verbs in the correct form. Add the helping verbs *do, be,* or *will* where necessary. More than one verb form may be possible. `13.1 B`

Soccer and the World Cup: FAQ

1. Q: _Is soccer the most popular sport in the world?_
   (**be** / soccer / the most popular sport in the world)
   A: Yes, it is. Soccer is the most popular sport—both to watch and to play.

2. Q: _____
   (how many people / **play** / soccer)
   A: About 300 million people around the world play soccer!

3. Q: _____
   (how often / the World Cup / **take** place³)
   A: It happens every four years.

4. Q: _____
   (when / **be** / the first World Cup)

   _____
   (where / **be** / it)
   A: It was in 1930, in Uruguay. Uruguay beat Argentina 4–2 in the final.

5. Q: _____
   (**be** / there / a World Cup for women)
   A: Yes, there is.

6. Q: _____
   (when / the Women's World Cup / **begin**)
   A: It began in 1991. The first Women's World Cup was in China.
   The United States beat Norway 2–1 in the final.

7. Q: _____
   (how many teams / **play** / in the World Cup)
   A: Thirty-two teams usually play. There are eight groups, each with
   four teams.

8. Q: _____
   (the number of teams / **increase** / in the future)
   A: It might increase to 40 teams.

9. Q: _____
   (the host country⁴ / always / **play** / in the World Cup)
   A: Yes, it does. The host country always has a team.

10. Q: _____
    (soccer / **become** / more popular / in the United States)
    A: Yes, it probably will. Americans are more interested in soccer today
    than in the past.

11. Q: _____
    (**be** / the World Cup / on TV in every country)
    A: Yes, it is. You can even watch it in Antarctica!

12. Q: _____
    (how many people / **watch** / the 2014 World Cup)
    A: About 1 billion people!

13. Q: _____
    (when / **be** / the first World Cup in Asia)
    A: In 2002. This was also the first World Cup with two host countries—
    Japan and South Korea.

³ **take place:** to happen   ⁴ **host country:** the country that has the games

6 | Error Correction Find and correct the errors. (Some sentences may not have any errors.)

1. Yuki talks to her brother right now.
2. Who did they got the keys from?
3. Meera and Anna are leaving tonight.
4. That hat was on sale and only cost $10.
5. We're not really knowing the neighborhood yet.
6. I have my own business in ten years.
7. Who going to take the kids to school tomorrow?
8. Aisha is usually studying on the weekends.
9. We finally finish the homework!
10. Felipe didn't came to class yesterday.
11. Our study group is meeting this morning.
12. I take you to the mall this weekend.
13. Look! It snows now!
14. Did you ate dinner already?
15. There won't be any more tickets tomorrow.
16. The bus never more than a few minutes late.

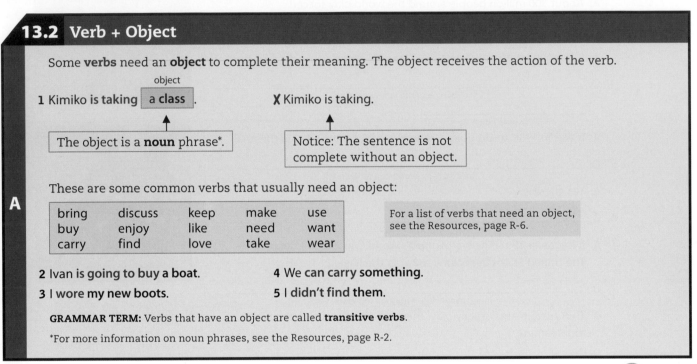

13.2 Verb + Object

Some **verbs** need an **object** to complete their meaning. The object receives the action of the verb.

object

1 Kimiko **is taking** a class .   ✗ Kimiko is taking.

The object is a **noun** phrase*.

Notice: The sentence is not complete without an object.

A

These are some common verbs that usually need an object:

bring	discuss	keep	make	use
buy	enjoy	like	need	want
carry	find	love	take	wear

For a list of verbs that need an object, see the Resources, page R-6.

2 Ivan **is going to buy** a boat.   **4** We **can carry** something.

3 I **wore** my new boots.   **5** I **didn't find** them.

GRAMMAR TERM: Verbs that have an object are called **transitive verbs**.

*For more information on noun phrases, see the Resources, page R-2.

7 | Noticing Verb + Object Underline the main verbs in these conversations. Then listen and complete the conversations with the object that follows each verb. **13.2 A**

TRAVELING

1. A: Did you <u>find</u> _____ *your passport* _____ ?
   B: Not yet. But I will.

2. A: Do you need _____ ?
   B: No, thanks. I'm OK.

3. A: Should I bring _____ ?
   B: You won't need _____ .
      A light jacket should be enough.

4. A: Can I bring _____
      on the plane?
   B: I'm sorry. It's too large.

5. A: Are we forgetting _____ ?
   B: Oh! Bug spray[5]!

6. A: Can I take _____ ?
   B: No. It's not going to fit in the car.

[5] **bug spray:** a liquid you put on your body to keep bugs away

7. A: I can carry _____ in
   my backpack.
   B: Thanks. Mine is really full.

8. A: I think we can take _____ to
   San Francisco.
   B: Let's do it. I love _____.

9. A: Can I use _____?
   B: Sure. There's just a little left. Keep
   _____.

10. A: I love _____! Where did
    you buy _____?
    B: Thanks. I bought them at Athletic World.

Talk about It Discuss the conversations in Activity 7 with a partner. Where are the speakers or where are they going?

8 | Writing Sentences with Verb + Object Complete each sentence with an object. Share your answers with a partner. `13.2 A`

SOME INTERESTING FACTS ABOUT ME

1. On a trip, I always take *a comfortable jacket with lots of pockets.* _____.

2. My friends and I often discuss _____.

3. My friends and I really like _____.

4. In school, I enjoy _____.

5. In (cold/warm) weather, I often wear _____.

6. In the grocery store, I usually buy _____.

7. In the morning, I often want _____.

8. After a long day, I need _____.

9 | Usage Note: Common Phrases with *Make* and *Take* Read the note. Then do Activity 10.

We often use *make* and *take* with certain objects.

MAKE +		TAKE +	
an appointment	I'd like to make an appointment with the doctor.	a picture	John **took** beautiful **pictures** on his trip.
plans	They're **making plans** for their summer vacation.	a long time	This train ride **is taking a long time.**
a decision	Jack finally **made his decision.**	a minute a few minutes an hour / all day . . .	This **is going to take a few minutes.**
a mess	You kids **are making a mess!**	a taxi / bus / train . . .	Did you **take the train** here?
a mistake	You're **making a big mistake!**	a walk	Let's **take a walk.** We can go through the park.
a good / bad impression	Dress nicely. You want to **make a good impression**[6].	a break	Let's **take a break.** We'll come back in ten minutes.
		a class / a course	How many **classes are** you **taking?**

[6]**impression:** feelings or thoughts you have about someone or something

10 | Using Objects with _Take_ and _Make_ Complete the sentences below with the form of _make_ or _take_ in parentheses and a word or phrase from the box. **13.2 A**

an appointment	classes	a plan	a picture

1. A: Alice is ___*taking*___ four ___*classes*___ next semester. What about you?
   (making / taking)

   B: I don't know yet. I have to _____ _____ with my adviser.
   (make / take)

2. A: What should we do this weekend?

   B: I don't know. Let's _____ _____!
   (make / take)

3. A: Can you _____ _____ of us?
   (make / take)

   B: Sure!

a break	a decision	a long time	a mess

4. A: Which apartment are you going to rent?

   B: I don't know. I really like them both. I have to _____ _____.
   (make / take)

5. A: Did you finish your paper?

   B: No. It's _____ _____. I'm exhausted. I can't think anymore.
   (making / taking)

   A: Then you should _____ _____. Let's watch a movie.
   (make / take)

6. A: Did you fix the kitchen sink⁷?

   B: Yeah. The sink is OK now. But I _____ _____ in the kitchen.
   (made / took)

a good impression	a mistake	a taxi

7. A: How did you do on the quiz?

   B: I don't know. I think I _____ _____ on the last question,
   (made / took)

   and it's worth a lot of points.

8. A: Is this a good outfit⁸ for a job interview?

   B: Yeah, you look great.

   A: Are you sure? I have to _____ _____.
   (make / take)

9. A: How did you get here so fast?

   B: I _____ _____.
   (made / took)

⁷**kitchen sink:** a large container in a kitchen where you wash dishes

⁸**outfit:** a set of clothes you wear together

13.3 Verbs with No Object

Some **verbs** are complete without an object.

1 Diego **is waiting**.   ✗ Diego **is waiting** me.

↑
Notice: It is incorrect to use an object here in this way.

These are some common verbs that usually do not take an object:

arrive	fall	happen	sit	stay	walk
come	go	laugh	sleep	wait	work

For a list of verbs that do not take an object, see the Resources, page R-6.

A

2 The children **are sleeping**.   **4** I **can't work** this evening.

3 Your package **arrived** yesterday.   **5** Jennifer **will go** with you.

Notice: We can use a **prepositional phrase** or **time expression** after these verbs.

↓   ↓

6 Diego **is waiting** for me.   **7** We're **leaving** tomorrow.

GRAMMAR TERM: Verbs that do not have an object are called **intransitive** verbs.

GO ONLINE

11 | Using Verbs with No Object Underline the main verbs in this survey. Then check (✓) your answers to the survey. **13.3 A**

Time Survey

1. When do you usually <u>arrive</u> . . .

   . . . for class?   ☐ on time ☐ early ☐ late

   . . . for a doctor's appointment?   ☐ on time ☐ early ☐ late

   . . . for dinner with a friend?   ☐ on time ☐ early ☐ late

2. During the semester, how often do you work in the library?

   ☐ almost every day   ☐ about once a week   ☐ less than once a week

3. On the night before a test, do you usually sleep a lot or study late?

   ☐ I sleep a lot.   ☐ I study late.

4. You are waiting in a long line for tickets. You'll probably wait for an hour or more. Do you wait patiently[9] or impatiently?

   ☐ I wait patiently.   ☐ I wait impatiently.

5. You are waiting for your friend at a restaurant. After 30 minutes, your friend doesn't come. Do you stay and wait? Or do you go home?

   ☐ I stay and wait.   ☐ I don't wait any longer. I go home.

6. You are sitting at your desk and studying for a test tomorrow. Some friends come to your door. They're all going out to dinner. What happens?

   ☐ I go with my friends.   ☐ I stay at my desk and work.

waiting impatiently

Talk about It Ask and answer the survey questions above with a partner. Compare your answers.

[9] **patiently:** staying calm and not getting angry while waiting

12 | Usage Note: Verb + Object vs. No Object Read the note. Then do Activity 13.

We can use many **verbs** with an **object** OR without an object. Some of these verbs include:

| begin | break | leave | move | study |

VERB + OBJECT	VERB WITH NO OBJECT
1a Noor **studies law** at my school.	**1b** Noor **studies** at my school.
2a We **began our project** today.	**2b** Classes **began** today.
3a I **broke something**.	**3b** Something **broke**.
4a Daniel **left his phone** in your car.	**4b** Daniel **left** yesterday.

For more verbs that can be used with or without an object, see the Resources, page R-6.

13 | Noticing Verb + Object or No Object Look at the **bold** main verbs. Which verbs are followed by an object? Which are NOT followed by an object? Check (✓) the correct column. If there is an object, underline the object. 13.3 A

	VERB + OBJECT	NO OBJECT
1. A: Is Dillon still at school? B: No, he's here. But he's **studying**.	☐	✓
2. A: I'll help you clear the table¹⁰. B: It's OK. **Leave** the dishes. I'll take care of them later.	✓	☐
3. A: What's wrong? B: My printer **broke** again. This time I'm getting a new one!	☐	☐
4. A: What's for lunch? B: Ramen noodles. I'm **boiling** the water now.	☐	☐
5. A: Is your son **studying** law? B: Either law or political science. He's not sure yet.	☐	☐
6. A: Do you want to go out for lunch? B: Unfortunately, I can't. I have to **leave**.	☐	☐
7. A: Can you **move** your things? I need to put these boxes here. B: Sure. Sorry about that!	☐	☐
8. A: Did you **begin** the new project yet? B: No, we're still waiting for some information.	☐	☐
9. A: What did the doctor say? B: Good news! I didn't **break** my wrist¹¹. It will be better soon.	☐	☐
10. A: Do you go to the gym a lot? B: No, not really. But I **run** every day.	☐	☐
11. A: When are you **moving**? B: In just a couple of weeks. I'm so excited!	☐	☐
12. A: When do classes **begin**? B: A week from Monday.	☐	☐

Talk about It Listen to the conversations above. Then practice them with a partner.

¹⁰ **clear the table:** to remove the dirty dishes from the table   ¹¹ **wrist:** the part of your body where your arm joins your hand

13.4 Be and Other Linking Verbs

We do not use objects after **linking verbs**. We use other words and phrases. *Be* is the most common linking verb.

A

BE + ADJECTIVE PHRASE, NOUN PHRASE, OR PREPOSITIONAL PHRASE

subject	*be*	**adjective** phrase
1	Amir	is	very **busy.**

subject	*be*	**noun** phrase
2	My brother	was	a **lawyer.**
3	Hong Kong	is	an amazing **city.**

subject	*be*	**prepositional** phrase
4	My parents	are	**in** Korea.

The verb *be* can be followed by:

- an adjective phrase

- a noun phrase

- a prepositional phrase

B

LINKING VERB + ADJECTIVE PHRASE

subject	linking verb	**adjective** phrase
5	The soup	is looks smells tastes	**great.** really **good.**

Other linking verbs are usually followed by an adjective phrase.

Some common linking verbs are:

be	get	seem	sound
feel	look	smell	taste

For more linking verbs, see the Resources, page R-5.

GO ONLINE

14 | Identifying Linking Verbs Underline the linking verbs before the **bold** phrases. Then label the **bold** phrases *A* (adjective phrase), *N* (noun phrase), or *P* (prepositional phrase). `13.4 A–B`

CONVERSATIONS IN SUMMER

lilies

1. A: These chairs <u>are</u> **so comfortable**. And the sun <u>feels</u> **wonderful**!
   A ... *A*

   B: Yeah. We're in a perfect place. And it's a perfect day.

2. A: These are **for you**. They're **from my garden**.

   B: Lilies! They're **my favorite flower**. They smell **amazing**!

3. A: Come in the water!

   B: No, it's **too cold**!

   A: It's not **cold**. It's **perfect**!

4. A: Did the kids finish school yet?

   B: Yeah, they finished last week. They're **at home**. They're **really bored**,

   but their summer camp will start next Monday.

5. A: Should we go to the outdoor concert tonight?

   B: That sounds **lovely**. It seems **so hot** right now, but it will be **nice and cool** this evening.

6. A: It's **so dark** and it's only 5:00!

   B: I know. It's getting **dark** really early these days!

7. A: You weren't **in class** today. Do you still feel **sick**?

   B: Yeah. Actually, I feel **worse** this week. This cold is **terrible**!

8. A: A ski trip sounds **really fun**. Colorado is **a beautiful state**.

   B: Yeah. I'm **excited**!

9. A: I need some new boots.

   B: Try these on. They're **really popular** this year. I think they'll look **good** on you.

10. A: Let's go sit by the fireplace.

    B: Good idea. The fire smells **great**.

15 | Using _Be_ vs. Other Linking Verbs Look at these sentences with _be_. Rewrite some sentences with a different linking verb from the box. Write _X_ if the change is not possible. **13.4 A–B**

AT SCHOOL

1. So far my classes are pretty good. _So far my classes seem pretty good._

2. The cafeteria food is OK. _____

3. My new roommate is interesting. _____

4. She's from Mexico. _____

5. We're in the best dorm. _____

6. We decorated our room, and it's beautiful now. _____

7. My friend Lisa is across the hall. _____

| look |
| seem |
| sound |
| taste |

13.5 Comparing Different Types of Verbs

We use different words and phrases after different types of **verbs**. Review Charts 13.2, 13.3, and 13.4 for more information about types of verbs.

A

VERB + OBJECT

		object (**noun** phrase)
1	He wants	some **ice cream.**
2	I bought	a new **sofa.**

✗ He wants.

VERB WITH NO OBJECT

3	The package **arrived.**	
4	The package **arrived**	at 3:00. (prepositional phrase)
5		yesterday. (time expression)

✗ The package arrived **us.**

BE + ADJECTIVE PHRASE, NOUN PHRASE, OR PREPOSITIONAL PHRASE

6		really **beautiful.** (adjective phrase)
7	Shanghai is	a big **city.** (noun phrase)
8		in China. (prepositional phrase)

✗ Shanghai is.

OTHER LINKING VERB + ADJECTIVE PHRASE

		adjective phrase
9	The music sounds	**beautiful.**
10	You seem	really **tired.**

✗ That music sounds.

16 | Noticing Different Types of Verbs Read this interview. Underline the main verbs in the bold phrases. Then write the verbs in the chart below. `13.5 A`

○ ○ ○

Interview with a Restaurant Reviewer

1. Q: Your job **sounds fun**. Do you **<u>enjoy</u> it**?
   A: Yes, but it's hard work, too. My job **seems easy**, so I always explain this.
2. Q: How do you **do your job**?
   A: Well, first, I **find some friends**. We **go to a restaurant**. I don't say my name.
3. Q: But do people **recognize[12] you**? You probably **look familiar**.
   A: That *is* a problem. I change my look—sometimes I **have a beard**, but sometimes I don't have a beard. I even wear disguises[13]. . . . Anyway, we all **order different things**. And we each try everything.
4. Q: What's your usual experience?
   A: There is no usual experience. Anything **can happen**. Sometimes food **looks great** and **smells great**, but it **doesn't taste very good**. Or it **looks terrible** but **tastes great**.
5. Q: After a meal, do you write your review?
   A: No. I return to the restaurant two or three more times, always with other people. This way, I **try many things** on the restaurant's menu. Then I **stay in my office** all day and write my reviews.
6. Q: And on your days off[14]—do you go to restaurants?
   A: Almost never. Restaurants **are great**, but I **get tired** of them. And on my days off I usually **don't feel very hungry**!

> **F Y I**
> Prepositions include:
>
> | at | in | to |
> |---|---|---|
> | for | on | |
>
> Remember: A prepositional phrase is NOT an object.

Verbs followed by an object	Verbs with no object	Linking verbs
enjoy		*sounds*

17 | Forming Sentences with Different Types of Verbs Use words from each box to form sentences. Write five sentences for each group of words. (Ø means no words.) `13.5 A`

1. Bob	is seems works	a lawyer. every day. in Chicago.	really nice. tired these days. Ø.

Bob works every day.   Bob works.

2. The students	discussed sounded worked	a little bored today. at their desks. in the library.	the questions. their plans for the semester. Ø.

[12] **recognize:** to know who someone is because you saw them before
[13] **disguises:** things you wear so people don't know who you are
[14] **days off:** days when you don't go to work

3.	This car	is looks uses	a Fiat Panda. a lot of gas. kind of dirty.	mine. really new. Ø.

4.	The children	got seemed slept	a lot of attention from everyone. dessert after dinner. every afternoon.	for a long time. tired at the end of the day. Ø.

Write about It Write six sentences about yourself or events in your life. Use two verbs from each of these groups. Use past, present, or future forms of the verbs.

GROUP 1		GROUP 2		GROUP 3	
buy	take	go	stay	be	look
enjoy	wear	sleep	work	feel	seem

I bought a new car a few years ago.

13.6 *Be* + Adjective Phrase + Preposition

We often use *be* + **adjective phrase** + **preposition**. We use certain prepositions after certain adjectives.

	be (+ *not*)	adjective phrase	preposition	noun phrase
1	I	'm	nervous	about	the test.
2	They	're not	very good	at	tennis.

Here are some common adjective + preposition combinations:

ADJECTIVE + *ABOUT*	**angry about (something)***	**3** He was **angry about** the bill.
	excited about	**4** We're **excited about** our trip to China.
	nervous about	**5** She's **nervous about** the test.
ADJECTIVE + *AT*	**angry at (someone)***	**6** I'm **angry at** my roommate.
	bad at	**7** My brother is **bad at** math.
	good at*	**8** He's really **good at** chess.
ADJECTIVE + *FOR*	**bad for**	**9** Too much sugar **is bad for** you.
	good for*	**10** Water **is good for** you.
	easy for	**11** Languages **are easy for** some people.
	hard for	**12** Languages **are very hard for** me.
ADJECTIVE + *IN*	**interested in**	**13** He's **interested in** sports, especially soccer.
ADJECTIVE + *OF*	**afraid of**	**14** I'm **afraid of** spiders.
	proud of	**15** Your parents **are so proud of** you.

*Notice: With some adjectives, we use different prepositions for different meanings.

16a My sister **is good at** math. (She can do math well.)

16b Vegetables **are good for** you.
(Vegetables have a good effect.)

17a Lisa **is angry at** me. (*angry at* + person)

17b Lisa **is angry about** the bill.
(*angry about* + thing or situation)

For more adjective + preposition combinations, see the Resources, page R-5.

A

18 | Noticing *Be* + Adjective Phrase + Preposition Listen and complete the sentences with the words you hear. Then practice the conversations with a partner. ▸ **13.6 A**

1. A: _____Are_____ you _____angry about_____ something?

   B: No, I'm just in a bad mood¹⁵ today. Sorry!

2. A: Are you starting your new job tomorrow?

   B: Yeah. _____ _____ it now, but I'll be fine in the morning.

3. A: How are your son's swimming lessons going?

   B: Great! A month ago he _____ the water. Now I can't get him out of the pool.

4. A: I heard your new album¹⁶. Congratulations!

   B: Thanks. _____ _____ it.

5. A: I'm going to the Indian music festival next weekend. Do you want to come?

   B: Definitely! _____ _____ Indian music.

6. A: _____ coffee _____ you?

   B: I'm not sure. I think maybe one or two cups a day are OK.

7. A: Why _____ those customers _____ you?

   B: They wanted to return some stuff. But they didn't have a receipt¹⁷.

8. A: My classes this semester seem hard.

   B: Hard classes _____ you. You'll learn more.

9. A: How can you do those problems? They seem impossible!

   B: They _____ me. I love math!

10. A: Thanks for the ride. I really appreciate it.

    B: Sure. _____ us. We go right by your house.

Think about It Look at the sentences you completed above. Do they use past, present, or future verb forms?

19 | Using *Be* + Adjective Phrase + Preposition in Sentences Look at these pictures. Complete the sentences below with *is/are* + an adjective from the box + *about*, *at*, *for*, *in*, or *of*. ▸ **13.6 A**

1.

Julio | Juan

a. Julio _____

   _____ sports.

b. Juan _____

   _____ sports.

| good |
| not interested |

2.

Nadia | Berta

a. Nadia _____

   the trip to New Zealand.

b. Berta _____

   the trip to New Zealand.

| excited |
| nervous |

¹⁵**in a bad mood:** feeling bad at a particular time
¹⁶**album:** a collection of songs on one CD, etc.

¹⁷**receipt:** a piece of paper that shows you paid for something

3.

a. Many people _____ math.

b. Math _____ Jeanine.

| bad |
| easy |

4.

a. Soda _____ you.

b. Water _____ you.

| bad |
| good |

5.

a. Marta _____ her son.

b. She _____ the broken lamp.

| angry |
| angry |

6.

a. Nighttime _____ Ethan.

b. He _____ the dark.

| afraid |
| hard |

20 | Using *Be* + Adjective Phrase + Preposition Compare your life in the past with your life today. Ask and answer these questions with a partner. Write down your partner's answers. **13.6 A**

	When you were a child . . .	Today . . .
Your interests	1a. What school subjects were you interested in? 2a. What other activities were you interested in?	1b. What academic subjects are you interested in today? 2b. What other activities are you interested in?
Your skills	3a. What were you good at? 4a. What were you bad at? 5a. What subjects or activities were easy for you? 6a. What subjects or activities were hard for you?	3b. What are you good at now? 4b. What are you bad at? 5b. What subjects or activities are easy for you? 6b. What subjects or activities are hard for you?
Your passions[18]	7a. What were you often excited about?	7b. What are you excited about now?

A: *What school subjects were you interested in?*
B: *I was interested in art and music.*

[18] **passions:** things you like a lot or are very interested in

Talk about It Tell the class about your partner's present interests, skills, and passions.

"Alexa is interested in birds and animals. At school she's really interested in biology and other science classes. She goes on hikes and looks for unusual birds."

13.7 | Multi-Word Verbs (Part 1)

Sometimes verbs have two or more words. They can include a verb + a preposition. These are some common **verb + preposition** combinations:

<table>
<tr><td>A</td><td>

VERB + PREPOSITION	EXAMPLE
look at	**1** We're **looking at** some pictures of Mika's family.
look for	**2** I'm **looking for** a one-bedroom apartment.
look like	**3** You really **look like** your brother.
talk to (someone)	**4** I **talked to** Sylvie yesterday.
talk about (something)	**5** We **talked about** our plans for the summer.
listen to	**6** We're **listening to** some new music.
write to	**7** Who are you **writing to**?
think about	**8** I'm **thinking about** my interview.
know about	**9** Did you **know about** Ted's problems at work?
worry about	**10** Don't **worry about** the dishes. I'll wash them later.
pay for	**11** Where can I **pay for** this shirt?
wait for	**12** **Wait for** Eduardo. He's coming, too.

</td></tr>
</table>

For more multi-word verbs, see the Resources, page R-6.

21 | Identifying Verb + Preposition Combinations Read this article. Underline the verb + preposition combinations from Chart 13.7. **13.7 A**

THE GREATEST ART THEFT[19]

On Tuesday, August 22, 1911, Louis Beróud went to the Louvre museum in Paris, France to see the *Mona Lisa*. He <u>looked for</u> the painting in its usual place, but it wasn't there. Beróud immediately told the museum guards. They didn't know about the disappearance of the painting. But they didn't worry about it. Probably the museum's photographers had the painting.

The photographers did not have the painting. Soon the police arrived and closed the Louvre. For a week they looked for the *Mona Lisa* everywhere in the museum. They didn't find it. They talked to all the museum's workers. One thing became clear: The theft happened on Monday morning. On Mondays the museum was closed. Did a worker steal the *Mona Lisa*? The police investigated[20] and thought about the possibilities.

Time passed. The police waited for more information. There was none.

Then, one day in 1913 (almost two years later), a man named Vincenzo Peruggia went to Florence, Italy and wrote to the owner of an art store there. He had the *Mona Lisa* for sale.

[19]**theft:** the crime of stealing something   [20]**investigate:** to try to find out about something

Was this painting real or just a copy? The owner of the art store met with Peruggia and looked at the painting. It looked like the *Mona Lisa*. After a closer look, he was sure: It *was* the *Mona Lisa*.

How did Peruggia steal the *Mona Lisa*? He hid in the Louvre on Sunday, and he stayed in the museum overnight. On Monday the museum was closed. He took the painting and left the museum.

Why did Peruggia steal the *Mona Lisa*? There were two reasons. First, Peruggia wanted this Italian painting for an Italian museum. Second, he wanted money for the painting. The art store owner did not pay for the *Mona Lisa*. Instead, Peruggia went to jail for six months.

The *Mona Lisa* traveled to museums around Italy for a year, and then it returned to the Louvre. Every year millions of visitors look at the *Mona Lisa*.

22 | Using Verb + Preposition Combinations Complete the conversations below with the correct preposition from the box. Then listen and check your answers. **13.7 A**

about	at	for	like	to

1. A: I'll pay ___*for*___ it.
   B: No, you paid last time. It's my turn.

2. A: Who are you looking _____?
   B: That guy in the brown jacket. Do you know him? He looks really familiar.

3. A: I'm sorry. I can't help you.
   B: Maybe someone else can help me. Can I talk _____ your supervisor, please?

4. A: There's still lots of time. We'll wait _____ you.
   B: It's OK. You don't have to wait. I can meet you there.

5. A: You worry _____ everything!
   B: There's a reason for that: You don't worry _____ anything!

6. A: I can't believe you're not her. You really look _____ her!
   B: I know. People always ask me for an autograph[21].

7. A: Did you know _____ the missing[22] money?
   B: No. No one said anything to me.

8. A: What are you thinking _____?
   B: Our plans for the summer. I'm really excited!

9. A: I'm sorry. I looked _____ it everywhere. I asked everyone. But no one found it.
   B: OK. Thanks for looking.

10. A: What did you and Sam talk _____?
    B: The usual. He still feels homesick.

Talk about It Who are the speakers in each conversation above? What are they talking about? Discuss your ideas with a partner.

"In conversation 1, I think two friends are having lunch together at a restaurant."

Talk about It Ask and answer these questions with a partner.

1. Who in your family do you look like? Do you look like any famous people?
2. What topics do you know a lot about?
3. What things do you often think about?
4. What things do you sometimes worry about?
5. What do you and your friends often talk about? What do you and your family often talk about?
6. Who do you talk to often? Who do you talk to about problems or important decisions?

[21] **autograph:** a famous person's name, which they themselves write

[22] **missing:** lost, or not in the usual place

23 | Error Correction Find and correct the errors. (Some sentences may not have any errors.) More than one correction may be possible for some sentences.

1. My younger brother Davi is afraid from bees.
2. I worry of my children all the time.
3. We're flying tonight, and I'm very nervous for it.
4. Don't be angry about me. I'm really sorry!
5. Gabriel is very interested at modern art.
6. We're looking at pictures from our vacation.
7. My friend Valeria is really good for chess.
8. Don't rush! We can wait to you.
9. Children should listen their parents and obey them.
10. I didn't pay the concert tickets. My friend bought them.
11. What are you listening to?
12. I'm easy at math.

13.8 Multi-Word Verbs (Part 2)

Some multi-word verbs include a verb + another small word like *along, back, down, off, on, out, over,* and *up*. The two words work together to form a new meaning.

MULTI-WORD VERBS WITH NO OBJECT

MULTI-WORD VERB	MEANING	EXAMPLE
come back	return	1 We'll **come back** after the appointment.
come over	visit someone in their house	2 **Come over** anytime!
get along	behave in a friendly way	3 Everyone in our group **gets along**.
get up	move to a standing position	4 **Don't get up**. I'll answer the door.
	get out of bed	5 We **got up** late this morning.
sit down	move to a sitting position	6 Grab a chair and **sit down**.
wake up	stop sleeping	7 I **woke up** in the middle of the night.
work out	exercise	8 She **works out** at the gym every day.
	have a good result	9 We had some problems at the meeting, but everything **worked out**.

MULTI-WORD VERBS + OBJECT

Some multi-word verbs need an **object** to complete their meaning.

MULTI-WORD VERB	MEANING	EXAMPLE
figure out	understand how to do something after trying	10 I finally **figured out the answer**.
fill out	complete a form	11 He's **filling out the application**.
look up	look for information	12 Let's **look up the directions**.
pick up	take something and lift it up	13 I can't **pick up this box**. It's too heavy.
	go get something or someone, especially in a car	14 We'll **pick up the children** after school.
turn down	make something lower, for example, in loudness	15 Can you please **turn down the music**?
turn on	make something start	16 Did you **turn on the TV**?
turn off	make something stop	17 Can I **turn off the TV**?

For more multi-word verbs, see the Resources, page R-6.

GRAMMAR TERM: some multi-word verbs are also called **phrasal verbs**.

A

GO ONLINE

24 | Understanding Multi-Word Verbs Listen and complete these conversations with the words you hear. Then practice the conversations with a partner. 13.8 A

1. A: Can I _____turn on_____ the light? Or will it bother you?

   B: Go ahead. It won't bother me at all.

2. A: I can't _____ the answer.

   B: I can't either. Let's _____ it _____ online.

3. A: I had a great time. Thanks for everything.

   B: We did, too. _____ and visit us again soon.

4. A: Can you _____ the TV? It's too loud.

   B: I can _____ it _____. I'm not really watching it.

5. A: Please _____ these forms. The doctor will be with you shortly.

   B: OK. Thanks very much.

6. A: How's your day going?

   B: Really good so far. I actually _____ early this morning and _____.

7. A: What time is your plane tomorrow?

   B: Ugh. It leaves at 6 in the morning. I have to _____ really early.

8. A: Are you still vacuuming?

   B: Yeah. Can you _____ for a minute? I need to vacuum under the couch.

9. A: Did you register for classes yet?

   B: Yeah, I did. There were some schedule problems, but in the end everything _____.

10. A: Do you live here in London?

    B: Not anymore. But I studied here, and I often _____ to visit people.

> **FYI**
>
> Sometimes we use an **object pronoun** with a multi-word verb. We put the pronoun between the **verb** and the **small word**.
>
> Let's **look it up**.
> I'll **pick you up** at 6:00.

25 | Using Multi-Word Verbs Complete these conversations with the multi-word verbs from each box. Change the form of the verb if necessary. 13.8 A

1. A: You're home already.

   B: Yeah. The game was boring. So we _____came back_____ early.

2. A: _____! It's 9:00.

   B: Oh, no! I didn't hear my alarm!

3. A: What did you do last night?

   B: Some friends _____ and we made dinner together.

4. A: I'm worried about my schedule. I won't have much time between classes.

   B: Don't worry. It will _____. You'll see.

> come back
> come over
> wake up
> work out

5. A: Would you like to _____?

   B: Thanks very much, but it's OK. I'm getting off at the next stop.

6. A: How often do you _____?

   B: Almost every day. I ride my bike or run in the park.

7. A: I'm hungry.

   B: Me too. Let's _____ some Chinese food.

8. A: How's your new job?

   B: I really like it. The people are great. Everyone _____ really well.

> get along
> pick up
> sit down
> work out

9. A: Can you give me a ride to the airport tomorrow?

   B: OK. What time should I _____ you _____?

10. A: Can you _____ the music? I'm trying to do my homework.

    B: OK. . . . Is that better?

11. A: Can you please _____ this form and then bring it back to me?

    B: Sure.

12. A: Are you leaving?

    B: Yeah, it's getting late. I have to _____ early tomorrow.

fill out

get up

pick up

turn down

Write about It Work with a partner. Choose two of these situations. Write a short conversation for each. Use one of the multi-word verbs from Chart 13.8 in each conversation.

1. Your friends stayed with you for a week. Now they are leaving.

2. You're going to the gym. You want your friend to go with you.

3. You want to invite a friend to your apartment for dinner.

4. You are talking to friends. It's very late. Tomorrow you have an early morning class.

Situation 1
A: It was great to see you. Come back soon!
B: Thanks. We will!

WRAP-UP

A | GRAMMAR IN READING Read the graduate school application essay below. Label the **bold** verbs with the verb forms in this box. Then answer the questions on page 356.

Simple present: *SPr*	Present progressive: *PP*	Simple past: *SPa*	Future with *will*: *F*	Imperative: *I*

Graduate School Application Essay

Marcus Johnson

                        PP
Why **am** I **applying** for the master's program in Emergency and Disaster Management[23]? The answer **is** a long story, and here it is.

Six years ago, I **graduated** from college with a degree in film studies. I **had** a plan: I wanted to make movies and become a famous director. Well, that **didn't happen**.

After college I **went** to New York City, and soon I began to work on movies. I'm still working on movies today. This **sounds** perfect for me, but it's not. These days I'**m writing** schedules and **planning** budgets. Am I making art? No, I'**m making** phone calls and giving advice to actors. "Don't **get** nervous," I tell the actors. "And, remember, **get** a good night's sleep before work!"

[23] **emergency and disaster management:** the field that helps people plan for and deal with dangerous situations (emergencies) and disasters (bad events that can hurt many people)

I may not be happy with my work, but I **am** good at my job. I can organize and plan projects. I can help people feel better about themselves and their situations. I don't want to be in the film business, but I do want to use those skills. A year ago, I **volunteered**[24] for the American Red Cross. They **trained** me in disaster response[25]. I'm still doing this volunteer work, and I love it. I like to help people. A family's house burned down, and we **found** a hotel room for them. They **thanked** me again and again. I **felt** good.

disaster relief after a hurricane

I want to continue in disaster response. This master's program **will give** me important skills and knowledge. Through my studies in the program, I **will become** a better disaster responder. Disasters like hurricanes and tornadoes **are** big challenges. To save people's lives, we need to plan before, during, and after disasters. This planning **takes** a lot of skills. I want to learn these skills and save lives.

Circle all the answers that are correct.

1. What did Marcus study in college?
   a. film
   b. painting
   c. business
   d. emergency and disaster management

2. What is Marcus doing now?
   a. He's in a film studies program.
   b. He's in an emergency and disaster management program.
   c. He's working on movies.
   d. He's doing volunteer work for the Red Cross.

3. When did Marcus become interested in emergency and disaster management?
   a. in college
   b. after graduation, six years ago
   c. during the last year
   d. after a tornado

4. What work does Marcus do for movies?
   a. He writes schedules.
   b. He plans budgets.
   c. He is an actor.
   d. He films with a camera.

5. Why does Marcus want to study emergency and disaster management?
   a. He wants to help people.
   b. He wants to work for the Red Cross.
   c. He wants to use his planning skills.
   d. He wants to film hurricanes and tornadoes.

Think about It Look again at the **bold** verbs in the reading. Why did the writer use these verb forms? What other words in the sentences tell you about past, present, or future meaning?

Think about It Which **bold** verbs in the reading are followed by an object? Which verbs are followed by an adjective phrase?

[24] **volunteer:** to do work without pay   [25] **disaster response:** helping people after a disaster

B | GRAMMAR IN WRITING Write a paragraph of about five or six sentences. Imagine that you are applying for a program of study or a job that interests you. In your paragraph, answer some of these questions.

- What program or job are you applying for?
- What are you interested in?
- What things in your past led to this interest?
- What related things are you doing now?
- What will you do in the future?

I am applying for the master's program in architecture. I am interested in the design of apartment buildings. In high school, I learned about the history of art and architecture. This was always my interest. Now I am studying for a bachelor's degree in engineering. In the future, I'll design interesting and comfortable buildings for people.

13.9 Summary of Types of Verbs

VERB FORMS

SIMPLE PRESENT

I work here. / We work here. / He works here.
They don't work here. / She doesn't work here.
Do you work here? / When do you work? Does he work here? / Where does he work? Who works here?

FUTURE WITH *BE GOING TO*

I'm going to leave. / He's going to leave. / They're going to leave.
I'm not going to leave. / She's not going to leave. / They're not going to leave.
Am I going to leave? / Is she going to leave? / Are they going to leave? Where am I going to work? / Where is he going to work? / Where are they going to work? Who is going to work?

PRESENT PROGRESSIVE

I'm working. / She's working. / We're working.
I'm not working. / She's not working. / We're not working.
Are you working? / Why are you working? Who is working?

FUTURE WITH *WILL*

I'll work.
He won't work.
Will it work? Where will you work? Who will work here?

SIMPLE PAST

We worked. / She left.
We didn't work. / She didn't leave.
Did you work? / Did she leave? What happened?

IMPERATIVE

Come here.
Don't forget your lunch!

TYPES OF VERBS

VERB + OBJECT	
Mina often wears	red sneakers. (object)
We bought	a new car. (object)

VERB WITH NO OBJECT	
Tina is sleeping.	
Tina is sleeping	on the couch. (prepositional phrase)
James is going to arrive	this evening. (time expression)

LINKING VERBS			
Abel	is	really nice. (adjective phrase)	*be*
		a good friend. (noun phrase)	
		in the kitchen. (prepositional phrase)	
Abel	looks seems	really nice. (adjective phrase)	other linking verbs

14

Sentence Patterns

WARM-UP 358

14.1 What Is a Sentence? 360

14.2 Subjects and Verbs in Questions 362

Pronunciation Note: Statements as Questions 364

14.3 Common Sentence Patterns 365

Usage Note: Placement of Adverbs of Frequency 368

14.4 Connecting Clauses with *And, But,* and *So* 370

14.5 Clauses with *Because* 373

14.6 Past and Present Time Clauses 375

14.7 Future Time Clauses 378

14.8 Using Sentence Patterns in Writing 381

WRAP-UP 382

Grammar in Reading 382

Grammar in Writing 382

14.9 Summary of Sentence Patterns 383

IN THIS UNIT, WE STUDY sentence patterns.

1. I bought some fruit at the market.

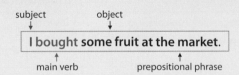

subject   object

I bought some fruit at the market.

main verb   prepositional phrase

2. Did you cook breakfast this morning?

subject   object   time expression

Did you cook breakfast this morning?

helping verb main verb

GO ONLINE

For the Unit Vocabulary Check, go to the Online Practice.

3. It's a cold day, but the sun is shining.

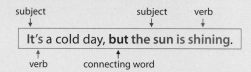

4. I always wear a hat when it's cold outside.

I always wear a hat | **when it's cold outside** .

time clause

Think about It Read these sentences. What is true about you? Check (✓) *True* or *False*.

	TRUE	FALSE
1. I bought some fruit yesterday.	☐	☐
2. I cooked breakfast this morning.	☐	☐
3. It's cold out now, but the sun is shining.	☐	☐
4. I usually wear a hat when it's cold outside.	☐	☐
5. I often watch TV when I get home.	☐	☐
6. I usually read before I go to bed.	☐	☐

14.1 What Is a Sentence?

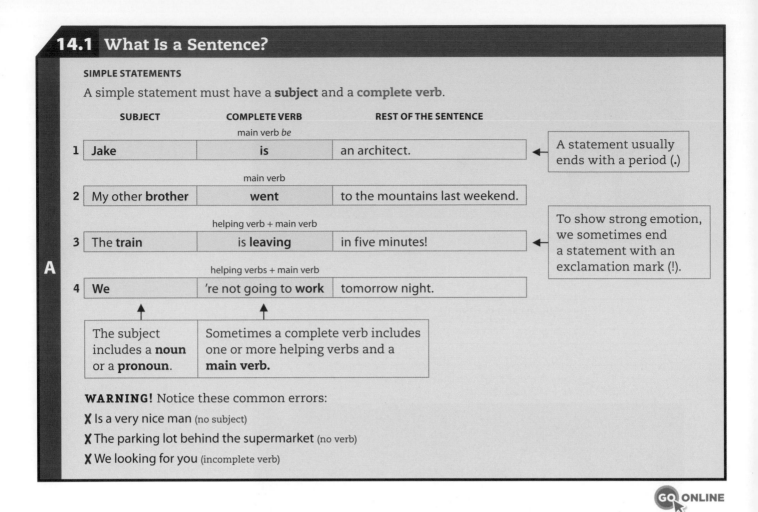

A

SIMPLE STATEMENTS

A simple statement must have a **subject** and a **complete verb**.

SUBJECT	COMPLETE VERB	REST OF THE SENTENCE	
	main verb be		
1	Jake	**is**	an architect.
	main verb		
2	My other **brother**	**went**	to the mountains last weekend.
	helping verb + main verb		
3	The **train**	is **leaving**	in five minutes!
	helping verbs + main verb		
4	We	're not going to **work**	tomorrow night.

A statement usually ends with a period (**.**)

To show strong emotion, we sometimes end a statement with an exclamation mark (**!**).

The subject includes a **noun** or a **pronoun**.

Sometimes a complete verb includes one or more helping verbs and a **main verb.**

WARNING! Notice these common errors:

✗ Is a very nice man (no subject)

✗ The parking lot behind the supermarket (no verb)

✗ We looking for you (incomplete verb)

GO ONLINE

1 | Noticing Subjects and Verbs Circle the subject in these sentences. Underline the complete verb.

`14.1 A`

ABOUT ME

1. (My best friend) is studying English.

2. I'm living on campus this year.

3. Yesterday was an excellent day.

4. I watched TV for several hours last night.

5. My classes started in September.

6. I'll get home around 9 p.m. tonight.

7. My hometown is a large city.

8. My family is going to take a vacation next summer.

9. My parents live in another country.

10. History is my favorite subject.

11. I can play the guitar.

12. I have an interesting job.

Write about It Rewrite the sentences above to make them true for you. Change the subject and/or the verb in each sentence. Don't change the other parts of the sentence.

*1. **My sister** is studying English.*

*2. I'm **not living** on campus this year.*

2 | Error Correction Some of these sentences are not complete. Label the incomplete sentences *NS* (no subject), *NV* (no verb), or *IV* (incomplete verb). If the sentence is correct, write a checkmark (✓) on the line and add a period (.) or exclamation mark (!) to the sentence. **14.1 A**

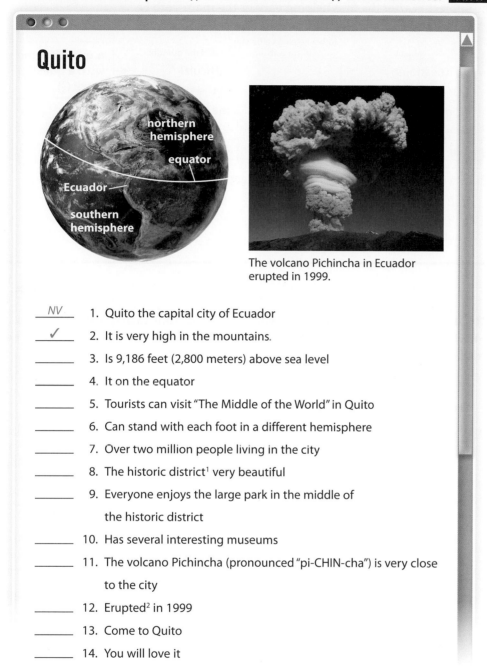

Quito

northern hemisphere

equator

Ecuador

southern hemisphere

The volcano Pichincha in Ecuador erupted in 1999.

F Y I

In imperative sentences, the subject (*you*) is invisible.

(You) **Come** back next week.
(You) **Stop** that!

For more information about imperative sentences, see page 19.

_NV_ 1. Quito the capital city of Ecuador

_✓_ 2. It is very high in the mountains.

_____ 3. Is 9,186 feet (2,800 meters) above sea level

_____ 4. It on the equator

_____ 5. Tourists can visit "The Middle of the World" in Quito

_____ 6. Can stand with each foot in a different hemisphere

_____ 7. Over two million people living in the city

_____ 8. The historic district[1] very beautiful

_____ 9. Everyone enjoys the large park in the middle of the historic district

_____ 10. Has several interesting museums

_____ 11. The volcano Pichincha (pronounced "pi-CHIN-cha") is very close to the city

_____ 12. Erupted[2] in 1999

_____ 13. Come to Quito

_____ 14. You will love it

Write about It Correct the incomplete sentences above. Add a period (.) or an exclamation mark (!).

1. Quito is the capital city of Ecuador.

Think about It Compare your answers with a partner. Did you use an exclamation point (!) in any of the sentences above? Why?

---

[1] **historic district:** an area in a city with old structures or buildings that are important in history

[2] **erupt:** When a volcano **erupts**, smoke, hot rocks, or liquid rock (called lava) suddenly come out.

14.2 Subjects and Verbs in Questions

In most questions, the **subject** is after the **first helping verb** or the **main verb be**.

A

	wh- word	be / first helping verb	subject	(other helping verbs +) main verb	rest of the question
1	-	**Were**	the questions	-	difficult?
2	-	**Are**	your computer classes	continuing	in the summer?
3	-	**Can**	Thomas	hear	me?
4	When	**did**	the eye doctor	call?	
5	Where	**are**	your parents	going to go	on vacation?

> A question ends with a question mark (?).

In some questions with *who* and *what*, the *wh-* word is the subject. It comes before the complete verb.

	wh- word (= subject)	complete verb	rest of the question
6	Who	called	yesterday?
7	What	is happening?	

3 | Identifying Subjects and Verbs in Questions What is missing from each question? Look at choices a–e in the box. Write the correct letter above each conversation. Then listen and complete the questions with the words you hear. Correct your labels if necessary. 14.2 A

1. _d_
   A: _Is_____ Tom in his office?
   B: I think so. He usually comes in at 8:00.

2. _b_
   A: When is the _____*new building*_____ going to open?
   B: In September, I think.

3. ____
   A: Could you _____ the door for me?
   B: Of course. No problem.

4. ____
   A: _____ does the book club meet?
   B: Usually at my house.

5. ____
   A: _____ he wear a uniform every day?
   B: Yeah. He has to.

6. ____
   A: Are _____ expensive?
   B: A little, but I got them on sale.

7. ____
   A: Was _____ a farmer?
   B: Yeah, he was. He grew corn and squash.

a. *wh-* word
b. subject
c. helping verb
d. *be* (main verb)
e. main verb (not *be*)

F Y I

Notice that we often do not answer questions with complete sentences.

A: Where are you going?
B: To the store.

A: How's your mom doing?
B: Pretty well.

A: Who ate the cake?
B: Brian.

squash

8. ____

    A: Who _____ that poem?

    B: I'm not sure. I found it online.

9. ____

    A: _____ is Alan leaving?

    B: He got a new job.

10. ____

    A: What time _____ the show?

    B: 3:00.

11. ____

    A: Who _____ the night class?

    B: Stevenson, I think.

12. ____

    A: Who _____ I talk to?

    B: Why don't you start with the counselor?

4 | Forming Questions Look at these statements. Rewrite each statement as a question in the chart below. Change the words *I* and *my* to *you* and *your* where necessary. `14.2 A`

TALKING ABOUT FOOD

Statements

1. My favorite food is fried chicken.
2. My mother cooks dinner at our house.
3. I ate at a restaurant last night.
4. My friend and I are going shopping tomorrow.
5. My school cafeteria has pretty good food.
6. I'm going out to eat tonight.
7. I like spicy food.
8. My brother is a good cook.
9. I shop at Kelly's Market.
10. I can't eat peanuts.
11. My parents pay for my groceries.
12. My family will eat dinner at 6:00 tonight.

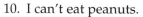

peanuts

Questions

	Wh- word	Helping verb or *be*	Subject or *wh-* word as subject	Main verb (not *be*)	
1.	What	is	your favorite food?		
2.			Who	cooks	dinner at your house?
3.	Where	did	you	eat	last night?
4.					shopping tomorrow?
5.					good food?
6.					out to eat tonight?
7.					spicy food?
8.					a good cook?
9.				shop?	
10.					peanuts?
11.					for your groceries?
12.					dinner tonight?

Talk about It Ask and answer the questions with a partner.

1. A: What's your favorite food?   *B: My mother's chicken soup.*

🔊 **5 | Pronunciation Note: Statements as Questions** Listen to the note. Then do Activity 6.

Sometimes we use a statement with rising intonation as a *yes/no* question. We often do this when we aren't 100% sure that the statement is true. Compare:

REGULAR STATEMENT

1a My brother's name is Bob.

STATEMENT AS A QUESTION

1b A: Your brother's name is Bob?
    B: That's right.

ANSWERING STATEMENT-QUESTIONS

When we use a positive statement to ask a question, we often expect a positive answer.

   2 A: You're from Argentina?
      B: **Yes**, I am.

When we use a negative statement to ask a question, we often expect a negative answer.

   3 A: Sal's **not** at home?
      B: **Nope**. He'll be home in about an hour.

🔊 **6 | Listening for Statements and Questions** Listen to each sentence. Add a question mark (?) or a period (.). `14.2 A`

AT WORK

1. You aren't finished yet?
2. Someone called this morning
3. They didn't leave a message
4. The packages are ready to go
5. Mark doesn't work today
6. This call is for you
7. The meeting is at 2:00
8. Kiera didn't call back
9. Break time is over
10. You're leaving early
11. Kim wasn't here yesterday
12. The customers are waiting

> **F Y I**
>
> Sometimes we use statements as questions to express surprise or disbelief.
>
> A: He's 70 years old?
> B: I know! He looks really young for his age.
>
> Sometimes we use statements as questions to check our understanding of something we heard.
>
> A: Today's Jerome's birthday.
> B: Today's Jerome's birthday?

Talk about It Look at the sentences above where you added a question mark (?). Ask a partner each of these "statement" questions. Give an "expected" response.

   1. A: *You aren't finished yet?*
      B: *No, I'm not.*

14.3 Common Sentence Patterns

Some sentences only have a **subject** and a **verb**. Many sentences have other elements as well.

STATEMENTS

Notice: We often use a **prepositional phrase** or a **time expression** at the end of a sentence.

A

	subject	complete verb	prepositional phrase
1	This computer	isn't working.	-
2	My parents	live	in a small town.

	subject	complete verb	object (= noun phrase**)	prepositional phrase
3	His assistant	answered	the phone.	-
4	Joanne	is taking	her daughter	to work.

	subject	linking verb (*be* or other)	adjective phrase	time expression
5	We	are	excited!	-
6	The runners	look	really tired.	-
7	You	seemed	happy	last night.

	subject	*be*	
8	Mr. Sato	is	a great manager. (noun phrase)
9	The boxes	were	in the back room. (prepositional phrase)

*A **prepositional phrase** starts with a preposition (such as *at, from, in, of, on,* or *to*) and includes a noun.

A **noun phrase includes a noun or a pronoun. For more information, see the Resources, page R-2.

QUESTIONS

B

	wh- word	first helping verb	subject	(other helping verbs +) main verb	object (= noun phrase)	prepositional phrase / time expression
10	-	Does	Antonio	work	-	at the mall?
11	-	Is	the teacher	going to correct	the papers	tonight?
12	When	did	the class	start?	-	-

			wh- word (= subject)	complete verb	object (= noun phrase)	prepositional phrase / time expression
13	-	-	Who	works	-	on Tuesday nights?
14	-	-	Who	can take	the money	to the bank?

	wh- word	*be*	subject	
15	-	Is	Julie	a new student? (noun phrase)
16	-	Are	you	hungry? (adjective)
17	-	Was	the new student	in class today? (prepositional phrase)
18	Where	are	your keys?	-

7 | Noticing Statement Patterns Read these sentences about an artist. Label the underlined words and phrases. Use the labels in the box. 14.3 A

ANDY GOLDSWORTHY

          S   *V*   *NP*

1. <u>Andy Goldsworthy</u> <u>is</u> <u>an artist</u>.

2. <u>He</u> <u>grew up</u> <u>in England</u>.

3. <u>He</u> <u>lives</u> <u>in Scotland</u> <u>now</u>.

4. <u>He</u> <u>has</u> <u>four children</u>.

5. <u>Goldsworthy</u> <u>uses</u> <u>natural materials</u> <u>for his art</u>.

6. <u>Most of his artwork</u> <u>is</u> <u>temporary</u>[3].

7. <u>He</u> <u>makes</u> <u>sculptures</u>[4] <u>from snow, leaves, and flowers</u>.

8. <u>The sun, wind, and water</u> <u>erase</u> <u>his work</u>.

9. <u>He</u> <u>has</u> <u>permanent</u>[5] <u>sculptures</u>, too.

10. <u>His sculptures</u> <u>are</u> <u>at museums around the world</u>.

11. <u>He</u> <u>takes</u> <u>photos</u> <u>of his temporary work</u>.

12. <u>You</u> <u>can see</u> <u>the photos</u> <u>on the Internet</u>.

> *S* = subject
> *V* = verb
> *O* = object
> *A* = adjective
> *NP* = noun phrase after *be*
> *PP* = prepositional phrase
> *T* = time expression

F Y I

We sometimes use *too* at the end of a sentence to show added information.

temporary artwork by Andy Goldsworthy

permanent sculpture by Andy Goldsworthy

Write about It Write five sentences about a famous person or a person you know. Use these sentence patterns.

subject	*be*	noun phrase
1.		
Pele	*is*	*a famous soccer player.*

F Y I

For a list of verbs that are followed by an object, see the Resources, page R-6.

For a list of linking verbs, see the Resources, page R-5.

subject	verb	prepositional phrase/ time expression
2.		

subject	verb	object	prepositional phrase/ time expression
3.			

[3] **temporary:** lasting for a short time
[4] **sculptures:** works of art often made from stone or wood
[5] **permanent:** lasting for a long time or forever

	subject	linking verb	adjective
4.			

	subject	*be*	prepositional phrase / time expression
5.			

8 | Using Statement Patterns Complete these statements to make them true for you. Use the sentence elements in parentheses to add information. Then share your sentences with a partner. **14.3 A**

OPINIONS AND DESIRES

1. Someday I want to live _____ *in Costa Rica* _____ .
   (prepositional phrase)

2. I would like to visit _____ .
   (object)

3. I would like to see _____ every day.
   (object)

4. The best cities have _____ .
   (object)

5. I like to bring _____ _____ .
   (object)   (prepositional phrase)

6. I don't _____ _____ .
   (main verb)   (prepositional phrase)

7. Fresh vegetables _____ _____ .
   (*be*)   (adjective)

8. I shouldn't _____ _____ .
   (main verb)   (prepositional phrase)

9. Reporters[6] should _____ _____ .
   (main verb)   (object)

10. I will never _____ _____ .
    (main verb)   (object)

Talk about It Compare your sentences as a class.

9 | Using Question Patterns Look at this chart. Follow the instructions on page 368 to write eight questions with words and phrases from the chart. Change the form of the main verb where necessary. **14.3 B**

Wh- words	Helping verbs or *be*	Subjects	Main verbs	Other sentence parts
When	do	you	bring	to school
Where	does	your friends	buy	to work
What	did	your town	clean	interesting
Who	is	your school	come	nice
Why	are	who	go	your bills
How	was	what	happen	your car
	were		have	your home
	can		make	your lunch
	will		pay	now
			start	tomorrow
			work	yesterday

> **F Y I**
> For an overview of past, present, and future verb forms, see Unit 13, page 334.

[6] **reporters:** people who write for newspapers or speak on the radio or television about things that happened

1. Write four *yes/no* questions. (You will NOT use words from every column in every question.)

   Are you coming to school tomorrow?
   Did you work yesterday?

2. Write four *wh-* questions. Include one question where the *wh-* word is the subject. (You will NOT use words from every column in every question.)

   When did you buy your car?
   Who makes your lunch?

Talk about It Ask and answer your questions with a partner. Write down your partner's answers.

Write about It Choose three of your partner's answers and write complete sentences about your partner. Share your sentences with the class.

   Bae works at a Chinese market.
   She's coming to school tomorrow.

10 | Usage Note: Placement of Adverbs of Frequency   Read the note. Then do Activity 11.

Notice the common location of **adverbs of frequency** in statements and questions.

STATEMENTS

	subject	first helping verb / be	adverb of frequency	(other helping verbs +) main verb	rest of the sentence
1	Jill	–	hardly ever	walks	to school.
2	Brent	can	usually	come	on time.
3	I	'm	never	going to fix	this problem.
4	Those cookies	–	always	smell	delicious.
5	Alan	is	sometimes	–	late.
6	My father	wasn't	always	–	an architect.

7	**Sometimes** Alan is late.
8	We take the train **sometimes**.

← We can also use *sometimes* at the beginning or end of a statement.

QUESTIONS

	wh- word	first helping verb / be	subject	adverb of frequency	(other helping verbs +) main verb	rest of the question
9	Where	does	Anna	usually	sit?	
10		Are	you	always	going to live	here?
11		Were	the meals	usually	–	pretty good?

12	Do you come here **often**?

← We often use *often* at the end of a question.

For more information on adverbs of frequency, see Unit 3, page 53.

11 | Using Adverbs of Frequency Add the adverb of frequency in parentheses to each sentence. Then check (✓) *Agree* or *Disagree*. `14.3 A`

MODERN TIMES	AGREE	DISAGREE
1. In the past, people were ∧ more polite. (usually) *usually*	☐	☐
2. Nowadays, students come late to class. (often)	☐	☐
3. Technology improves our lives. (always)	☐	☐
4. Older people don't understand the younger generation[7]. (always)	☐	☐
5. Popular music is good. (hardly ever)	☐	☐
6. Video games are bad for children. (usually)	☐	☐
7. The government can solve people's problems. (never)	☐	☐
8. Young people have the best ideas. (often)	☐	☐
9. Technology causes serious problems. (hardly ever)	☐	☐
10. Children don't respect[8] their parents. (always)	☐	☐

Write about It Rewrite the statements you disagreed with in the survey above. Change the adverb of frequency to write about your opinion. Share your ideas with a partner.

In the past, people were sometimes more polite.

Write about It Write four questions. Use the patterns below. Then ask and answer your questions with a partner. `14.3 B`

	first helping verb	subject	adverb of frequency	(other helping verbs +) main verb	(rest of the question)
1.			always		

	first helping verb	subject	(other helping verbs +) main verb	(rest of the question)	adverb of frequency
2.					often?

	wh- word	first helping verb	subject	adverb of frequency	(other helping verbs +) main verb	(rest of the question)
3.				usually		

	be	subject	adverb of frequency	adjective phrase / prepositional phrase / noun phrase	(rest of the question)
4.			usually		

1. Does Vicky always eat cereal for breakfast?
2. When does your family usually go on vacation?

---

[7]**generation:** people who were born at around the same time

[8]**respect:** to have a good opinion of someone or something

14.4 Connecting Clauses with *And*, *But*, and *So*

A

SENTENCES WITH ONE CLAUSE

A simple sentence has one **clause**. A clause includes a subject, a complete verb, and other words. (Charts 14.1–14.3 are about simple sentences.)

CLAUSE		
subject	complete verb	rest of the clause
1 Some people	are standing	outside the store.

SENTENCES WITH TWO CLAUSES

Many sentences contain more than one clause. We can use the **connecting words** *and*, *but*, and *so* to connect two clauses.

	CLAUSE			connecting word	CLAUSE		
	subject	complete verb	rest of the clause		subject	complete verb	rest of the clause
2	Maria	left	at 7:30,	and	she	is going to return	at 4:00.
3	I	love	apples,	but	I	don't like	pears.
4	We	have to work	late tonight,	so	we	can't come	to dinner.
5	Greg	isn't going	on vacation,	so	he	'll watch	our house.

> Notice: We sometimes use a comma (,) before the connecting word if the sentence is long.

B

USING *AND*, *BUT*, AND *SO*

6 I looked in the closets, **and** Tim searched the living room.

7 It rained yesterday, **but** today it's really sunny.

       cause   result

8 We needed more paper, **so** Tim went to the store.

We use *and* to add information and to connect related ideas.

We use *but* to show contrast.

We use *so* to introduce a result.

---

12 | Identifying Clauses   Underline the clauses in these sentences. Label the subject (*S*) and complete verb (*V*) in each clause. (Some sentences only have one clause.)   **14.4 A**

WORLD LEADERS

Benito Juarez

1. Benito Juarez was born very poor, but he became the president of Mexico.

2. Juarez' parents spoke an Indian language, so he didn't learn Spanish at home.

3. Juarez was a small man (only 4'6"/1.37m tall) with a big heart.

4. He became an important leader, and his birthday is now a national holiday in Mexico.

Sejong the Great

5. Sejong the Great was the king of Korea in the early 1400s.

6. He was very intelligent and creative, and he helped Korea in many ways.

7. At that time Koreans used the Chinese writing system, but it didn't work well for the Korean language.

8. King Sejong wanted a Korean writing system, so he created the Korean alphabet.

你好
Chinese writing system

안녕
Korean alphabet

Mahatma Gandhi

9. Mahatma Gandhi helped the poor people of India, and he changed the lives of many people.

10. Gandhi did not believe in violence[9].

11. His first name was Mohandas, but most people called him Mahatma.

13 | Using Connecting Words Complete each conversation with *and*, *but*, or *so*. Then listen and check your answers. `14.4 B`

VACATION QUESTIONS

1. A: Did you go to Mallorca?
   B: No. We wanted to go there, _____*but*_____ the flight was too expensive.

2. A: Where did you go?
   B: The tickets to Cancun were pretty cheap, _____ we went there.

3. A: What did you do in Cancun?
   B: We sat on the beach a lot, _____ one day we went to the pyramids. It was great!

4. B: How about you? Are you going on vacation soon?
   A: I'd love to take a vacation, _____ I'm really busy at work.

5. B: Will you have more time this summer?
   A: Yeah. I finish school in June, _____ I might take a vacation then.

6. B: Where do you want to go?
   A: I want to go to Europe, _____ my husband wants to go to Brazil.

7. B: Where in Europe do you want to go?
   A: I want to go back to Paris, _____ I'd love to see Switzerland, too.

8. A: I think you went to Europe a few years ago?
   B: I did! We stayed in Paris for a few days, _____ we didn't go to Switzerland.

pyramid in Cancun

[9]**violence:** behavior that causes physical harm to other people

9. A: How long did you stay in Europe?

   B: We stayed for two weeks, _____ we went to four different countries.

10. A: How was the food?

    B: The food was great, _____ the restaurants were really expensive.

11. A: Was the language a problem?

    B: No. I always try to speak the local[10] language, _____ people are usually friendly to me.

12. B: I went with World Tour Company. You should check their website.

    A: Thanks. I'll look at it, _____ we probably won't take a tour.

Talk about It Complete the answers below with your own ideas. Then ask and answer the questions with a partner.

1. A: What did you do last summer?

   B: I _____,

   and I _____.

2. A: What do you want to do next summer?

   B: I want to _____,

   but _____.

3. A: Are you going somewhere next weekend?

   B: I _____,

   so _____.

14 | Writing with Connecting Words Choose two phrases from each box. Combine the two ideas with *and*, *but*, or *so* to write sentences about your future plans. **14.4 A–B**

MY FUTURE

1.
go to graduate school
study business
finish my degree[11]

4.
live in another country
get a job in Asia
study Chinese

7.
improve my computer skills
design websites
become a programmer[12]

2.
get a good job
work hard
make a lot of money

5.
get plenty of exercise
become a professional athlete
be healthy

8.
become a teacher
work with small children
continue my education

3.
travel around the world
take a long vacation
save money

6.
learn to cook
open a restaurant
eat delicious food

9.
buy a house
move to a different city
save money

1. *I'm going to finish my degree, but I'm not going to study business.*
   OR *I want to go to graduate school, so I'm going to finish my degree.*
   OR *I don't want to study business, and I'm not going to go to graduate school.*

---

[10] **local:** of the place
[11] **degree:** a certificate from a university, such as a BA (Bachelor of Arts) or MA (Master of Arts)

[12] **programmer:** a person who writes computer programs

Write about It Write three more sentences about your future. Use your own ideas.

I'd like to _____, but I don't want to _____.

I want to _____, and I'd like to _____.

I want to _____, so I'm going to _____.

14.5 Clauses with *Because*

We can combine two clauses with the connecting word **because**.

The clause with **because** is called the **reason clause**. It answers the question *why*.

MAIN CLAUSE			REASON CLAUSE			
subject	complete verb	rest of the clause	*because*	subject	complete verb	rest of the clause
1 Tom	moved	to Mexico	**because**	his father	got	a job there.
2 Shaun	didn't get	the job	**because**	he	didn't have	any experience.
3 Kim	is working	extra hours	**because**	she	has to save	money.

A

This clause is called the **main clause**.

Notice: A main clause can be a complete simple sentence alone.

✓ Tom moved to Mexico.   ✓ Shaun didn't get the job.

WARNING! In writing, we don't use a reason clause alone. The sentence is not complete.

✗ Because we took the bus.

Notice: In conversation, we often use a reason clause alone when we respond to a question:

A: Why did it take you so long to get here?
B: **Because we took the bus.**

GO ONLINE

---

15 | Noticing Clauses with *Because* Underline the reason clause in each statement. Then check (✓) *Agree* or *Disagree*. **14.5 A**

Opinions

	AGREE	DISAGREE
1. Children misbehave[13] <u>because they're spoiled[14]</u>.	☐	☐
2. People don't write as well now because they text too often.	☐	☐
3. Many people are unhealthy because they eat too much sugar.	☐	☐

F Y I

Sometimes we put the **reason clause** before the **main clause**. When we do this, we add a comma after the reason clause.

Because people are online too much, they don't get enough exercise.

---

[13] **misbehave:** to act badly

[14] **spoiled:** A spoiled child gets everything he/she wants

	AGREE	DISAGREE
4. Sick people shouldn't go to work because other people will get sick.	☐	☐
5. Most people don't get enough exercise because they are online too much.	☐	☐
6. It's OK to take office supplies[15] from work because the company can afford[16] it.	☐	☐
7. A lot of people get into car accidents because they are on the phone.	☐	☐
8. Crimes happen because people are naturally violent[17].	☐	☐
9. Life is better today because we have technology.	☐	☐
10. Many people are poor because they don't want to work.	☐	☐

Think about It In the sentences above, label the subject (*S*) and the verb (*V*) in each clause (the main clause and the reason clause).

Talk about It Share your answers to the survey as a class.

16 | Writing Sentences with *Because* Complete the sentences with *because* and your own ideas. Then share your sentences with a partner. `14.5 A`

EXPLAIN YOURSELF

1. I left the door open _____ *because it was hot inside* _____.
2. I didn't finish my homework _____
   _____.
3. I forgot my lunch _____.
4. I was late _____.
5. I missed the bus _____.
6. I didn't clean the house _____
   _____.

7. I didn't come to class _____
   _____.
8. I ate too much _____.
9. I didn't call my friend _____
   _____.
10. I got sick _____.
11. I'm happy _____.
12. I'm studying English _____
    _____.

Think about It Label the subject (*S*) and the verb (*V*) in each reason clause you wrote above. Correct your answers if necessary.

Write about It Complete these sentences with your own ideas. Complete the main clause and add a reason clause with *because*.

Yesterday I _____.

Tomorrow I _____.

Sometimes I _____.

Yesterday I called my brother because it was his birthday.
Tomorrow I'm going to the mall because I need a new jacket.
Sometimes I stay up late because I have to study.

---

[15] **office supplies:** things you use in an office, such as pens, pencils, paper, etc.

[16] **afford:** to have enough money to buy or do something
[17] **violent:** strong and dangerous; causing physical harm

14.6 Past and Present Time Clauses

We can connect a main clause with a **time clause**. The time clause answers the question *when*.
We can begin a time clause with connecting words like **before**, **when**, or **after**.

A

	main clause	time clause	
1	Maria always eats breakfast	**before** she goes to work.	(First, she eats breakfast. Second, she goes to work.)
	(1)	(2)	

	main clause	time clause	
2	Ken checked his email	**when** he got to the office.	(First, he got to the office. Second, he checked his email.)
	(2)	(1)	

	main clause	time clause	
3	My roommate usually watches TV	**after** he eats dinner.	(First, he eats dinner. Second, he watches TV.)
	(2)	(1)	

B

TIME CLAUSES WITH THE SIMPLE PRESENT

We can use time clauses with the simple present to describe general habits and routines.
Notice that we use a **simple present verb** in the main clause and in the time clause.

	main clause	time clause
4	I always **do** the dishes	after I **eat** dinner.
5	The teacher usually **closes** the door	when class **begins**.

TIME CLAUSES WITH THE SIMPLE PAST

We can use time clauses with the simple past to describe when two past events happened.
Notice that we use a **simple past verb** in the main clause and in the time clause.

	main clause	time clause
6	Sarah **called** me	before she **left**.
7	She **broke** her arm	when she **fell**.

WARNING! In writing, we don't use a time clause by itself. The sentence is not complete.
✗ After you went to bed.

C

We often use a time clause after the main clause:

	main clause	time clause
8	I met some wonderful people	when I went to Russia.

We can also use a time clause before the main clause:

	time clause	main clause
9	When I went to Russia,	I met some wonderful people.

Notice: When the time clause is before the main clause, we use a comma (,) to separate the clauses.

17 | Noticing Time Clauses Read the information about Marie Curie and Enrico Fermi. Underline the time clause in each sentence. Then number the events in the correct order. **14.6 A**

FAMOUS SCIENTISTS

Marie Curie

1. Marie Curie began her scientific training in Poland <u>before she moved to Paris in 1891</u>.

    _1_ She began her scientific training.

    _2_ She moved to Paris.

2. She finished her degrees in physics and chemistry after she moved to Paris.

    ___ She moved to Paris.

    ___ She finished her degrees in physics and chemistry.

3. She and her husband Pierre won a Nobel Prize in physics after they discovered the element radium.

    ___ Marie and Pierre Curie discovered radium.

    ___ Marie and Pierre Curie won a Nobel Prize in physics.

4. She won another Nobel Prize in chemistry after she won the physics prize.

    ___ She won a Nobel Prize in chemistry.

    ___ She won the physics prize.

Marie Curie

Enrico Fermi

5. Enrico Fermi became interested in physics after his brother died.

    ___ He became interested in physics.

    ___ His brother died.

6. Other scientists discovered the parts of the atom[18] before Fermi began his work.

    ___ Scientists discovered the parts of the atom.

    ___ Fermi began his work.

Enrico Fermi

7. He moved to the United States after he won the Nobel Prize for physics in 1938.

    ___ He moved to the United States.

    ___ He won the Nobel Prize.

8. Fermi worked on the atomic bomb[19] after he came to the United States.

    ___ He came to the United States.

    ___ He worked on the atomic bomb.

9. He was very unhappy when he saw the results of the bomb.

    ___ He was unhappy.

    ___ He saw the results of the bomb.

10. He became a professor at the University of Chicago when he finished the atomic bomb project.

    ___ He became a professor at the University of Chicago.

    ___ He finished the atomic bomb project.

[18] **atom:** one of the very small things that everything is made of

[19] **atomic bomb:** a very powerful thing that explodes and causes a lot of damage. Two atomic bombs exploded in Japan in 1945 (in Hiroshima and Nagasaki).

18 | Using Time Clauses Complete these sentences with the phrases from the box or your own ideas. Underline the time clause in each sentence. Then share your answers with a partner. `14.6 B–C`

MY DAILY ROUTINES

1. I usually _____*drink coffee*_____ when I get up in the morning.

2. Before I go to bed, I always _____.

3. When I get home from school, I usually _____.

4. I usually _____ after I eat dinner.

5. When I'm sick, I usually _____.

6. I usually _____ when I have a day off.

YESTERDAY AND TODAY

7. When I woke up this morning, I _____*took a shower*_____.

8. I _____ before I came to school today.

9. Yesterday I _____ after I ate lunch.

10. I _____ when I went to bed last night.

11. When I got to school today, I _____.

12. Before I left the house today, I _____.

call my parents
take a shower
eat something
exercise
go online
do my homework
watch TV
see my friends
stay in bed
drink a lot of tea
go to the park
drink coffee
text a friend
take a nap
come to class
fall asleep

Write about It Write two present and two past sentences about your partner. Use time clauses.

Tom brushes his teeth before he goes to bed.

19 | Using Punctuation in Time Clauses Underline each time clause in the article below. Add a comma (,) where necessary. `14.6 C`

Negative Feelings

We all have negative feelings sometimes. Maybe you feel anxious[20] <u>before you meet new people</u>. Maybe you feel depressed[21] after you have a bad day. Or maybe you get angry at the customers at work. Here are some ways to deal with common negative emotions[22].

- When you start to feel anxious find a quiet place to sit. Close your eyes and take some deep breaths.
- When someone makes you angry count to 25 before you talk to them.
- After you get home from a hard day at work go outside. Get some exercise or work in the garden.
- Make a list of good things in your life. When you are feeling bad look at the list again.

When you have negative feelings you may not sleep well. Try these tips:

- Before you go to bed listen to calm music or take a warm shower.
- Don't get in bed before you are tired.
- Turn off your computer, phone, and TV 30 minutes before you go to bed.

These tips will help you sleep. When you get enough sleep it's easier to fight negative emotions!

[20] **anxious:** worried and afraid
[21] **depressed:** very unhappy

[22] **emotions:** feelings

Write about It Add a time clause to make each sentence true for you. Then rewrite the sentences and change the order of the clauses.

1. I get very anxious _____.   3. I was anxious _____.

2. _____, I feel really good.   4. _____, I was very angry.

I get very anxious when I fly. → *When I fly, I get very anxious.*

20 | Error Correction Find and correct the errors. (Some sentences may not have any errors.)

1. He got a promotion[23] because ^he^ worked very hard.

2. I took a shower after I went to bed.

3. He graduated from high school. Before he went to college.

4. After got the good news, she was very happy.

5. Before I made soup, we ate it in the kitchen.

6. I wanted to study English, but this semester I'm taking an English class.

7. I visited my family before I go on vacation.

8. Anton is worried about his grade because the test was very difficult.

9. They went out to dinner. After they went to the movie.

10. I saved money so I wanted to buy a car.

11. When he told us the good news. We were very excited for him.

12. After I take an exercise class, I felt a lot better.

14.7 Future Time Clauses

We can use connecting words like *when*, *before*, and *after* in **time clauses about the future**. Notice the different verb forms in each clause.

We use a **future verb form** (*will* or *be going to*) in the **main clause**.	We use a **simple present verb form** in the **time clause**. (Notice: The verb has a future meaning.)

	main clause	time clause
1	Bob **will make** dinner	when he **gets** home.
2	I **am going to talk** to the teacher	before I **register** for the class.
3	The manager **will lock** the doors	after the last customer **leaves**.

A

The time clause can also come before the main clause:

	time clause	main clause
4	When I **get** home tonight,	I'm **going to call** my brother.
5	After Mark **fixes** the car,	he'll **try to sell** it.
6	Before we **buy** a car,	I'm **going to do** a lot of research.

simple present form	**future form**

Remember: When the time clause is before the main clause, we use a comma (,) after the time clause.

WARNING! Use a simple present verb form in the time clause. DON'T use a future verb form.

✓ I'll call you when I **get** home.   ✗ I'll call you when I **will get** home.

GO ONLINE

[23] **promotion:** a more important job

21 | Noticing Future Time Clauses Complete these conversations with the verbs you hear. Underline the time clauses. Then read the conversations with a partner. `14.7 A`

MAKING PLANS

1. A: Are you going to make dessert?

   B: No, I _____'ll do_____ that <u>after we</u>
   <u>_____eat_____ dinner.</u>

2. A: When should we buy the flowers?

   B: I _____ them right before

   we _____.

3. A: When do you want to open your presents?

   B: I _____ that when my parents

   _____ home.

4. A: These chairs _____

   wet when it _____.

   B: They're plastic. They'll be fine.

5. A: I _____ you before the movie

   _____.

   B: Thanks.

6. A: Is he coming with us?

   B: No. He _____ after he

   _____ Anna home.

7. A: Do you have any free time this weekend?

   B: I'm not sure. I _____ you after

   I _____ to my boss.

8. A: When you _____ us,

   we _____ camping.

   B: Sounds fun!

9. A: She's not _____ happy

   when she _____ about our plan.

   B: I know.

10. A: What's Miguel going to do?

    B: I don't know. But he _____ to us

    before he _____ a decision.

11. A: I _____ some cash when I

    _____ to the store.

    B: Good idea.

12. A: I _____ you the directions before

    I _____ the office.

    B: OK.

Think about It In the sentences above, label the future verb forms *F* and the simple present verb forms *SP*. Are the present verb forms in the time clause or the main clause?

   F   SP
No, I'll do that after we eat dinner.

Think about It Which sentence has the time clause before the main clause?

22 | Using Future Time Clauses Circle the correct verb form in each sentence. Then practice the conversations with a partner. `14.7 A`

OFFICE CONVERSATIONS

1. A: Did Tina start the new project?

   B: Not yet. She (starts / ('ll start)) that one when she finishes this one.

2. A: We (begin / 'll begin) the meeting after the manager gets here.

   B: When is she coming?

3. A: I (call / 'll call) the customer when I get to the office tomorrow.

   B: OK.

4. A: When the IT person gets back from lunch, I (send / 'll send)

   him up to help you.

   B: Thanks.

5. A: I'll call you back after I (review / 'll review) your problem.

   B: Thanks.

6. A: Do I need to sign this?

   B: Not yet. We'll print a new copy before we (ask / 'll ask) you to sign it.

7. A: So what's next?

   B: We'll test the product before we (show / 'll show) it to customers.

8. A: Is he going to hire someone?

   B: Yes, but he (writes / 'll write) a new job description before he (interviews / 'll interview) anyone.

9. A: I need a new computer.

   B: Don't worry. When the new computers (arrive / 'll arrive), we (set / 'll set) them up right away.

10. A: When the manager (sees / will see) this, she (is / 's going to be) angry.

    B: I know.

11. A: After he (checks / will check) the meeting notes, I (make / 'll make) a copy for everyone.

    B: Thanks.

Write about It Complete these sentences with your own ideas. Add a comma (,) where necessary.

1. I'll call you before _____.

2. I'll go shopping after _____.

3. When I get home tomorrow _____.

4. Before I come to the next class _____.

23 | Understanding Past, Present, and Future Time Clauses Listen to each conversation. Then complete each sentence with information about the conversation. (See Chart 14.6 for help with past and present time clauses.) **14.7 A**

1. The woman _____*wants*_____ to have children after she _____*gets*_____ married.

2. The man _____ a nap after he _____ home yesterday.

3. The man _____ after Sandra _____ back.

4. The woman _____ to the gym in the morning before she _____ to school.

5. The man _____ to Mexico after he _____ from high school.

6. Martha _____ always happy when her children _____.

7. The man _____ lunch before he _____ to class.

8. The woman _____ her car before she _____ this job.

9. All students _____ the English test before they _____ for classes.

10. Terry _____ after she _____ off work.

11. The woman _____ her mom every night before she _____ to bed.

12. Ken _____ right after she _____.

Write about It Complete these statements with a main clause that is true for you. Share your sentences with a partner.

1. When I finish this English class, _____.

2. _____ when I have time.

3. Before I started at this school, _____.

14.8 Using Sentence Patterns in Writing

A

Good writers use a variety of sentence patterns. This makes writing more interesting.

Alicia Delgado is a nurse at Longwood Hospital in California. **She grew up in Oregon, and she graduated from Portland State University in 2007.** After she graduated, she moved to Chicago and worked in a medical office. She stayed there for a year and a half. Then she went to nursing school. **Alicia moved west in 2012 because she wanted to attend the University of Southern California.** Now she is studying and working part-time. She wants to become a nurse educator.

| Simple sentence (one clause) |
| Sentence with two clauses connected by *and, but* or *so* (two main clauses) |
| Sentence with main clause + time clause or reason clause (two clauses) |

24 | Noticing Sentence Patterns Read the student's paragraph. Label each sentence. Use a label (*A*, *B*, or *C*) from the box. `14.8 A`

| A Simple sentence (one clause) | B Sentence with two clauses connected by *and, but,* or *so* | C Sentence with main clause + reason or time clause |

An Important Person from My Childhood

(1) __A__ My grandmother (Nana) was an important person in my life. (2) ____ She lived with us when I was a child. (3) ____ My parents both worked, so Nana took care of my sister and me. (4) ____ She was very kind to us, but she was also very strict[24]. (5) ____ She wanted us to do well in school because she never had that opportunity[25]. (6) ____ We did our homework every day when we got home.

(7) ____ Nana always looked at each page carefully. (8) ____ The homework had to be complete, and it had to be neat! (9) ____ After we finished our work, Nana always made delicious food.

(10) ____ Nana got sick when I was 11 years old. (11) ____ She couldn't cook for us anymore, but she was always kind and loving. (12) ____ I will always be grateful to her.

25 | Using Sentence Patterns in Writing Rewrite this paragraph. Use *when, because, but, after, and, before,* or *so* to connect some of the sentences. More than one answer may be possible. `14.8 A`

I was 5 years old. We moved to the city. My father wanted to move. There were more opportunities in the city. Life in the city wasn't easy for us. My mother found a job. My parents were able to save some money. They saved money for a few years. They opened a bakery. I helped them in the bakery. I didn't enjoy working there. I worked at the bakery through high school. Then I went to college. I'm living far away now. I can't visit very often. I call every weekend. My parents will retire someday. They will move near me. We'll all be together again.

When I was 5 years old, we moved to the city....

Write about It Write a short paragraph about your past. Use a variety of sentence patterns.

[24] **strict:** not permitting people to break rules   [25] **opportunity:** a chance to do something

WRAP-UP

A | GRAMMAR IN READING Read the student essay. Underline the complete verb in each clause.

Assignment: Describe one of your heroes[26] and explain how the person influenced you.

Some of my heroes <u>are</u> famous people. They <u>are</u> world leaders or great artists or scientists. <u>I'm going to tell</u> you about another kind of hero. My dance teacher, Joy Galen, is not rich or famous, but she is a hero to me.

I started taking dance classes when I was very young. I was shy[27], and I always stood in the back of the class. After I studied dance for several years, I started Joy's class. Joy was not an easy teacher. I had to repeat the same moves again and again. Some steps[28] were easy for other students, but they were difficult for me. I often wanted to quit, but Joy never let me give up[29].

Joy saw the best qualities in every student. When one girl danced in front of the class, the others had to give feedback[30]. Joy was always honest, but she was also kind. We followed her example, and the girls in the class became close friends.

Because we were teenagers, we often had personal problems. Joy always listened to us. After the other teachers went home, Joy usually stayed at the studio with us. We told her all of our problems and she listened patiently.

My experience in Joy's class changed my life. When I started the class, I was very shy. Now I'm not nervous around new people. I feel confident, and I'm also a pretty good dancer!

Joy was a wonderful teacher, but she is also my hero for another reason. She had a full-time job in an office, and she didn't make much money as a dance teacher, but she danced because she loved it. People often say, "Follow your heart," and Joy really did that. I learned that lesson from her.

Think about It Answer these questions.

1. What connecting words does the writer use? _____

2. How many time clauses does the writer use? _____

3. How many simple sentences does the writer use? _____

4. How many reason clauses does the writer use? _____

5. There is one sentence with four clauses. What words connect the clauses? _____

B | GRAMMAR IN WRITING Write a paragraph about someone you admire[31]. Write 7 or 8 sentences. Answer some of these questions in your paragraph.

- When did you first meet/learn about the person?
- Why do you admire him or her?
- How did the person influence you?

I admire my friend Martin very much. I met him in high school. He was three years older than me, but he was always very kind to me. He was also an excellent student. After he graduated from high school, Martin went to a university in the United States. He wants to be a doctor. . . .

[26] **hero:** a person who did something brave or good
[27] **shy:** nervous with other people
[28] **steps:** the ways a dancer moves his/her feet

[29] **give up:** to stop trying to do something
[30] **feedback:** information about something you did (if it was good or bad)
[31] **admire:** to think that someone is very good

SENTENCES WITH ONE CLAUSE

Every clause must have a **subject** and a **complete verb**. A complete verb includes a **main verb**. (It may also include one or more helping verbs.)

SUBJECT + VERB (+ PREPOSITIONAL PHRASE / TIME EXPRESSION)

STATEMENT	-	-	Anthony	**works** doesn't **work**	at this restaurant.
YES/NO QUESTION	-	Is	the baby	**sleeping?**	-
	-	Did	JoAnn	**help**	with the housework?
WH- QUESTION	Where	are	the children	going to **go**	tomorrow?
	-	-	What	**happened?**	-

SUBJECT + VERB + OBJECT (+ PREPOSITIONAL PHRASE / TIME EXPRESSION)

STATEMENT	-	-	The students	will **buy** won't **buy**	their books	at Morey's Bookstore.
YES/NO QUESTION	-	Are	the students	going to **take**	the test	tomorrow?
WH- QUESTION	Where	did	Kim	**get**	that computer?	-
	-	-	Who	is **taking**	the exam	today?

SUBJECT + LINKING VERB + ADJECTIVE PHRASE

STATEMENT	-	-	Marcos	**is** isn't	Mexican.
YES/NO QUESTION	-	**Is**	the manager	-	really angry?
	-	Doesn't	the soup	**smell**	delicious?
WH- QUESTION	Why	does	Kathy	**look**	tired?
	-	-	Who	**was**	angry?

SUBJECT + BE + PREPOSITIONAL PHRASE / NOUN PHRASE

STATEMENT	-	-	The books	**are** aren't	in the living room.
	-	-	Sanam	**is** isn't	a student.
YES/NO QUESTION	-	**Is**	your brother	-	a doctor?
WH- QUESTION	When	**was**	the teacher	-	in her office?
	-	-	Who	will **be**	in class tomorrow?

SENTENCES WITH TWO CLAUSES

main clause	connecting word	main clause
He called last night,	**but**	we weren't home.

main clause	reason clause / time clause
I paid for dinner	**because** he didn't bring any money.
The meeting always starts	**before** you get here.

↑ connecting word

time clause / reason clause	main clause
After he finishes the report,	he will share it with everyone.
Because tomorrow is a holiday,	the school will be closed.

↑ connecting word

Resources

I Spelling Rules: Possessive Nouns R-2
II Common Noncount Nouns R-2
III What Is a Noun Phrase? R-2
IV Common Adjectives R-3
V Spelling Rules: Doubling the Final Consonant to Form -*ing* Verbs R-3
VI Spelling Rules: Doubling the Final Consonant to Form -*ed* Verbs R-4

VII Simple Past Form of Irregular Verbs R-4
VIII Non-Action Verbs R-5
IX Linking Verbs R-5
X Common Adverbs of Degree R-5
XI Common Adjectives + Prepositions R-5
XII Common Multi-Word Verbs R-6
XIII Common Verbs + Object or No Object R-6

I. Spelling Rules: Possessive Nouns

We sometimes add -**'s** or -**'** after a noun or name to show possession.

Rules	Examples	
We add -**'s** after a singular noun and most names.	one student's book	John's book
We add -**'** after a name that ends in -**s**.	Bess' family	Chris' book
We add -**'s** after an irregular plural noun.	the children's room	the men's group
We add -**'** after a plural noun that ends in -**s**.	all of the students' exams	my parents' house

II. Common Noncount Nouns

advice	coffee*	gasoline (gas)	information	money	rain	traffic
air	confidence	glass*	jewelry	music	rice	truth*
baggage	electricity	grammar	knowledge	news	safety	water
beauty	entertainment	hair*	literature	noise*	salt	weather
behavior*	experience*	happiness	luck	organization*	sand	work*
blood	flour	health	luggage	oxygen	smoke	
bread	fruit*	heat	mathematics	paint*	snow	
cash	fun	help	medicine*	pasta	soap	
clothing	furniture	homework	milk	peace	sugar	

*often has a count meaning or a noncount meaning

III. What Is a Noun Phrase?

A noun phrase can be (1) a single noun,
(2) a noun + any descriptive words (article, adjective, quantifier, etc.), or
(3) a pronoun.

(1) NOUN	(2) ARTICLE + NOUN	(2) ARTICLE + ADJECTIVE + NOUN	(2) QUANTIFIER + NOUN	(3) PRONOUN	
Canada	a friend	a big city	many friends	I / me	it
Thomas	a school	a nice place	much work	you	we / us
music	an animal	an unusual person	some news	she / her	they / them
money	the people	the best food	no books	he / him	

IV. Common Adjectives

These are the 100 most common adjectives in English in order of frequency.

other	little	human	full	current	serious	religious
new*	important	local	special	wrong*	ready	cold
good*	political	late	easy	private	simple	final
high	bad	hard*	clear	past	left	main
old*	white*	major	recent	foreign	physical	green
great	real	better	certain	fine	general	nice*
big*	best	economic	personal	common	environmental	huge
American	right*	strong	open	poor	financial	popular
small	social	possible	red	natural	blue	traditional
large	only	whole*	difficult*	significant	democratic	cultural
national	public	free	available	similar	dark	
young	sure*	military	likely	hot	various	
different*	low	true*	short	dead*	entire	
black*	early	federal	single	central	close	
long*	able*	international	medical	happy*	legal	

*common in conversation

V. Spelling Rules: Doubling the Final Consonant to Form -ing Verbs

The base form of some verbs ends in a **consonant** + **vowel** + **consonant**. For example:

win   for**get**   pre**fer**   vi**sit**

With some (but not all) of these verbs, we double the final consonant and add -ing. For example:

win → wi**nning**   forget → forge**tting**   prefer → prefe**rring**

Follow these rules to decide when to double the final consonant before you add -ing.

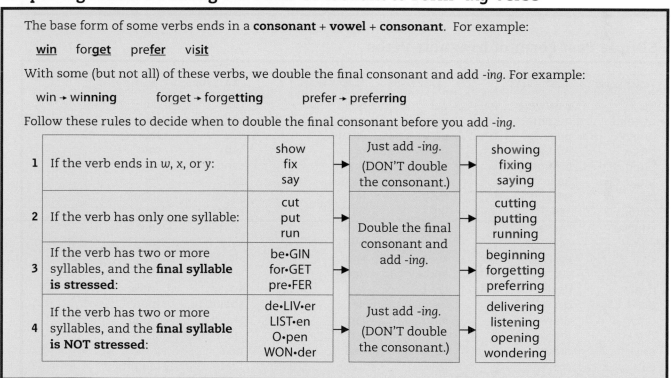

1	If the verb ends in *w*, *x*, or *y*:	show fix say	Just add -ing. (DON'T double the consonant.)	showing fixing saying
2	If the verb has only one syllable:	cut put run	Double the final consonant and add -ing.	cutting putting running
3	If the verb has two or more syllables, and the **final syllable is stressed**:	be·GIN for·GET pre·FER		beginning forgetting preferring
4	If the verb has two or more syllables, and the **final syllable is NOT stressed**:	de·LIV·er LIST·en O·pen WON·der	Just add -ing. (DON'T double the consonant.)	delivering listening opening wondering

VI. Spelling Rules: Doubling the Final Consonant to Form -*ed* Verbs

The base form of some regular verbs ends in a **consonant** + **vowel** + **consonant**. For example:

p<u>lan</u>   d<u>rop</u>   pre<u>fer</u>   deve<u>lop</u>

With some (but not all) of these regular verbs, we double the final consonant and add -*ed*. For example:

plan → pla**nn**ed   drop → dro**pp**ed   prefer → prefe**rr**ed

Follow these rules to decide when to double the final consonant before you add -*ed*.

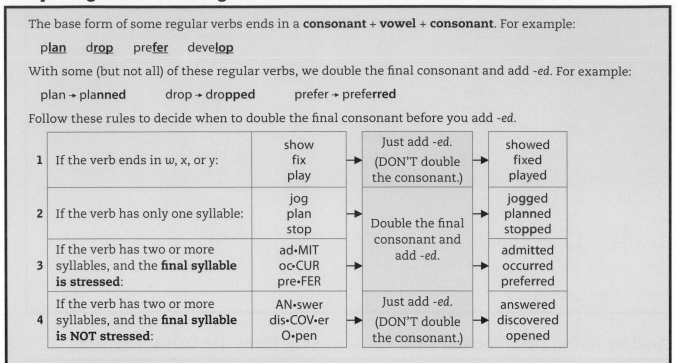

1	If the verb ends in *w*, *x*, or *y*:	show fix play	→	Just add -*ed*. (DON'T double the consonant.)	→	showed fixed played
2	If the verb has only one syllable:	jog plan stop	→	Double the final consonant and add -*ed*.	→	jogged planned stopped
3	If the verb has two or more syllables, and the **final syllable is stressed**:	ad·MIT oc·CUR pre·FER	→		admitted occurred preferred
4	If the verb has two or more syllables, and the **final syllable is NOT stressed**:	AN·swer dis·COV·er O·pen	→	Just add -*ed*. (DON'T double the consonant.)	→	answered discovered opened

VII. Simple Past Form of Irregular Verbs

BASE FORM	SIMPLE PAST
be	was/were
become	became
begin	began
break	broke
bring	brought
build	built
buy	bought
catch	caught
choose	chose
come	came
cost	cost
cut	cut
deal	dealt
do	did
draw	drew
drink	drank
drive	drove
eat	ate
fall	fell
feed	fed
feel	felt
fight	fought
find	found
fit	fit
fly	flew
forget	forgot
forgive	forgave

BASE FORM	SIMPLE PAST
get	got
give	gave
go	went
grow	grew
have	had
hear	heard
hide	hid
hit	hit
hold	held
hurt	hurt
keep	kept
know	knew
lay	laid
leave	left
lend	lent
let	let
lie	lied
lose	lost
make	made
mean	meant
meet	met
pay	paid
put	put
quit	quit
read	read*
ring	rang
rise	rose

BASE FORM	SIMPLE PAST
run	ran
say	said
see	saw
sell	sold
send	sent
set	set
shake	shook
shoot	shot
shut	shut
sing	sang
sit	sat
sleep	slept
speak	spoke
spend	spent
stand	stood
steal	stole
take	took
teach	taught
tear	tore
tell	told
think	thought
throw	threw
understand	understood
wear	wore
win	won
write	wrote

*The past form *read* is pronounced "red."

VIII. Non-Action Verbs

agree	contain	feel	involve	need	remember	understand
appear	cost	fit	know	owe	see	want
appreciate	dislike	hate	like	own	seem	weigh
be	doubt	have	look	possess	smell	wish
believe	envy	hear	love	prefer	suppose	
belong	equal	imagine	mean	realize	taste	
consist of	fear	include	mind	recognize	think	

Remember:

- A non-action verb describes a state (an unchanging condition).
- Non-action verbs are also called **stative verbs**.
- Some verbs have more than one meaning. They can be a non-action verb in one context and an action verb in another.

IX. Linking Verbs

Examples: *She looks tired. That seems interesting.*

appear	become	get*	look	seem	sound	turn*
be	feel	grow*	remain	smell	taste	

*with a meaning of *become*

Remember: A linking verb can be followed by an adjective.

X. Common Adverbs of Degree

Examples: *really big; pretty scary*

almost	exactly*	highly	perfectly	real*	so	too*
awfully	extremely	kind of*	pretty*	really*	somewhat	totally
completely	fairly	more	quite	slightly	terribly	very*
definitely	fully	nearly	rather			

*common in conversation

XI. Common Adjectives + Prepositions

Examples: *really afraid of snakes; different from her; good for you*

ADJECTIVE + *OF*	ADJECTIVE + *FROM*	ADJECTIVE + *ABOUT*	ADJECTIVE + *IN*	ADJECTIVE + *FOR*
afraid of	different from	curious about	common in	good for
full of	free from	excited about	important in	hard for
proud of	safe from	happy about	interested in	important for
tired of	tired from	nervous about	involved in	necessary for
		serious about	useful in	ready for
		sorry about		responsible for
		worried about		sorry for
				useful for

XII. Common Multi-Word Verbs

believe in	do without	get over	leave out	put away	throw out
bring up	dream of	get up	listen to	put on	try on
call off	eat out	give away	look after	shut down	turn down
call on	feel like	give up	look at	shut off	turn off
care about	figure out	grow up	look for	sit down	wait for
care for	fill out	hand in	look forward to	slow down	wake up
check out	fill up	hand out	look like	take out	worry about
check over	find out	help out	look up	talk about	write down
come back	finish up	hold off	make up	talk to	write to
come over	forget about	keep on	pay for	think about	work out
complain about	get along (with)	keep out	pick out	think of	
depend on	get off	know about	pick up	think over	
do over	get on	lay down	plan on	throw away	

Remember: Multi-word verbs include *phrasal verbs* and *prepositional verbs*.

XIII. Common Verbs + Object or No Object

VERB + OBJECT

Some verbs need an object to complete their meaning. Verbs that have an object are called *transitive verbs*.

Examples:

	verb	object
Please	bring	your computer.

	verb	object
I	love	coffee.

bring	describe	forgive	love	produce	receive	use
buy	discuss	keep	make	provide	send	want
carry	enjoy	lend	mean	put	take	wear
create	find	like	need	raise	throw	

VERB WITH NO OBJECT

Some verbs are complete without an object. Verbs that do not have an object are called *intransitive verbs*.

Examples:

	verb
My finger	is bleeding.

	verb	adverb
They	arrived	early.

agree	belong	cough	fall	laugh	look	sleep	swim
appear	bleed	die	go	lie	rain	snow	wait
arrive	come	disappear	happen	live	sit	stay	work

VERB + OBJECT OR NO OBJECT

Many verbs have more than one meaning. With one meaning the verb needs an object. With another meaning the same verb is complete without an object.

Examples:

	verb	object
We	rang	the bell.

	verb
Your phone	is ringing.

answer	call	finish	hurt	pass	start	watch
ask	close	follow	know	read	stop	win
begin	cut	forget	leave	remember	study	
believe	decide	hear	lose	ring	visit	
break	eat	help	meet	run	walk	
burn	end	hold	move	see	wash	

Index

A

Ability
  be able to for (past, present, and future), 290, 305
  can and *cannot/can't* for (present and future), 280, 305, 326
    with *very well*, *pretty well*, and *not at all*, 281
  could for (past)
    in negative statements, 286, 305
    in positive statements, 286, 305
Action verbs
  vs. non-action verbs, 336
  present progressive with, 336
  simple present with, 336
Adjective phrases
  be +, 345, 346, 357
  linking verbs with, 345, 346, 357, 365, 383
Adjectives, 220–249
  adverbs of degree with (e.g., *very*, *really*), 226
  after *be*, 222, 249
  common, R-3
    + prepositions, R-5
  ending in *-ing*, 225
  + *enough*, 226
  -er/more/less forms of (e.g., *larger*, *more important*), 233–236, 239, 249
    irregular (*better, worse, farther*), 233
    less, 239
    spelling *-er* forms, 234
    with *than*, 236, 237
  -est/most forms of (e.g., *the largest*, *the most important*), 242–246, 249
    irregular (*the best, the worst, the farthest*), 242
    prepositional phrases after, 246
    spelling *-est* forms, 244
  how +, 231
  less +, 239, 240
  after linking verbs, 222, 249, 345, 346, 357
  in sentence patterns, 365, 383
  placement of, 222
    after *be*, 222
    after linking verbs, 222
    before nouns, 222
  + preposition, 348, R-5
  pretty as, 227
  summary of, 249
  too +, 226
  uses of, 220–221

Adverbs
  of degree (e.g., *very*, *really*), 226, 227, R-5
  of frequency (e.g., *sometimes*, *never*, *always*)
    placement of, 368
Advice, with *should* and *shouldn't*, 308–311, 326, 331. See also *Should* and *shouldn't*

After
  in future time clauses, 378
  in past time clauses, 375
  in present time clauses, 375
A little + *-er/more* adjectives, 235
A lot + *-er/more* adjectives, 235
Am. See *Be*
And, connecting clauses with, 370
Are. See *Be*
At
  in time expressions (e.g., *at 5:00*), 196, 256
Auxiliary verbs. *See* Helping verbs

B

Be
  + adjective, 222, 249
    vs. other linking verbs, 222, 345, 346, 357
    + preposition, 348, R-5
    in sentence patterns, 365, 383
  as helping verb
    in *be going to*, 252, 259, 261, 334
    in present progressive, 334
  as main verb with *be going to*, 252
  + noun phrase, 345, 346, 357
    in sentence patterns, 365, 383
  vs. other verbs, 213, 346, 357
  + prepositional phrase (place), 345, 346, 357
    in sentence patterns, 365, 383
  simple past (*was/were*), 209–216, 219
    vs. other verbs, 213
  there + be
    there is/there are going to be, 255
    there was/there were, 216, 219
  wh- questions with, 365, 383
  yes/no questions with, 365, 383
Be able to, 290, 305
Because, 373
Before
  in future time clauses, 378
  in past time clauses, 375
  in present time clauses, 375

Be going to, 252–261, 277. *See also under* Future forms
Borrow vs. lend, 298
But, connecting clauses with, 370

C

Can
  for ability and possibility, 280–283
  negative statements with, 280
  for permission (with *I/we*), 293, 298, 305
  positive statements with, 280
  pronunciation of, 282, 284
  for requests (with *you*), 295, 298, 305
  short answers with, 283, 284
  vs. *should* and *have to*, 326
  uses of, 305
  wh- questions with, 283
  yes/no questions with, 283
Clauses
  defined, 370
  commas and, 370, 373, 375, 378
  connecting with *and*, *but*, and *so*, 359, 370
  main clause, defined, 373 (*See also* Main clause)
  reason clauses (*because*), 373
  time clauses (*before, after, when*), 375, 378, 383 (*See also* Time clauses)
Comma, 370, 373, 375, 378
Comparative form of adjectives, 233. *See also* *-er/more/less* adjectives
Comparisons with adjectives, 223–249. *See also* *-er/more/less* adjectives; *-est/most* adjectives
Complete verb, 360, 362
Connecting words (*and, but, so*), 359, 370, 383
Contractions
  with *not*
    be + not
      isn't/aren't as helping verb (e.g., *he isn't waiting*), 259
      wasn't/weren't, 209
    can't, 280
    couldn't, 286
    didn't, 204, 206
    don't/doesn't, 318
    shouldn't, 308
    won't, 269
  with *will* and pronouns (*'ll*), 269
  with *would* and pronouns (*'d*), 299

Could
negative statements with, 286
for past ability, 286
for permission (with *I/we*), 293
positive statements with, 286
for requests (with *you*), 295, 298
Count nouns
there was/there were with, 216

D

Degree, adverbs of (e.g., *very, really*),
226, R-5
with *well*, 281
Desires, *would like* for, 299
Did. See *Do*
Do
did as helping verb
in short answers to *yes/no*
questions, 206, 334
in simple past questions, 206, 334
vs. *was/were*, 213
didn't as helping verb
in negative statements, 204, 334
in short answers to *yes/no*
questions, 206, 334
do/does as helping verb
in questions
with *have to*, 321
pronunciation of *do you want to*
(*d'you wanna*), 302
simple present, 334
in short answers to *yes/no*
questions, 334
don't/doesn't as helping verb
in negative statements
with *have to*, 318
simple present, 334
in short answers to *yes/no*
questions, 334
as helping verb and main verb, 207

E

-ed form of verbs, 196, 197, 199, R-4.
See also Simple past
Enough
with adjectives, 226
with nouns, 255
-er/more/less adjectives, 233, 234,
235, 236, 249
irregular (e.g., *better*), 233
spelling *-er* adjectives, 234
with *than*, 236
-est/most adjectives, 242, 244, 246, 249
irregular (e.g., *best*), 242
prepositional phrases after, 246
spelling *-est* adjectives, 244
Exclamation mark, use of, 360

F

Future forms, 250–277, 334
be going to, 252–261, 334, 357
with *I think* and *probably*, 258
negative statements with,
252, 277, 334
vs. other verb forms, 334, 357
positive statements with,
252, 277, 334
vs. present progressive, 266
pronunciation of (*gonna*), 253
there is/there are going to be, 255
in time clauses, 378
wh- questions, 261, 277, 334
yes/no questions and short
answers, 259, 277, 344
may and *might*, 266
vs. present and past verb forms,
334, 357
present progressive, 263
for future plans, 263
for personal plans, 265
summary of, 277
time expressions with, 256, 334, 335
uses of, 250, 251
will, 269–274, 334, 357
contractions with (*'ll, won't*), 269
negative statements with,
269, 277, 334
vs. other verb forms, 334, 357
positive statements with,
269, 277, 334
questions with, 274
in time clauses, 378
wh- questions with, 274, 277, 334
yes/no questions and short
answers with, 274, 277, 334
Future time clauses, 378

G

Give vs. **have** (e.g., *could you
give me . . .*), 298
Going to, pronunciation of (*gonna*),
253. See also *Be going to*

H

Have/has in requests (e.g., *could I have
a glass of water?*), 298
Have to/not have to, 318–321,
324, 326
vs. *can* and *should*, 326
negative statements (*not have to*)
with, 318, 324, 326
vs. *must not*, 324
positive statements with, 318, 326
pronunciation of, 319
questions with, 321

Helping verbs, 360, 365, 383
defined, 334
be, 252 (See also under *Be*,
as helping verb)
vs. *do*, 213
can, 280
could, 286
do, 207, 334
vs. *be*, 213
did, 206, 207
didn't, 204, 206, 207
may, 266
might, 266
must, 323
overview of, 334
in sentence patterns, 360, 362, 365,
368, 383
should, 311
will, 269
would, 299
How, 231
+ adjective (e.g., *how hot is it?*), 231

I

Imperative sentences, 334, 357
subject in, 361
In
adjective + (e.g., *interested in*),
348, R-5
in time expressions (e.g., *in July*),
196, 256
-ing form of verbs
as adjectives, 225
spelling rules for, R-3
Intonation
in statements as questions, 364
in *yes/no* questions, 364
Intransitive verbs, 343, R-6. *See also
under* Verbs, with no object
Invitations (*would like* for), 299
saying yes or no to, 301
Irregular verbs, simple past forms of,
202, R-4
Is. See *Be*
I think/I don't think
in statements with *be going to*, 258
in statements with *should*, 310

L

Lend vs. **borrow**, 298
Less + adjective, 239, 240
Linking verbs, 222, 249, 345, 346,
357, R-5
defined, 222
be vs. other, 222, 345, 346, 357
vs. other types of verbs, 346, 357
in sentence patterns, 365, 383

M

Main clause
  defined, 373
  with reason clause, 373, 383
  with time clause, 375, 383
Main verbs, 334
  in sentence patterns, 360, 362, 365, 368, 383
Make, common phrases with, 341
May
  for future possibility, 266, 277
  for permission, 293, 305
Maybe + should (e.g., *maybe you should . . .*), 310
Might for future possibility, 266, 277
Modals, 266, 279–305, 306–331
  for ability
    be able to, 290, 305
    can, 280–283, 305, 326
    could, 286, 305
  for advice (*should*), 308–311, 331
  for desires (*would like*), 299, 305
  for necessity/no necessity
    have to and *need to*, 318–321, 326, 331
    must, 323, 331
    not have to and *not need to*, 318–321, 324, 326, 331
  for offers and invitations (*would you like*), 299, 302, 305
  for permission (*can, could, may*), 293, 305
  for possibility, 280–283, 305
    can, 280–283, 305
    may and *might*, 266
  for prohibition (*must not*), 323, 324, 331
  for requests (*can, could, would*), 295, 298, 305
  for suggestions
    should, 308–311, 326, 331
    why don't you/we, 314, 331
More + adjective, 233, 235, 236
Most + adjective, 242, 246
Much + *-er/more* adjectives (e.g., *much faster*), 235
Multi-word verbs (e.g., *look for, come back*), 351, 353, 354, R-8
  object pronoun with, 354
Must and *must not*, 323, 331
  must not vs. *not have to*, 324

N

Necessity/no necessity
  with *have to* and *need to*, 318–321, 324, 326
  with *must*, 323

Need to/not need to, 318–321, 324, 326
Negative statements
  with *be*, 334
  with *be able to*, 290, 305
  with *be going to*, 252, 277, 334
  with *can*, 280, 305, 326
  with *could*, 286, 305
  to deny things, 204
  with *have to* and *need to*, 318, 326, 331
  with *may*, 277
  with *must*, 323, 331
  with present progressive, 263, 334
  with *should*, 308, 326, 331
  with simple past, 204, 219, 334
    be (*wasn't/weren't*), 209, 211, 219
  with simple present, 334
  with *there + be*, 216, 219
  with *will*, 269, 277, 334
Non-action verbs
  vs. action verbs, 336
  list of, R-5
  simple present with, 336
Noncount nouns
  common, R-2
  there was with, 216
Not have to vs. *must not*, 324
Noun phrases
  defined, R-2
  after *be*, 345, 346, 357
    in sentence patterns, 365, 383
  I + would like + (e.g., *I'd like some tea*), 299, 302
  as objects of verbs (e.g., *take a class*), 340, 357, 365, 383
  want + (e.g., *do you want some tea?*), 302
  would you like +, 299, 302
Nouns
  adjectives in describing, 220
  after *be*, 345, 346, 357
    in sentence patterns, 365, 383
  count (*See* Count nouns)
  noncount (*See* Noncount nouns)
  possessive (e.g., *Jim's book*), R-2
  there with, 216

O

Object pronouns (e.g., *me, them*), 298
  in comparisons (e.g., *stronger than him*), 236
  placement in multi-word verbs (e.g., *I'll pick you up*), 354
Objects in sentences. *See also* Object pronouns
  in sentence patterns, 365, 383

verbs + object, 340, 344, 346, 357, R-6
verbs with no object, 343, 344, 346, 357, R-6
Offers (*would like* for), 299
  saying yes or no to, 301
On in time expressions (e.g., *on Monday*), 196, 256
One as pronoun
  in comparisons (e.g., *it's better than the other one*), 236
Opinions, with *should* and *shouldn't*, 308–311

P

Past time, 194–219, 375. *See also* Simple past
Past time clauses, 375, 376
Past verb forms. *See* Simple past
Period, use of, 360
Permission with *can, could,* and *may*, 293, 305
Phrasal modals, 290, 318
Phrasal verbs, 353, R-6.
  See Multi-word verbs
Phrases
  adjective (*See* Adjective phrases)
  common, with *take* and *make*, 341
  noun (*See* Noun phrases)
  prepositional (*See* Prepositional phrases)
Please, 295
Possessive nouns, spelling of, R-2
Prepositional phrases
  after *be* (e.g., *he's at school*), 345, 346, 357
  after *-est/most* adjective forms, 246
  in sentence patterns, 365, 383
Prepositional verbs, 351, R-6. *See also* Multi-word verbs
Prepositions, 347
  be + adjective +, 348, R-5
  in *wh-* questions (e.g., *who did you go with?*), 208
Present continuous. *See* Present progressive
Present progressive, 334, 357
  action verbs in, 336
  vs. *be going to*, 263
  for future plans, 263
  negative statements with, 263, 334
  vs. other verb forms, 334, 357
  positive statements with, 263, 334
  short answers with, 334
  time expressions with, 334
  wh- questions with, 263, 334
    about the subject, 334
  yes/no questions with, 263, 334

Present time. *See* Present progressive; Simple present
Present time clauses, 375
Present verb forms. *See* Present progressive; Simple present
Pretty, as adjective or adverb of degree, 227
Probably, 258
Prohibition, *must* for, 323, 324, 331
Pronouns
  object (e.g., *him, us, them*)
    after *than* in comparisons (e.g., *stronger than him*), 236
  possessive (e.g., *mine, hers, ours*)
    after *than* in comparisons (e.g., *better than mine*), 236
  subject (e.g., *I, he, we*)
    after *than* in comparisons (e.g., *stronger than he is*), 236
Pronunciation
  can vs. *can't*, 282
  contractions, *'ll*, 271
  do you want to (*d'you wanna*), 302
  -ed endings (simple past), 199
  going to (*gonna*), 253
  have to, 319
  intonation
    in statements as questions, 364
  need to, 319
  stress in, 211, 282, 308
  were vs. *weren't*, 211
  would you (*wouldju/wouldja*), 300
Punctuation
  comma, in sentences with two clauses, 360, 373, 375, 378
  exclamation mark, use of, 360
  period, use of, 360
  question mark, use of, 362, 364

Q

Question mark, use of, 362, 364
Questions
  adverbs of frequency in, 368
  with *how* + adjective, 231
  overview of, with verb forms, 334
  with prepositions (e.g., *who did you go with?*), 208
  question mark in ending, 362
  sentence patterns for, 362, 365
  statements as (e.g., *that's your brother?*), 364
  verbs in, 362
  wh- (See also *Wh-* words)
    about the subject (e.g., *what is happening? what happened?*)
    with *be going to*, 261, 334
    with *be* in simple past, 334
    with *be* in simple present, 334

    in present progressive, 334
    in simple past, 206, 213, 219, 334
    in simple present, 334
    with *will*, 274, 277, 334
   with *be*
    in simple past, 213, 219, 334
    in simple present, 334
   with *be going to*, 261, 277, 334
   with *can*, 283, 305
   with *did* (simple past), 206, 207, 219, 334
   with *do/does* (simple present), 334
    with *have to* and *need to*, 321
   with *might*, 277
   overview of, with verb forms, 334
   with prepositions (e.g., *who did you go with?*), 208
   with present progressive, 263, 334
   in sentence patterns, 362, 365, 383
   with *should*, 311
   with *will*, 274, 334
  yes/no
   with *be*
    in simple past, 213, 219, 334
    in simple present, 334
   with *be going to*, 259, 277, 334
   with *can*, 283, 293, 305
   with *could*, 293, 294, 305
   with *did* (simple past), 206, 219, 334
   with *do/does*, 334
    with *have to* and *need to*, 321, 331
   with *may*, 293, 305
   overview of, with verb forms, 334
   with present progressive, 263, 334
   in sentence patterns, 362, 365, 368, 383
   short answer (*See* Short answers to *yes/no* questions)
   with *should*, 311, 331
   with *will*, 274, 277, 334
   with *would*, 299, 305

R

Really, 226, 227
Reason clauses (with *because*), 373, 383
Requests (*can, could, would* + *you*), 295, 298, 305

S

Sentence patterns, 358–383
  adverbs of frequency in, 368
  and, but, and *so* in, 370, 383
  because in, 373, 383
  with one clause, 360–368, 383
  for questions, 362, 365, 368, 383
  time clauses in, 375, 378, 383

  with two clauses, 370, 383
  in writing, 381
Sentences
  defined, 360
  objects in, 340
  subjects and verbs in, 360
Short answers to *yes/no* questions
  with *be*
    as helping verb, 259, 277, 334
    as main verb, 213, 219, 334
  with *can*, 283, 284
  with *did*, 206, 219, 334
  with *do/does*, 334
    with *have to* and *need to*, 321, 331
  overview of, with verb forms, 334
  with *should*, 311
  with *will*, 274, 277, 334
Should and **shouldn't**, 308–314, 326, 331
  vs. *can* and *have to*, 326
  negative statements with, 308
  positive statements with, 308
  pronunciation of, 308
  questions with, 311
  short answers with, 311
  using *maybe* and *I think/I don't think* with, 310
  vs. *why don't you/we*, 314
Simple modals vs. phrasal modals, 290
Simple past, 194–219, 334, 357
  of *be*, 209–213, 219, 334
  irregular verbs (e.g., *ate, went*), 202, R-4
  negative statements with, 204, 209, 219, 334
  vs. other verb forms, 334, 357
  positive statements with, 196, 209, 219, 334
  regular verbs (e.g., *stopped, worked*), 196, 197, 199, R-4
    spelling of *-ed* endings, 197, R-4
  short answers, 206, 213, 219, 334
  summary of, 219
  there was/there were, 216, 219
  time clauses with, 375, 376
  time expressions with, 196, 202, 334
  uses of, 194–195, 203, 204
  wh- questions, 206, 213, 219, 334
    about the subject, 213, 334
    prepositions in (e.g., *who did you go with?*), 208
  yes/no questions, 206, 213, 219, 334
Simple present, 334, 357
  action verbs in, 336
  of *be*, 334
  negative statements with, 334
  vs. other verb forms, 334, 357

positive statements with, 334
short answers with, 334
time clauses with, 375
    about the future, 378
time expressions with, 334
    about the future, 378
wh- questions with, 334
    about the subject, 334
yes/no questions with, 334
Simple statements, 360
Singular and plural nouns
    with *there + be*, 216
So, connecting clauses with, 370
Spelling
    -ed verbs, 197, R-4
    -er adjectives, 234
    -est adjectives, 244
    -ing verbs, R-3
    possessive nouns, R-2
Statements
    defined, 360
    ending with exclamation mark, 360
    ending with period, 360
    placement of adverbs of frequency
        in, 368
    as questions (e.g., *Tim is your
        brother?*), 364
    sentence patterns for
        with one clause, 365, 368, 383
        with two clauses, 370–373
Stative verbs. *See* Non-action verbs
Subject pronouns
    in comparisons (e.g., *stronger than
        he is*), 236
    in subjects, 360
Subjects of sentences
    in imperatives, 361
    nouns in, 360
    in questions, 362, 365, 383
    in statements, 360, 365, 383
    subject pronouns in, 360
    wh- questions about the subject,
        334, 362, 365 (*See also under*
        Questions, *wh-*)
    wh- words as, 362, 365
Suggestions
    should for, 314, 326
    why don't you/we for, 314
Superlative form of adjectives, 242.
        See also *-est/most* adjectives

T
Take, common phrases with, 341
Than, in comparisons, 236
There + be
    there is/there are going to be, 255
    there was/there were, 216, 219

This in time expressions
    (e.g., *this evening*), 256, 257
Time clauses (with *before, after, when*)
    defined, 375
    comma with, 375, 378
    future, 378
    with simple past, 375, 376
    with simple present, 375
        simple present form in future
            time clauses, 378
Time expressions
    with future forms, 256, 257, 334, 335
    overview of, with verb forms, 334
    with present progressive, 334, 335
    in sentence patterns, 365, 383
Tonight, 256, 257
Too
    before adjectives, 226
    at end of sentence, 366
Transitive verbs, 340, R-6. *See also
    under* Verbs, + object

V
Verb forms
    future, 250–277, 334 (*See also*
        Future forms)
        with *be going to*, 252–261, 277,
            334, 357
        with present progressive,
            263, 265, 334
        with *will*, 269–277, 334, 357
    imperative, 334, 357, 361
    modals, 266, 279–305, 306–331
        (*See also* Modals)
    overview of, 334
    present progressive, 334, 357
        (*See also* Present progressive)
    simple past, 194–219, 334, 357
        (*See also* Simple past)
    simple present, 334, 357 (*See also*
        Simple present)
        of *be* (See also *Be*)
        of *have* (See also *Have/has*)
    summary of, 357
Verbs, 332–357. *See also* Verb forms
    action, 336
    be (See also *Be*)
    complete, 360, 362
        defined, 360
    -ed form of, 196, 197, 199, R-4
    have (See also *Have/has*)
    helping, 360, 364
    -ing form of, R-3
        as adjective, 225
    intransitive, 343 (*See also under*
        Verbs, with no object)
    irregular, 202, R-4

linking, 222, 345, R-5 (*See also*
        Linking verbs)
    main, 334 (*See also* Main verbs)
    multi-word, 351, 353, 354, R-8
    non-action, 336, R-5
    with no object, 343, 344, 346,
        357, R-6
    + object, 340, 346, 357, R-6
        vs. no object, 344, R-6
    in sentence patterns, 365, 383
        (*See also* Sentence patterns)
    stative (*See* Non-action verbs)
    transitive, 340 (*See also under*
        Verbs, + object)
    types of, 346, 357
    uses of, 332–333
Very, 226, 227

W
Want
    + noun phrase (e.g., *do you want a
        cup of tea?*), 302
    + *to* + verb (e.g., *do you want to go
        somewhere?*), 302
    vs. *would like*, 302
Was, 209–216, 219. *See also under*
        Simple past
Was born in, 209
Well as adverb, 281
Were, 209, 211, 213, 216, 219, 334
Were vs. **weren't**, pronunciation of,
        211
When in time clauses, 375, 376, 378
Which, 233
Wh- questions. *See under* Questions,
        wh-
Wh- words
    as subjects, 362
    which, 233
Why don't you/we for suggestions,
        314
Will, 269–277, 334, 357. *See also under*
        Future forms
Would for requests, 295, 305
Would like
    for desires (*I'd like*), 299, 305
    vs. *like*, 302
    for offers and invitations (*would you
        like*), 299, 305
    pronunciation of (*wouldju/wouldja*),
        300
Writing, sentence patterns in, 381

Y
Yes/no questions. *See under* Questions,
        yes/no

ELEMENTS *of* SUCCESS
Online Practice

How to Register for Elements of Success Online Practice

Follow these steps to register for *Elements of Success Online Practice*:

1. Go to www.elementsofsuccessonline.com and click **Register**

2. Read and agree to the terms of use. **I Agree.**

3. Enter the Access Code that came with your Student Book. Your code is written on the inside back cover of your book.

    Enter

4. Enter your personal information (first and last name, email address, and password).

5. Click the Elements of Success 1 Student Book.

   > It is very important to select the Elements of Success 1 book. Please click the **RED** Elements of Success 1 cover.

   If you don't know which book to select, **STOP**. Continue when you know the book cover to click.

6. Enter your class ID to join your class, and click NEXT. Your class ID is on the line below, or your teacher will give it to you on a different piece of paper.

   _____ **Next**

   You don't need a class ID code. If you do not have a class ID code, click Skip. To enter this code later, choose Join a Class from your Home page.

7. Once you're done, click Activities to begin using *Elements of Success Online Practice*.

Next time you want to use *Elements of Success Online Practice*, just go to www.elementsofsuccessonline.com and log in with your email address and password.